The Vowed Life

The Vowed Life

by

ADRIAN VAN KAAM, C.S.Sp.

DIMENSION BOOKS
DENVILLE, NEW JERSEY

Published by Dimension Books
Denville, New Jersey

Imprimatur: ✠ Most Reverend Vincent M. Leonard, D.D.
Bishop of Pittsburgh

Nihil Obstat: William J. Winter, S.T.D.
Censor Librorum

Imprimi Potest: Francis P. Trotter, C.S.Sp.
Provincial

TABLE OF CONTENTS

PART THREE

PART FOUR

PART FIVE

PART SIX

The Vowed Life

Preface

This book concludes the trilogy on the fundamental meaning and structures of religious life. It brings to an end reflections which began tentatively in the first two books of this series, PERSONALITY FULFILLMENT IN THE SPIRITUAL LIFE and PERSONALITY FULFILLMENT IN THE RELIGIOUS LIFE.

While this third volume can stand on its own and may benefit the reader who did not read the former two volumes, it would deepen his insight and understanding if he would study carefully the preceding works. Similarly, a prolonged reflection on this final volume will deepen the understanding of the ideas expressed formerly, for these reach greater clarity and precision in the considerations developed in the chapters to follow.

Because the trends of thought expressed here may sound rather new, it may be helpful for some readers to dip into the book at any chapter that seems to them more familiar and more in tune with other readings they may have done already on this subject by the author or other authors. Each chapter blends in so much with the central ideas that underlie all chapters that the reading of one chapter aids the understanding of any other chapter. Especially for some, the first chapter may seem at first sight rather technical. In that case the reader should feel free to begin with one of the later chapters. It would be advisable, however, at the end to read the whole book through from the beginning to its conclusion so that a clear and comprehensive understanding of the continuation of the line of thought may be gained.

Like the two former publications in this series, this book is written not from the viewpoint of theology but from that of Religion and Personality. Religion and Personality in this context means for us the discipline of a fundamental lived spirituality as developed over the centuries and enlightened by some of the relevant insights of the human sciences insofar as they deal directly or indirectly with the personal and spiritual unfolding of mankind and man.

The science of fundamental lived spirituality could be called pre-theological and post-theological. It is pre-theological insofar as it deals with matters that are not or not yet open to the theological method, such as certain psychological and biopsychological dynamics and structures which, while the object of study of other sciences, can be integrated within a study of the spiritual unfolding of man.

We call this study post-theological insofar as theologians have contributed to the expansion and formulation of the living faith of the Church to which they belong. As soon as the Church has made theological opinion its doctrine, it is no longer mere theological opinion but belongs to the living faith of the Church. Fundamental Spirituality can be called post-theological insofar as it deals with the concrete living of the fundamental tenets of faith in such a way that it leads to personal and spiritual unfolding in Christ.

It is advantageous for the study of lived spirituality to take into account the dynamics and structures of spiritual living as lived by the naturally religious man and the religious man in other religions, not enlightened by the Revelation of God in Christ and His Church. A considerable part of our study of religious life is dedicated to this search. We conclude then with a consideration of the way in which Christian religious life took up, deepened and perfected pre-Christian forms of religious life in the light of the basic tenets of the Christian faith.

Finally, it is our pleasant task to express our gratitude to the staff, faculty and students of the Institute of Man at Duquesne University, who contributed in numerous ways to the finalization of this book by discussion and dialogue, by taking dictation, and by assistance in typing of the manuscript. Our special thanks are also extended to the executive director of the Institute of Man, Father Bert van Croonenburg, C.S.Sp., and to the assistant director, Miss Susan Muto, who both critically read the original drafts of this work and improved and enriched the manuscript by valuable suggestions in regard to its thought and expression.

November, 1968

I

The Emergence of Religious Life in the History of Human Unfolding

In a time of transition, there is an inclination among many to question all areas of church and society, including the consecrated life. Modern man is in the midst of a crisis of meaning. Such periods of crisis are excellent times in which to live. All of us are invited to plunge deeply into the wellsprings of our lives and the foundations of our institutions so that together we may discover anew their meaning and value. In times when there is no doubt or crisis, our awareness of the foundations of our lives may be dimmed by involvement in daily routines. Life begins to be lived in its functional sense only. We labor in the dark, as it were, no longer inspired by the deepest meanings of our life structures and institutions. However, during periods of doubt and crisis, it is impossible to succumb wholly to the blindness of daily functioning. Survival demands that we immerse ourselves once again in the foundations of human life and history.

An initial immersion in the wellsprings of religious life reveals, in the first place, that Christianity is not a destruction of the natural and cultural-historical structures of life, evolved by man over the millennia. Christianity, on the contrary, is a respectful assumption of such structures which are then permeated by the light of Revelation. It may be valuable to reflect on the natural and cultural-historical foundations of the celibate religious life form in order to understand how the Lord took up this mode of life transforming it with His light and His grace.

Human Attitudes Foreshadowed in the Highest Forms of Animal Life

When we try to find all possible sources of the emergence of a fundamental life form like religious life, it may be enlightening to return not only to the beginnings of human life and of the spiritual transformation of that life by man but also to go even farther back to a man-centered interpretation of the highest forms of prehuman animal life. Could there be something in the highest manifestations of animal life which might be regarded, from the viewpoint of man, as a dim foreshadowing of man's life to come with its own biopsychological orientations and of the various fundamental life forms within which his life would articulate and unfold itself? To be sure, the final human and spiritual transformation of all biopsychological orientations of man can never be reduced to these biopsychological roots themselves. On the other hand, we are in danger of a deceptive mysticism when we consider all humanized and spiritualized attitudes of man as mere angelic phenomena totally isolated from and without any possible reference to certain biopsychological orientations anchored in man's bodily organism.

Any fundamental form of human life can be related somehow to some underlying biopsychological structure in which the human self or spirit can incarnate itself, transforming but never totally obliterating the faint initial pointing of this biopsychological structure. Such structures represent the most primitive outline of the basic orientation of man's organism. Man as self or spirit reads this outline in an experiential way and endows it increasingly with human and spiritual meanings which are not contained in the initial biopsychological outline itself.

The human self or spirit in its movement of humanization and spiritualization cannot ignore this fundamental pointing of man's biopsychological organism. Already in man there is a spontaneous directedness which, for example, makes him sensitive to the presence of members of his own species in a way that is different from his sensitivity to members of another species. When the human person deepens and transforms what is given here into love for humanity, he develops a human orientation which is not a denial of his initial biopsychological orientation. In other words he does something that is not totally at odds with his biopsychological structures.

In this regard the study of the life orientations of the highest animals is interesting because we find there, in a more integral and highly elaborated form, fundamental biopsychological structures and orientations which seem to foreshadow dimly similar structures in man. In man, however, these structures are less elaborated and always permeated by the light of reason and spirit, by acculturation and learning. Therefore it is difficult to see them clearly in man without discovering them first in the higher animals where they are present and operative in a far more pure way. So we may theorize that the biopsychological life orientations and structures in animal life are somehow a dim foreshadowing of analogous structures in human life which underlie the highest transformed modes of human living, modes which themselves can never be reduced to these underlying biopsychological orientations.

When we reflect on instinctive principles that make the survival and unfolding of a higher species of animal possible over a long period of time, we are dealing with instinctive conditions that guide the animal organism and animal behavior in their overall interaction with appearances in the life space of the species. Survival and development are always threatened by certain factors in the life space of the animal and promoted by other factors in the same environment. Survival and development are therefore dependent on the instinctive ability of the animal to cope with the conditions within which it has to grow and live. For example, biochemical conditions within the animal, such as proper blood pressure, proper digestion and right functioning of the glands under stress, are dependent for their effective functioning within various life situations on the vital instincts which adapt the functioning of all biochemical structures to environmental demands. In other words, the relational instincts enabling the animal to cope with its environment are the main conditions for the survival and development of the higher species concerned.

When we ask ourselves what are these main relational instincts or coping abilities, we may look first at the life space of the animal and ask whether or not there are different aspects to its environment which demand different types of adaptation, implying in turn different kinds of instinctive abilities. We are not looking here for all possible differentiations of the field of the animal. What we are interested in is the most primordial differentiations of this field which may lead us to a few fundamental relational orientations of the animal under which all other instinctive differentiations can be subsumed.

Exploring in this way the life space of the animal, we can distinguish immediately three quite different primordial dimensions. There are first of all changes and events in its overall environment, such as variations in climate and in the rise and fall of other species; secondly, there is the presence of animals of the same species to be met in such a way that they can promote the survival of the species; and thirdly, there is the presence of biologically relevant things that have to be used for shelter, nourishment and protection if the species is to survive. Obviously each one of these dimensions imposes its own demands, eliciting a quite different type of response which must be somehow written in the instinctive make-up of the animal organism. Each one of these challenges of the environment implies the presence of an original biopsychological orientation related to the other biopsychological orientations but still different in some respects. It may be worthwhile to consider these three fundamental orientations and later on to ask ourselves whether they foreshadow in some dim way an analogous threefold biopsychological orientation in man that can be taken up and transformd by him as self or spirit.

Let us look first at the relational orientation of higher animal life that insures sufficient coping of the animal species with changing events in its life space. In order to survive and evolve, the animal species must cope with biologically relevant events and changes in its surroundings. The instinctive ability to cope with change implies the ability to set in motion other relational instinctive patterns, such as effective adaptation, aggression and withdrawal. The ability to cope with changing environmental events presupposes necessarily that the animal is in a certain way aware of biologically relevant changes and events in its life space. While the higher animal species does not have the free, enlightened insight man has into reality, the species is instinctively open and attentive to biologically relevant events in its world. The species listens, so to speak, with its whole biological being to various changes in its surroundings and learns instinctively to cope with these changes in a way that protects and fosters its survival.

Over the millennia, animals have coped and adapted so well that higher forms of animal life evolved continuously. Thus it would seem that a necessary condition for survival and development of an animal species is the principle of listening to environmental events combined with the readiness to behave in accordance with the messages communicated in that listening. This elementary guiding principle in animal life could be called an instinctive organic obedience.

The term "obedience" is derived from the Latin *ob* and *audire* which in English means "listening to." The principle of listening to, built into the relational structure of animal life, was a main condition for its survival and evolvement and, as we shall see, this biopsychological relational structure seems to foreshadow an analogous biopsychological structure in man that is then taken up and transformed by man as self or spirit.

Another relational biopsychological orientation in the animal relates it to other animals of the same species. The higher species of animals could not survive if each single member of the species would live always in total isolation from the other members of the same species. Species survive often because a certain instinctive drive leads the members of the species to come together for mating at certain periods. In other species this instinct of gregariousness leads also to the formation of loose periodical groups, such as families. Other higher animals may live in herds or packs. There seems thus to be built into the biological structure of the higher animal some inclination and ability for some kind of bio-affective gregariousness. Along with this gregariousness, there is always operative a structure or principle of instinctive moderation of this gregariousness, which, like all instincts, is rooted in the instinct of survival. If the animal were driven only by its need for togetherness, other necessary biological functions would remain unfulfilled, and it would be impossible for the species to survive. The built-in structure of moderation and modulation of gregariousness prevents animals from overpowering one another in their strong drives for the same gregariousness.

Bio-affective gregariousness takes two forms. The first is an inclination to be together with a group of animals of the same species. This is accompanied by an instinctive protective attitude toward the species even at the risk of survival. For example, if one buffalo within a group of buffaloes realizes that a hunter is stalking the herd, it may risk its own survival to protect the herd by making conspicuous noises and movements. As a result the herd as a whole may escape while the buffalo that gave the warning may be shot. Secondly, instinctive gregariousness expresses itself in an inclination to seek togetherness with a mate so that the species may be procreated.

Instinctive love or gregariousness as manifested in species of animals that stand on the highest level of the biopsychological evolution of animal life can be considered from the viewpoint of man as a foreshadowing of analogous biopsychological orientations underlying his transformed forms of human gregariousness. Any form of human love is somehow related to some original biopsychological orientation in man that is sublimated and profoundly transformed into a love that is truly human and spiritual.

Human love can assume many forms, but two main forms of human love seem to be celibate love and marital love. When we speak here of celibate love, we do not yet speak of its divine dimension but we restrict ourselves, for the moment, to the human dimension of celibate love. This dimension is one possible transformation of a biopsychological orientation in man which fosters his concern for members of his own species in a way that does not necessarily limit itself to those he encounters in marital love. Celibate love in its human dimension is a generous nonexclusive respect and concern for other human beings as they appear within the life situation, simply because they are human beings. Respectful love for human beings is an expression of man as spirit. The spontaneous directedness of man toward other members of his species, transformed later in celibate love, must be linked with some biopsychological orientation written into man's bodily presence in the world. Otherwise his spiritual love would in no way be anchored in man as embodied and as concretely appearing in the cosmos. He would no longer be an incarnated spirit but a pure spirit totally separated from his organism.

Briefly, man's spontaneous concern and special sensitivity to members of his own species, as opposed to his spontaneous attitude toward members of other species and toward plant life, is not merely the fruit of a spiritual illumination totally alien from and at odds with his biopsychological make-up. The biopsychological orientation of animal life toward members of the same species foreshadows an analogous biopsychological orientation of man toward his fellowman which can be transformed into the human dimension of celibate love.

The other form of animal love or gregariousness, union for the sake of procreation, can be seen also as a foreshadowing of certain bio-affective structures in man which can be transformed by man as spirit into marital love. In both forms of animal gregariousness, as we have seen, there is also an innate principle of instinctive moderation and modulation rooted in the instinct for survival, a principle of nonviolating respect for one's biological integrity and the biological integrity of the other. This principle foreshadows a similar moderation in the analogous biopsychological structures in man that orient him toward his fellowman and his mate. As we have mentioned earlier, these biopsychological orientations in man are already changed by man's free decisions and cultural learning. Therefore man can unlearn the art of behaving in accord-ance with this built-in moderation. On the other hand, man can transform this built-in moderation into free, human respect which dominates his love for fellowman and marriage partner.

So far we have considered two main conditions for the survival and development of higher species of animals in relation to their life space, namely the structures of instinctive obedience and instinctive modulated togetherness. However, these two instinctive orientations toward appearances in the environment cannot explain how the species relates effectively to other aspects of the same life-world which have to be dealt with in a way that will not endanger the survival of the species. If animals were obedient only to the events that change the physical and biological scene surrounding them, if they were only to sustain each other in a restrained gregariousness, they would still be hard pressed for survival. Something more is needed.

An animal has to utilize the material aspect of its life space wisely and effectively to make its nest, to obtain nourishment, and to find cover from its enemies. Therefore, built into the biological structure of animal life is an instinctive orientation for the right selection and use of those things that make survival and biological development possible. Like the instinct of gregariousness, the ability to select and use rightly things in the environment also has a component of built-in modulation that is rooted in the overall instinct for survival.

Imagine for a moment that the instinct of right selection and use were not regulated by the inner instinctive wisdom of maintenance and survival that guides all the partial instincts of the animal. The drive to select, gather, collect and use would take over totally. As a result there would be no time, energy and attention left over for the manifold other biological functions necessary for health, survival, and procreation. Without a degree of moderation, rooted in the larger instinct for survival or, so to speak, without a certain sobriety or poverty in the movement toward things in the life space, the animal would destroy itself.

22

Three main life space relations of animal life in relation to the outside world have thus far been considered. These are an instinctive obedience, an instinctive moderate togetherness and an instinctive moderate use and enjoyment of things. These three relational attitudes seem to cover all the other attitudes which the animal assumes instinctively in relation to its life space. The outside world, as it appears to the higher species, seems to divide itself into three main types of biologically relevant appearances, which, in review, are environmental changes and events, including the rise and fall of other species; other members of the same species; and environmental things to be used. As we delve deeper into the biopsychological structures of man which underlie man's spiritual attitudes toward his life space, we can ask ourselves whether or not these three biopsychological orientations of animal life are not in some way pointing to analogous biopsychological structures in human life, albeit, permeated and transformed by spirit and culture.

Biopsychological Orientations as Taken up by Man

The emergence of man does not imply that all the original biopsychological orientations guiding the higher organisms in relation to their environment will not be present in his organism. The coming of man does mean the entrance of a whole new element into the unfolding of life — that of freedom and insight. Man is a call to transcend instinctiveness. Transcendence implies that there is something in man that can be transformed and transcended. Man seems to be not merely intellect or spirit but a spirit that is incarnated in a body which already carries biopsychological orientations. It seems that such biopsychological orientations are present in man in a new way and that they are open to spiritual and cultural transformation. With the coming of man as freedom, insight or spirit, the unfolding of life becomes a process of humanization or spiritualization. In service of this process, the threefold relational orientation found in animal life assumes a specifically human or spiritual character and therewith a new terminology. This terminology differs from culture to culture and from one period of history to another. Moreover it is always open to change, improvement and refinement. For instance, we are living within a temporal tradition which calls these three necessary attitudes obedience, chaste love, and poverty. Let us now see in what way the threefold path of human and spiritual unfolding is, on the one hand, foreshadowed in animal evolvement, and, on the other hand, different from the unfolding of animal life when taken up by man.

Obedience

Evolvement was only possible for animals because they had an instinctive openness to the biologically relevant aspects of events and situations within which they had to maintain and adapt themselves. Man is no longer blindly dominated by that instinctive animal appreciation of what happens around him. Nevertheless, he needs to be open to happenings that affect his becoming. He can only survive, grow and become by allowing himself to be fully open with his whole being to the events that he meets in daily life, by being open with his spirit and intelligence, his feelings and emotions, his experience and learning; with his prayerful, scientific, practical and poetic attitude; with his eyes and ears, his sense of touch, his body, hands and feet.

Obedience in the widest sense is the total openness of the whole man to the meaning of all events in his life situation. This respectful reading of events is the safeguard and basis of human development. Because obedience is no longer instinctive and unavoidable, man can refuse to open himself fully to the meaning and reality of the natural and cultural events that influence his life. Man's freedom grants him the possibility to destroy himself by closing himself off from the message of events and situations or by resisting their meaning. Disobedience is the proud stand of a free human being who isolates himself willfully from the flow of events and situations in a foolish attempt to unfold his life outside the differentiations of the very reality in which he is immersed.

Because man is spirit, freedom and insight, his obedient listening to events attains a depth and variety incomparably richer than the instinctive obedience of animal life. Animal obedience is pre-set in advance, fixated, and focused in few directions. Man's

obedience is not limited once and for all. His obedience is dynamic. Man's ability to listen to the hidden
meanings and potentialities of natural and historical
events is never closed and finished but ever ongoing
and expanding.

Obedience, as we have said, involves the whole
man, that is, all a man is at a certain moment of his
life and all he can become. Every past experience can
affect his obedience insofar as it has expanded his
openness and refined his sensitivity. For instance,
when my life experience has truly become mine, all of
me comes into play. I am fully present here and now
in obedience to a certain event or situation. Growth
in experience thus implies growth in my potential for
obedience.

Because I am incarnated spirit, listening to the
possible meaning of events implies my willingness to
listen to the whole and Holy to which all events
are related. The simple biological focus of obedience
makes it impossible for the animal to listen to the
presence of the whole and the Holy in situations and
events. The obedience of animal and man has to be
lived on different wavelengths. Again, because man's
obedience is fundamentally free, he is able to tune in
or out of the many wavelengths that become available
to him during the history of his personal development.
In this process of option for a wise and balanced stance
toward reality rests man's destiny within the limits of
his concrete life situation. He alone decides on the

fullness, indigence and balance of his growth and development.

Chaste Love

As we have seen, animals can only survive and evolve if they live in some kind of togetherness, at least within the same species. If it is true that an animal needs other animals for survival of the species, it is even more true that man needs man. We cannot survive and grow alone. From the first to the last day we stand together. Survival and evolvement of the human race are therefore dependent on some form of community.

Instinctive gregariousness in the higher mammals is expressed in a bio-affective attraction which leads in certain cases to mutual instinctive support in group behavior and in other cases to mating behavior. When this attraction is sublimated and transformed in human lives, it leads in certain *humanly* relevant situations to celibate love for other humans and human groups and, in other *humanly* relevant cases, to marital love. Both forms and expressions of instinctive gregariousness are thus foreshadowings of the two sublimated forms of human love.

In man, blessed as he is with insight and freedom, the instinctive gregariousness of higher animal life makes possible the sublimation of a bio-affective attraction to human love. Love in humans is free. It is no longer an inescapable, compelling force like the gregariousness of animal habitation. Again, because

27

man is free, he can choose to love or not to love. His freedom enables him to destroy in himself this fundamental condition of harmonious self-maintenance and balanced self-unfolding. This no animal can do. Man has the option to destroy or create himself insofar as he can prevent or prepare for the emergence of these attitudes of love in his life. Without them, the chances for wholesome human and spiritual unfolding are nonexistent.

Animal gregariousness has its own built-in moderation. Human togetherness, on the contrary, is no longer modulated automatically by the instinctive regulation typical of animal life. Togetherness for man can become human love only when it is freely modulated by respect for self and others. Here again I should realize that the respectful modulation of human love shares in the dynamic of the evolving openness that man is. Respectful presence to self and others, a presence to be incarnated in sensitive, reverential behavior, presupposes deepening understanding of the evolving uniqueness of myself and of the other.

To the degree that I do not increasingly sense and understand the other's uniqueness, to that degree my well-meant love may violate his unique calling, dignity and integrity. Unwittingly my loving counsel may hamper or destroy what he is most fundamentally. In regard to myself, lack of loving self-respect may lead to self-inflicted violence. The latter usually takes the form of a misguided self-love which makes me strive to become what I cannot be. In this sense self-love, untempered by self-respect and self-acceptance, may lead to the sin of self-abuse, not in the more peripheral sense of mere bodily self-abuse but in the most profound and pernicious sense of abusing my true self by repressing it and forcefully falsifying its expression. This psychological and spiritual self-abuse is the worst form of self-abuse possible.

To speak of the free modulation of human love, we use the term "chaste love," a term common to the linguistic tradition of a long period of Christian explication of the threefold path to self-unfolding for all men. In general, we should carefully avoid limiting the expression "chaste love" to a mere bio-sexual preoccupation. The same is true for the word "morality," which has sometimes been applied only to those principles that govern bio-sexual movements.

"Chaste love" is too wide a concept for us to naively believe that our love is automatically human and spiritual, provided we do not abuse another bodily. Chaste or respectful love is infinitely more comprehensive and deeper than the mere avoidance of bodily imposition on others. It is a lifelong effort to be respectfully present to the other in marriage or outside marriage with a love that in no way violates his integrity, that in no way ravishes his dignity, his right to privacy, and his unique personal and spiritual calling.

The principle of chastity or non-violation of the integrity of the other is so fundamental in human love

29

that its absence, or its pretense, contains potentially the greatest power of destruction. Love also grants me the greatest power for self-unfolding and for fostering the unique unfolding of the other. Love invites me to lower my defenses and to trust another person unconditionally. It respectfully grants me the freedom to bring into the light of day my world of meaning with its strengths and weaknesses, its joys and sorrows, to put myself at the mercy of another human being, and to experience the personal growth such loving acceptance makes possible.

But the pretense of love, violence which masquerades as love, opens me to the greatest possibility of abuse. If love is not modulated by cautious respect for one another, it tends to falsify what I am and what the other is; it tends to violate his unique calling as well as my own. This realization alone may explain the lifesaving necessity of chastity or respectful love at the heart of human unfolding. The very condition for humanization and spiritualization, for the full growth of human personality and community, is the steady emergence of a love that is not needy, imposing, begging, and overpowering.

In the movement of growth toward maturity, our love is mixed initially with self-centered needs and drives; it is not respectful but passionate and demanding. As children, we are so dependent on our parents that we cannot yet temper love with respect. It takes time for us to grow to a love that really represents the

unconditional gift of self to others and an unconditional reception of their love in return. In other words,
to become fully human, love has to be "chastened" or
purified of self-centered purposes, anxious needs, over-
dependency and isolated passions. Only when our love
is chaste can we diminish the tendency to use and
abuse ourselves and others in a disrespectful manner.

Poverty

A third principle of balanced human unfolding was
foreshadowed in the biological instinct for the right
selection and use of things. This drive in the animal
was kept within bounds by other aspects of the instinct for survival. Man also needs to use things in a
wise and respectful way to survive and unfold himself. In animal life the right selection and effective use
of things was conditioned by instinctive structures of
moderation. Man is no longer compelled by such an
instinctive wisdom. Rather he is guided by the growing wisdom of the spirit drawing upon the expanding
experience of man in history.

Because man is not fixated on the dimension of
mere biological relevance of things for organic survival, his presence to things covers an inexhaustible
range, moving from their immediate material and utilitarian meaning to their highest spiritual significance.
Various meanings are also uncovered in light of the
situations and persons for whose unfolding these
things can be used.

Man's wise and respectful presence to culture and nature is thus as dynamic as his respectful presence to events and people, expressed in obedience and chaste love. The three fundamental attitudes of human and spiritual unfolding participate in the dynamic openness to life and reality that the maturing man is. The man who is truly alive grows daily in presence to the possibilities and limitations of the gifts of culture and nature. Increasingly, he comes to a deep comprehension of the manifold ways in which they can be used by him and others without destroying the harmonious unfolding of human life.

In the course of his life, man can assume a presence to things that demeans him as a humane and spiritual being. Man can become so attentive to things that caring for them, collecting them and hoarding them becomes his main preoccupation. All other modes of presence he is called to unfold are then paralyzed. Similarly, man lessens his possibilities for growth when he becomes fixated on only one dimension of the many meanings things natural and cultural can convey, such as a fixation on their utilitarian or material meanings only.

In animal life we observed a built-in protection against self-destruction. For example, an instinctive moderation prevented total absorption of animal functioning in the selection, use or hoarding of things. Man's care and enjoyment of cultural and natural possessions should likewise be moderated by means of a recurrent movement of freely distancing himself from preoccupation with possession, when such collecting threatens to take precedence over everything else. The same movement of moderation should spontaneously emerge when one isolated dimension of things, like the pragmatic, threatens to drain the richness and depth of all other meanings.

Respectful, modulated presence of man to culture and nature, in the language of the Christian tradition, has been called poverty. Poverty in its deepest sense signifies the wise use and celebration of things. It aids my openness to all dimensions of their meaning. Poverty of spirit prevents the human person from being overwhelmed by possessing things, from being tied permanently to them, and from being fixated on only one dimension of their potentially infinite significance.

If I allow myself to become a hoarding, possessive, greedy person, I lose my possibilities for human and spiritual growth through culture and nature. Therefore I, and all men, have to develop the ability of serenely distancing ourselves from things when personal unfolding demands joyful and relaxed restraint. I am called to be fully present to culture and nature, to enjoy its treasures immensely, and yet to never become trapped in an isolated aspect that presents itself to me as merely a thing to be hoarded or used for purely pragmatic purposes. Without affirmation of the wide horizon against which things natural and cultural arise in their ultimate meaning, I may neither seek the whole and Holy nor accept my share of responsibility for the humanization and spiritualization of man.

The person freed from mere possessiveness may find the Holy in a sunset, in the smile of a child, in a painting, in a sip of mellow wine, a crust of bread, an evening of good company. Everywhere in culture and nature the mystery of the Holy is waiting to reveal itself to the man no longer burdened by the need to possess things disrespectfully. Unfortunately, all of us are inclined to forget our most fundamental tending toward the Sacred and to see only the glass of wine, the lovely face before us, the house in which we live. Our inclination is not to go beyond the shell of things into the mystery they contain. We easily fall away from our innermost calling, from the message of reality which is open to the Holy, and from our mission to convey this meaning. By our anxious and possessive preoccupation with things in isolation from their deepest ground, we may lose our joyful presence to things in poverty.

In our analysis thus far, we have seen that any evolvement of higher animal life presupposes an instinctive obedience, moderate togetherness and poverty. Moreover, we saw that man also had to follow the paths of obedience, chaste love and poverty, only now as rooted in the spirit. No other way of humanization and spiritualization is given to man but this threefold path. No other attitudes can substitute for these three. Obedience, respectful love and poverty are the most fundamental and primordial differentiations of what man is as spirit. And this pathway to spiritualization corresponds to the fundamental conditions for survival and evolvement of higher forms of biopsychological life as we know it in this world.

While we have meditated on the road men must follow to find human and spiritual fulfillment, we have not yet considered the relationship of religious life itself to the maintenance and evolvement of this threefold path. Already we can see that the three religious vows, traditionally called obedience, chastity, and poverty, point toward the main pathway given to man for human unfolding. In the course of human history, countless men and women, representing a variety of cultures and religions, felt compelled to make themselves free in a special way for the living of these three basic human attitudes.

Celibate religious life, like marital life, is first of all a special life form. Like the life form of marriage, religious life began to emerge with the break-up of tribal life and the beginnings of urbanization. With the end of tribal life two principles began to guide the evolvement of mankind. Both principles are rooted in the necessity of specialization. Due to the very richness of life possibilities open to him after the isolation of tribal cultures, man has to select and unfold some aspects of post-tribal life explicitly while others will remain implicit.

The first principle of post-tribal cultural unfolding is the choice of a life form. The second principle is that of value radiation. In order to understand the emergence of religious life in history, we have to clarify both principles of post-tribal cultural unfolding. For, as we shall see, religious life is both a fundamental lasting life form and a center of religious-cultural value radiation.

Lasting Life Form

What can we say about the emergence of fundamental life forms in the course of the development of mankind? In differentiating the basic attitudes of obedience, respectful love and respectful presence to things natural and cultural, we have stressed that man is an increasing openness to reality. His dynamic openness to events, people and things leads necessarily to the discovery of a vast multitude of possible ways in which to live his life. The styles and modes of living human life are so overwhelming and disparate that I could be torn apart by the bewildering multiplicity arrayed before me. I must be able to harmonize these various modes into some kind of unity.

Man is not only spirit or openness to the whole and Holy as its underlying ground; he is also finite spirit, limited openness. Man's finitude compels him to select only certain possibilities of living his life. Most likely these will be in tune with his predispositions and personal history. The same finitude—which also limits him in time and space — makes it impossible for one man, or even for a few generations of men, to find out how such selected possibilities of living can be integrated most harmoniously and sustained by a life style which promotes this kind of living. This radical limitation may explain in part why the cultural unfolding of man led gradually to the emergence of fundamental lasting life forms.

Life forms emerge in humanity following upon the experience of generations of men and women who attempted seriously to live such forms in a sustained and harmonious way. One such fundamental lasting life form, developed over the millennia, was the religious life form. Religious life became the life form of those men and women who wanted to live the threefold path in a concentrated way. They chose to be free from the pressures and limitations of marital life in order to be more fully present to the Holy as revealed in events, self and others, culture and nature. Slowly but definitely this fundamental life form took shape. The manifold experiences of numerous men and women of religious cultures, who felt predisposed to express their life in this style of experience and participation, contributed to the growth of the religious life form. Thus it is the outcome of a living tradition, one which implies the spiritual communion of people in any time, place, religion and culture who attempted to live this specific form of worship and witness.

Any life form is an expression of a complex, differentiated totality of living concretely rooted in experience. Therefore, a life form can never be reduced to a brief analytical definition. A life form by its very nature is infinitely more meaningful than any reductive description of its main characteristics. Such summaries may objectively identify the life form and distinguish it in a categorical way from other life forms. But they can never describe it fully, for a life form is precisely a lived form of life. It contains the mystery of the lived experiences of countless men and women, who have tried to incarnate its meaning in a particular time and place.

Entrance into the religious life form is always an entrance into dialogue with the experiences of those who lived this life over the millennia. At certain periods of history, this communion may have led to the emergence of collectively organized communities or religious corporations. Such corporations in and by themselves are not of the essence of the religious life form. Rather they represent temporal-cultural condensations of the far wider spiritual community composed of all the men and women who developed and lived the religious life form over the millennia.

Condensation of the world community of the religious life form into a specific temporal corporate articulation may be most useful or necessary in certain historical periods and in certain organizational types of civilization. But again, organizational community is not the only possible expression of the religious life form. In other civilizations and in other periods of history, there have been and still are men and women who vow their lives in celibate presence to the Sacred and strive to live in intense dialogue and communion with masters of religious living in their own and past ages without congregating into strictly organized collective corporations. Their mode of communion and dialogue with the wisdom contained in the religious life form begins regularly with a period of initiation during which they and other initiates grow in spirituality under the guidance of a master of religious living. At some future time, they may establish communion with other people living the religious life form without, however, establishing with them a specific organizational community or legal corporation. When such an establishment seems necessary — and this is prone to be the case when the religious life form emerges in an organizational civilization — the legal corporation which results by no means constitutes the essence of the religious life form.

This form of life is far older than any specific corporate community which has been lawfully established. Later in history, however, especially in an organizational civilization, overemphasis on the aspect of community as corporation may have led to a fatal misunderstanding and consequent perversion of this life form. At times the concern for corporate efficiency and organization may have reduced the wide scope of the original religious life form to the one narrow meaning of membership in a smoothly running organizational unit efficiently serving one or the other contemporary need.

It is especially necessary in light of the functional bent of twentieth century western culture to clarify once again the meaning and magnitude of the religious life form. Over the millennia it has been lived at different periods inside or outside an organizational community structure. No proof exists in history that the religious life form as lived inside a spiritual community but outside an organizational legal corporation was necessarily less intense, less religious, less celibate or less spiritual than the same life form when periodically lived within legal corporations. A study of the hermits, desert fathers and traveling holy men and monks in the Far East and periodically in the West reveals, for example, a well-integrated, deeply experienced religious life lived *outside* an organizational community but always *in* profound spiritual communion with past and present representatives of this life form.

The religious life form can be viewed as one of those special life forms which emerge when human culture becomes increasingly rich and complex. This life form is the response of those men and women who by predisposition desired to unfold their lives in concentrated presence to the Holy unencumbered by family duties. Theirs is an explicitly lived openness to the transcendent as revealed in events, people and things. So long as some people feel predisposed to live this life style, they will be ready to assume the religious life form in dialogue with those who have lived it over the centuries.

Centers of Value Radiation

As we have seen, the first principle of cultural differentiation is that of differentiation of the life form. The second principle involves differentiation of the culture into centers of value radiation. Man is an openness to values which are revealed to him in his encounter with nature and culture, people and events. In and through a lived articulation of these values man unfolds personally and spiritually.

At the beginnings of humanization, tribal man was able to live the main values of life in such a way that his presence to one value, like the religious, did not obscure for him other values, like the practical and the æsthetic. This situation changed considerably as man moved toward urbanization by forming the first small collective units housing members of different tribes. Along with this move came the need for specialization. Modes of presence to certain aspects of reality became so complex that people were needed who would spend the major portion of their day in dedication to the unfolding of these highly elaborated dimensions of human life.

For example, craftsmen became involved in practical enterprises, but they often had less time to devote to æsthetic and religious values. Artists in turn were so dedicated to preservation of æsthetic appreciation that they neglected practical values. Other modes of value-orientation evidence the same concentration in one area of value radiation to the diminishment of others. It may be noticed here that the religious value orientation is nearly always the first one to reach this level of cultural specialization. The religious specialist of later cultural development already emerges as such in the more advanced forms of tribal life.

In a former book, PERSONALITY FULFILLMENT IN THE RELIGIOUS LIFE, we argued that the only way for post-tribal culture to safeguard the actual or at least potential presence of its members to fundamental human values was for this culture to foster the emergence in its midst of centers of value radiation. People predisposed to develop a specific human value may free themselves from other interests to witness for this value in a special intensity. They keep its wealth alive for other members of the same culture who, while involved in certain values, nonetheless need the complementary influence of other values witnessd for in centers of radiation of these values. Thus in a given culture we might find people set free for scientific endeavors, for the arts and for religious presence, to mention only a few areas of concentration.

Post-tribal culture can thus be seen as a field of value forces which keep each other actually or potentially in balance. The culture fluctuates in accordance with the intensity or diminishment of these value centers. Because culture is a dynamic field of human unfolding in time and space, the field of value forces can be regarded both vertically and horizontally. That is to say, the vitality of a culture, its balance and fullness is not necessarily present at any one moment in its history. Horizontal fullness of a culture at a certain moment in time is an exceptional event. Usually a culture can only be called full and balanced in a potential sense. The culture which contains in itself the potentiality for a balanced presence of its members to the main values of human life is one in which all the centers of value radiation, representing the different fundamental values of human life, are actually present, even if one or the other value radiation is not appreciated at that moment by the population at large.

Usually, the changing historical and national situation of a culture leads to the emergence of cultural periods that are characterized by the prevalence of involvement in one or the other set of values. The actual radiation power of centers which sustain these values is parallel to their popularity at this moment of history. By the same token, value centers which represent values that are less popular in view of the felt contemporary needs of the population exert less influence in such a period and consequently their actual radiation power is dimmed.

From the viewpoint of the culture as a dynamic potentially balanced unfolding of a population over a long span of time, a paradox presents itself. Temporarily unpopular centers of value radiation are infinitely more crucial for cultural unfolding in the future than those centers of value radiation popular in the same period. The reason for their vital significance for the future is not hard to find. The culture as a dynamic whole does not have to be concerned about values that are highly popular. These take care of themselves, as it were. They are lived and articulated enthusiastically in a given cultural period, which by its very nature tends to be onesided.

The real long range concern should be for those values that for the time being are unpopular, neglected, and perhaps ridiculed and rejected. Due to the necessary onesidedness of every cultural period, the danger is always present that the culture may destroy not only the actuality but even the potentiality which is indispensable to keep alive the temporarily underestimated value, if this value is to be renewed in later generations. For later a change may take place in the historical situation which allows for this once hidden value to recapture the desire and imagination of the population.

Thus the future balanced unfolding of the culture as a whole always calls for the continuation of presently, seemingly unneeded and ineffective centers of value radiation. The survival of the temporarily neglected human value is of vital importance. There may be a time in history, for instance, when many chance factors foster the development of technical knowledge and spontaneously stimulate increasingly complex technical breakthroughs. In such a time people and institutions alike are liable to be carried away by the scientific, technical and practical values of human unfolding. The centers that radiate these values become more popular than ever. Many cooperate in this advancement of technical knowledge, partly because of genuine interest in these values and partly because cooperation with such popular centers of value radiation usually assures some increase in status, power and possession. At the same time centers that radiate other values, like the æsthetic and the religious, may lose popular support, diminish drastically in numbers and become less and less able to promise its adherents tangible remuneration and reward. The light such centers may have shed in time past is dimmed by other stars appearing now brightly in the firmament of the culture.

Those people who, despite a decline in interest in a specific value, still join this temporarily rejected center of value radiation may be more deeply and sincerely dedicated to this value than those who lived it when it was popular. They may see that each cultural period, their own included, is at the same time a threat and a promise of purification. On the one hand, cultural onesidedness threatens the survival of certain essential values. On the other hand, it purifies the radiation center of the threatened value from those adherents who may have come originally because radiation of this value promised them not only spiritual growth through selfless presence to this value, but also the possibility of status, power, pleasure and possession. In times when these values were highly popular, the latter incentive may have outweighed the former.

Purification is a blessing. Those in popular value radiation centers may have been unwittingly contaminated by their unconscious needs for power and status. Moreover, the values they affirmed may have been falsified in an attempt to please and placate those in power. Each culture may need just such a succession of onesided cultural periods in order to purify in turn the periodically rejected centers of value radiation and their representatives from the perversions and falsifications popularity may bring to the value concerned.

An in-depth analysis of the meaning of centers of value radiation is necessary for full understanding of religious life and of its particular place in the culture. From what we have said, it may be clear that the significance of religious life has nothing to do with its popularity or its rejection, with a rise or fall in the number of people dedicated to it. It is to be expected that there will occur prolonged cultural periods when people will be unable to understand or appreciate the primordial significance of religious value radiation. It might even be said that its popularity at certain times is a bad omen. It may mean that religious life is badly in need of rejection and of the purification that follows.

Unpopularity, ridicule and rejection of truly spiritual values are at times unavoidable in a broken world. Religious life profits from such times to the degree that it engages in the process of purification and brings itself back to its original value and meaning. It might even be said that this purification is a blessing for the culture within which it functions. For religious life is not *a* center of value radiation on par with all other centers; it is *the* center of value radiation in the culture.

As we have seen, the unfolding of man and his culture is dependent on his willingness to live the threefold path of humanization and spiritualization. Religious life frees people to witness for this sole pathway to true self-unfolding. In his threefold presence to reality, man would be torn apart if he had no means to unify all that reveals itself to his openness. What harmonizes his life is his experience of the whole and of the Holy as its underlying ground. Religious life, therefore, not only witnesses for the threefold path of self-unfolding; it also finds the beginning and end of this threefold presence in the Sacred. Without religious presence, a balanced and harmonious self-un-

47

folding and unfolding of the culture is virtually impossible. In this sense it may be clear that religious life is the most fundamental center of value radiation known to man.

We have spoken about the fact that historical situations tend to mobilize the imagination of a population in one or the other direction. Incidental excitement for a partial aspect of life threatens to alienate man from his presence to the deepest meaning of life and living. This is not to imply that engagement in a partial aspect of life and reality cannot be integrated with presence to the whole and Holy. On the contrary, this possibility of union of partial aspects of reality with the whole led to the emergence of that specific dimension of religious life known as participative religious life.

Participative religious life as a center of value radiation tries to be a living witness for the integration of partial cultural endeavors with presence to the Holy. The very life of the religious cultural participant demonstrates that this integration is possible, that it can lead not only to greater wholeness and happiness for the cultural participant but also increase the effectiveness of the cultural endeavor in which he is engaged.

It may be wise to pause here and briefly resume our line of thought up to this moment. First of all, we have seen that the highest forms of animal life foreshadow three attitudes transformed by man. In the organism of the higher animals these include an instinctive obedience to biologically relevant events; an instinctive and at least periodical gregariousness of the higher mammals with those of the same species; and a well-modulated, biologically relevant use of surrounding nature. Then we found that man's biological survival and development, as well as his human and spiritual unfolding, demand the same threefold openness to reality, now centered in man as incarnate spirit. Subsequently, we demonstrated that the openness of mankind — since it is a free and dynamic openness — leads, on the one hand, to an inexhaustible range and discovery of possible modes of being and leads, on the other hand, to the possibility of man's freely limiting himself to one or the other aspect of reality revealed in this openness. In the case of deliberate closure, we tend to idolize and deify one dimension of life, to live it in exclusion and repression of all other dimensions, and thus to seriously damage our possibilities of harmonious self-unfolding.

To counter this problem, human culture became a dynamic field of centers of value radiation, each one of which reminds the members in that cultural field of a fundamental human value. Each center has the responsibility to prevent people from becoming satellites circling blindly around only one center of value radiation totally out of touch with all other centers.

Finally, returning to our initial discovery, we realized that the most crucial value for man is his threefold presence to the whole and Holy which ultimately can redeem and save him from his constant inclination to become fixated on only one or the other isolated dimension of reality. From this we concluded that the religious life form is not only a fundamental life form like other life forms but is also by its very nature *the* most fundamental center of religious-cultural value radiation that emerged in human history.

We may now proceed to discuss in more detail the religious life as life form and as a center of value radiation. Having spoken about the religious life form as it emerged historically in several cultures and religions, we should add that its emergence is always influenced by the specific religion and culture in which it it found. The same can be said of the marital life form. While in its fundamental outline, the marital life form is the same in most cultures, its concrete appearance still varies in accordance with different religions, cultures and civilizations.

We gave previously an example of the effect an organizational civilization like ours can have on the religious life form. This example illustrated the specific emphasis of western religious life. While it is essential for people living this life form to be in profound communion and dialogue with those who have lived it in past and present, it is not essential that this deep communion take on the hierachical form and corporate structure of legally established organized communities. However, in western civilization, which has evolved primarily as an organizational culture, well-structured hierarchical communities also developed. Their development made it possible for the average person called to religious life to live this call in relative ease and in regular communion and dialogue with past and present communities.

Organizational communities in this case attempted to embody historical experience and wisdom into rules, constitutions and customs. The advantages of such systematic structures are clear, provided western communities maintain as primordial the aim to foster in their initiates continual dialogue and communion with the great representatives of the religious life form, for their insights in religious living elucidate the fundamentals of this life form and have become classics.

A written expression of religious life becomes a classic when it has been accepted by numerous religious of many generations as a true expression of their life's meaning, an expression which at least partially presents the truth of this life as discovered and lived by many over the centuries. The person who intends to live the religious life form cannot neglect respectful dialogue with these religious classics if he wants to

51

understand and live religious life in a profound sense. Therefore, a considerable part of the period of initiation into religious life should be spent in reading, meditating and discussing these classics under the guidance of a master of religious living.

This latter central person in personal and spiritual initiation must be deeply aware of the essential meaning of these writings as distinguished from their local language and cultural accretions. Moreover, he must be truly at home in the psychology of the persons whom has has to initiate into the religious life. In this way he may be able to make classical writings relevant for contemporary initiates and perhaps prevent these initiates from the futile attempt to base their life form only on writings of contemporaries. No matter how excellent the writings of one or two generations may be, they can never equal the accumulated insights and experiences expressed in the best writers of the centuries and implicitly affirmed by countless generations of men and women who granted to these writings the stature of classics.

Religious Life and Threefold Presence

Deepening reflection on the religious life form brings to light another question. What is the difference between the way in which the threefold path is lived by the celibate religious and the way it is lived by those who are not celibate religious? As we have seen, the threefold path is the main condition for the humanization of mankind and man. All people, married or single, Christian or non-Christian, can only grow by being faithful in their own way and style to these basic conditions of human and spiritual living. What then is the difference between the style in which I as a religious choose to live this threefold path as distinguished from the style in which other people are called to live it in like manner?

In the first place, all people implicitly follow the threefold path when they desire to be their best selves, but I and my fellow religious also follow it explicitly. I vow explicitly to make this road mine and to concentrate on living its implications in my daily life. I make it my central concern and declare publicly that I have done so. Moreover, I accept a whole set of rules and customs formulated primarily to protect and promote my explicit living of this threefold path. In other words, I vow to attempt daily to be my best self. Like any other man or woman, I can only do so the degree that I follow the threefold path of humanization. My vowed concentration, incarnated in a set of life customs, enables me to stand among my fellowmen as a witness for this path to humanization and spiritualization.

The threefold path of respectful openness to culture and nature, people and things in all their dimensions finds as its most fundamental dimension the implicit relationship of people, things and events to the Holy. As a vowed religious I consecrate my life to a lived awareness and conscious actualization of a three-fold presence to the Holy in people, things and events. My fellowmen, living other life forms, also need to develop this presence. They are less explicitly dedicated to it as a way of life. They have fewer means available in their life structures and customs to keep this mode of prayerful presence in the forefront of their attention and action.

A next main difference is that I live this concentrated presence in communion and dialogue with others who historically have attempted to live in vowed concentration on these fundamental attitudes as celibate religious. If I happen to be a religious in the later periods of western civilization, this communion and dialogue may be protected by administrative structures of a legal religious corporation. It is clear that the average man living other life forms has neither the time nor the means to concentrate so intensely on this dialogue.

Finally as a religious I am called to live this life form in such a way that I, together with my fellow religious, can transcend to some modest but real degree the incidental and temporal limitations inherent in my cultural period. The religious life form sets me free from administrative and emotional involvement in family life and allows me to live in intense dialogue with the great spiritual masters of all times and all cultures, thus liberating me from some of the pressures which weigh down my cultural counterparts.

It would be far more difficult for me to live in this transcending freedom if I were obliged to find and establish a family economically and socially within the frame of contemporary enthusiasms and interests. Even as a celibate religious, I may be tempted, of course, to become so overinvolved in my work that I allow it to interfere with my periods of recollection, meditation, and solitude. If this is the case, I may become unfaithful to the religious life form and unable to profit from its essential benefits.

To be sure, a certain number of exceptional men and women can perfectly transcend the limitations and pressures of society in spite of their family involvement, but when dealing with fundamental life forms we must address ourselves necessarily to the average man, not to the exceptional one. For the average man it seems more difficult to transcend his times when deeply involved with his family than for the average man who is set free to a degree from his times by his celibate life — a life lived in communion with the great representatives of spirituality over the centuries and ideally supported by his local legal religious corporation.

A last difference to be mentioned, especially in regard to participative religious life, is the greater availability of the participative religious to cultural participation. This availability again is due to the fact that his celibate life frees him more than the average person who has to shape his participation in accordance with the primary demands imposed on him by his family. This seems to reemphasize that the style and character of religious life is very much bound to the celibate dimension of this life. Thus we may turn briefly to a discussion of the meaning of celibacy in relation to the religious life form.

Celibacy and Celibate Love

Celibacy witnesses for a specific attitude of love for God and man which we call celibate love. Celibacy is more than relinquishing my right to establish and maintain a new family unit in society. This freedom from family care is only a condition which enables me to live in a special way the celibate mode of love for God and man. Celibacy therefore is not an inhibition or diminution of human love. For celibacy is not only a special style of love for God but also a special style of love for man. It is true that celibacy implies some limitation in the expression of the human dimension of celibate love. But this is true of all human love. For human love is meant to be incarnated and expressed in a mode of behavior which makes this love real, concrete and acceptable within the limited life situation in which I find myself. Each life situation, marital or celibate, calls for an appropriate expression of human love in tune and in harmony with that situation. Adaptation of the manifestation of my love to the situation does not diminish my love itself. In regard to the specific life situation of celibacy, the human love of the celibate focuses on a field of incarnation that differs in its primordial structure from the field of incarnation of marital love. However, this difference does not prevent celibacy from being not only a special mode of love for God but also a special mode of love for man. Well-developed celibate life is not only a life of intimate solitary presence to God but also a cordial, gentle, human love life, outgoing and tender.

While the contemplative religious witnesses more pointedly for the solitary presence of the celibate to God, the participative religious brings to this solitary presence a more explicit witness to the human dimension of celibate love. As we shall see, celibate love is necessary for any true human love. The celibate love attitude is so basic to the structure of human love that no true love, inside or outside of marriage, is possible without this attitude. Thus the question arises why is a celibate attitude necessary in all forms of human love?

Human love life begins in early childhood with a kind of love that is demanding, possessive and imposing. This childish love may still be with me. I may manifest love in order to gain something. My growth toward full humanity must go beyond this. I must move toward a mode of love that is for the other, for his own sake, a life of love in which I not only receive in loving gratefulness but in which I am also able to love the other as the person he really is. The height of this growth of other-centered presence is reached at the moment that I can experience the other as not merely the isolated, painfully limited, imperfect person he necessarily is but also as endowed with the mystery of the Holy calling him forth for time and eternity in his uniqueness. This is the precious moment of distancing myself temporarily from the peripheral immediacy of the other and encountering him in his true and mysterious uniqueness.

The lifelong movement from self-centered to other-centered love is difficult, demanding constant effort and attention. At its most sublime heights, it repeatedly demands a recollected presence to God as the mysterious ground of the other. Daily concerns may invade my awareness in such measure that I forget that my chief call, the reason for my being, is love, is to be for God and others. In my forgetfulness of this call, my love may regress to its earlier structure of mere need-love. For example, tired from my daily preoccupations, I may turn to the other merely for relief or to engage him in my worries. If relief becomes my main reason for loving the other, it may be most difficult for me to be non-possessive, non-demanding and to refrain from imposing on him. It becomes then almost impossible to respect him and to care for him as the unique gift of God which he is, valuable and infinitely worthwhile in himself, independent of what he means to me.

A truly loving person is not a demanding but a facilitating person, one who appreciates the other and tries to help him to be what he can be best. Full growth to a deeply respectful other-centeredness in selfless love is a movement beyond one's self to the mystery of the whole and Holy from which the other emerges and by which he is called to unfold himself in a unique way. I may harm or foster this unfolding, depending on the self-centeredness or selflessness of my love.

The sacred human dimension of celibate love can only emerge in me to the degree that the mystery of the whole and Holy from which the other emerges means something to me. The Holy can mean something to me only when I find its meaning by a steadily renewed celibate solitary presence to God in solitude. This is the divine dimension in which the human dimension of celibate love should be rooted. The last flows forth from the first and cannot be maintained for long without recurrent recollection and centeredness in the Divine Love for me. Any attempt to reach the fullness of celibate love merely by loving other human beings directly and exclusively in God is doomed to failure and based on self-deception and illusion.

Understandably, human love wants to receive, to be cared for by the other, to command his attention and appreciation. This desire of human love is not demeaning provided it does not paralyze the possibility of selfless presence to which the aspect of receiving love should be subordinated. Human love needs some reciprocity, but it does not need every possible form of reciprocity, at every moment from all people. The kind of reciprocity of love to be expected depends on the situation within which human love is incarnated whether it is mere celibate love or primordially marital love.

Celibate love, both inside and outside of marriage, represents that moment of presence to the other in which I experience him in his uniqueness as a manifestation of the whole and Holy independent of what he means to me. Celibate love is unconditional. I delight in the other's sacred uniqueness whether or not he can serve my needs. I love him not for what he can do for me but for what he is. My delight at such moments is to promote his being and to bless his becoming.

The average human being, despite his best intentions, could not maintain this sublime attitude without finding some reciprocity in another at some time. Also the religious celibate, who is called to live a love life among men that symbolizes primordially the celibate moment of all divine and human love, is in need of some reciprocity at some time by some person. It is true that the divine dimension of his celibate love makes him experience the reciprocity of divine love in his solitary loving presence to God. Nevertheless, the average celibate is in need of at least some reciprocity at some time when he has to live daily the human dimension of celibate love. This is especially true of the participative religious who, more than the contemplative religious, witnesses for this specific aspect of celibate love. In this respect, the vow of celibacy implies not an absolute but a relative relinquishing of the need for human reciprocity.

The participative religious witnesses not only for man's calling to be a solitary presence to God in the solitude of his uniqueness but also for the fundamental humanizing attitude of celibate love to which all men are also called. In service of both kinds of testimony, the religious freely relinquishes the possibility of the secure and steady presence of a source of human reciprocity that one finds in principle in marriage, though even this established lasting occasion does not always guarantee steady reciprocal need-fulfillment. The celibate person, by giving up this possibility of continuous human reciprocity, freely accepts the risk that he may have to incarnate his love in situations in which he will find little or no human reciprocity. In such periods he can only save and truly live his human love by living it in the celibate dimension.

The readiness to live at such moments in the celibate dimension of human love is what makes him a true witness for this necessary dimension of all human love. The same situation invites him to deepen his solitary presence to the always present reciprocity of divine love. At such moments the celibate who is Christian grows in celibate solitary presence to Christ, his Savior and Redeemer. In this way he becomes at the same time a witness for the divine and the human dimension of celibate love, for human love becomes more possible when celibate love is deepened.

The witnessing of the religious celibate is not necessarily less effective when at certain moments human reciprocity may come to him as an unexpected gift. It may happen that his superior shows gratefulness for something he has done. A fellow religious may spontaneously compliment him. Sometimes people or patients may tell him how much they like him, or he may meet families or friends who are truly kind to him.

There is no reason for the celibate to be ashamed of his feeling of joy and contentment when his celibate love is reciprocated not only by divine love in the precious moments of solitude but also by human love in the moments of participation in human community. He should gratefully accept these manifestations of human sympathy. Even as a human being who in a special way lives the celibate aspect of divine and human love, he still needs some human reciprocity from time to time. He would only be unfaithful to his calling if he were to bind himself once and for all exclusively and primordially to such sources of reciprocity, for example, in the relationship of marriage. Vowing celibacy is vowing *not* to secure legally, lastingly and exclusively the certainty of lifelong presence to a potential source of reciprocity of human love.

Celibate love is first of all a love responsive to the prompting of the Spirit. It is altruistic, non-exclusive and, like divine love, it is freely given and seeks no recompense. When his love is returned in a manner which does not betray his primordial commitment to God and others, the celibate accepts it gracefully, allowing it to deepen and enlarge his humanity without becoming bound exclusively to it or becoming alienated from divine love which he finds in celibate solitude.

While delighting in loving appreciation and recognition by fellow-religious, friends, cultural participants and others, a religious preserves his readiness to live unreciprocated celibate love the moment his life history would force upon him a situation of non-reciprocity on the human level. An attitude of celibate love that is ready to transcend repeatedly the human need for reciprocity is simultaneously a love that makes a person more free to meet cultural needs, cares and concerns, and to take stands which are less popular and do not always bring with them the opportunities for attention, appreciation and gratitude all of us hope for. Celibate love enables us to keep incarnating our lives in social, scientific and artistic pursuits, which, no matter how right or necessary they may be, are still misunderstood, ridiculed and rejected.

It is clear then that the vow of celibate love enlarges the possibilities of the religious to become an effective cultural participant within the limits of his life situation and personal limitations. The seriousness of his attempt to participate in the culture depends on the depth of his celibate love. For fostering the emergence of true culture means fostering the dynamic event of humanization and spiritualization as a preparation for full redemption and divinization of humanity and culture in all realms of human life. The religious celibate, who lives primordially the solitary divine dimension of his celibate love, and who anchors in this solitary presence the human dimension of celibate love, experiences an unusual freedom to meet needs in spite of rejection and opposition.

It may be worthwhile to digress for a moment to clarify what we mean when we say that non-exclusive celibate love is a love for humanity as emerging from the Holy. The term "humanity" in this context is not used in an abstract, philosophical or theological sense. Terms employed by Religion and Personality or Fundamental Spirituality are valuable insofar as they point to concrete life situations. When we speak about celibate love for humanity, we mean humanity not as an abstraction but concretized humanity or humanity as concretely appearing in concrete individual persons and groups within the successive actual life situations of the religious. The vow of celibate love for humanity as emerging from the Holy means therefore the readiness to love *all men* as they may appear on the horizon of my life. In each case, celibate love life presupposes the willingness to honor each one of these persons appearing in one's life situation with dignified respect.

If the gift of friendship does come to the religious celibate — always an exceptional circumstance — his primordial respect for others is deepened by the rare mutual understanding friendship brings. In friendship, loving respect for the other as unique can express itself in encouragement, reproach, advice and request which affect the unique core of the personality. The same loving respect would forbid one to attempt a like incarnation with persons for whom he would not have any affinity. Affinity will not necessarily lead to friendship, for while it is true there can be no friendship without a certain degree of affinity, there can be affinity without friendship. The absence of any affinity, makes it highly improbable that I shall be able to sense the unique movement of personal and spiritual unfolding which the other is. Without a certain affinity, any advice, request or proposal on my part, which touches his uniqueness, would risk distortion and falsification of his true unfolding.

The celibate religious, in his love for humanity as appearing in his life situation, should realize that the most exquisite expression of loving respect is in most cases a dignified distance in regard to the unique core of the other. He should maintain this distance as long as the other does not invite him to share in his unfolding and as long as he does not experience the affinity which will guard him from falsifying the life of the other in the name of well-meant love.

Because the vow of celibate love implies also respectful love for himself, the celibate religious should also insist that others keep a dignified and respectful distance in regard to his own interiority and inner motivations and the unique mystery of his personal unfolding. As he grows in faithfulness to the aspect of respectful self-love, to which he has also vowed himself, the celibate religious may develop gradually a dignified manner, firm but flexible, which enables him to deal effectively with potential violators of his unique self-emergence.

When we say that celibate love is a love for humanity as concretely appearing in the celibate's life situation, we thus do so for good reasons. Another is the necessity to distinguish the focus of a primordially celibate love life from that of a married love life. The latter, especially in western culture, is a dedication to one's partner and to one's children. Celibate love life, on the contrary, never lastingly concentrates itself exclusively on certain loved persons for a lifetime. It may happen that the life situation of the celibate happens to evolve in such a way that the same persons to whom he is dedicated keep appearing for his whole life. Even this chance situation, however, does not mitigate the reality that his vow of non-exclusive love makes him, in principle, ready and willing to grant full respect to any new persons who may appear unexpectedly in his life situation.

Fundamental readiness to love, as expressed in the phrase "celibate love for humanity," thus implies that insofar as any person may potentially appear on the horizon of the life of the celibate, he will be granted a love which is not potentially curtailed by the obligation of primary love for one's family. Humanity, as it appears in the life-space of the celibate religious, includes not only those men who actually appear in the flesh, but also all those for whom he is called to be in some way a meaningful influence within the limits of his personality and life situation.

For example, it is quite possible that a religious will write letters to servicemen whom he has never seen. Another religious may engage in research, writing or artistic creation for the benefit of persons whom he may never meet. He tries to write so that his readers will benefit from work that is unclouded by sensational expressions and coy divulgations. These people are included in his loving concern for them as persons. He makes their welfare a concrete motive for his endeavors, for they are an intimate part of his celibate love for humanity. This concrete motive modifies his writing style.

After this brief digression, we may return to our discussion of the pure moment of the human dimension of celibate love. An interesting illustration of this moment can be found in the good counselor or therapist. The latter is a person able to become involved in a most intimate relationship with many others without receiving always and necessarily love in return. He is ready to care for clients even when there is no response or only a negative response during long periods of time. The celibate love of the therapist consists in his full knowledge and acceptance of the fact that he may not in any primary sense receive a loving reciprocation from his clients. Still he is able to be totally present to them in a loving concern that transcends the frustration naturally felt when our love meets only a wall of indifference or hostility.

The counselor's celibate love is maintained even when the client becomes aggressive, tries to seduce him, ridicules him, is jealous of other patients, demands exclusive attention, and only slowly gains sufficient confidence and stability to stop imposing on the therapist. The therapist's unconditional love for the patient could only be called a celibate love in the fullest sense if the human dimension of his celibate love would be rooted in a respect for the sacred ground of this unique counselee. This may well be in the case of a therapist who has a religious life orientation.

Even from this brief illustration, it becomes increasingly clear that all forms of love for mankind as unfolding can only reach perfection and be protected when a strong component of celibate love is present in those engaged in cultural and social endeavors. If we recall for a moment the principle of the necessity of centers of value radiation in post-tribal culture, we can also see the necessity and value of a radiation center of celibate love which can at times transcend the need for human reciprocity.

The human dimension of celibate love relates to the total development of mankind. It is the core of every form of true human love. It is that dynamic center of human love that makes the ongoing humanization of mankind and man possible, especially when this movement demands the resistance of human inertia and hostility and therewith the necessity to love without reciprocity.

A culture without witnesses for the celibate component of human love would be an impoverished culture. All modes of human love including marital love would suffer. We are speaking, of course, of an authentic celibacy and of an authentic celibate love which is not negative and which realizes that relinquishing the right of an exclusive reciprocal marital love would be meaningless if it would not make the celibate more available for a true but non-exclusive love.

If authentic celibacy is found at the core of non-Christian religions, where monastic life flowered so immensely, it is no less the core of Christian culture and of Christian life and marriage. This unspoken dim awareness has perhaps been one of the unknown roots of the true Christian couple's desire to have one of their children enter religious life. They may have felt vaguely, without ever being able to conceptualize or verbalize this experience, that this child, who will be dedicated to the life of celibate love, will witness to the most beautiful component of their own love.

Moreover, once we begin to think of celibacy as a heightened and special form of human love, we are no longer halted by a seeming opposition between celibate and married life. Both are specialized expressions of the harmonious totality of human love. A depreciation of celibate love is a depreciation of the best in married life. A condemnation of celibate love is a rejection of the best of married love. Indeed married life reaches its heights, when the component of celibate love is sufficiently developed.

Finally, celibacy, which makes the religious free in a special way for presence to the Holy and for cultural participation, can be related to religious life in its fundamental structures as symbolized by the threefold path of human and religious living. Religious life, as we have disclosed, is a fundamental life form within which a person can find a serene and harmonious road to self-unfolding centered in a threefold religious presence. Secondly, religious life is a center of religious-cultural value radiation which keeps alive in the culture the awareness of man's primordial need to live the threefold path of presence to the Sacred. Viewed in light of religious life, celibacy can be seen in relation to obedience as a road to self-unfolding and obedience as part of a fundamental life form.

One condition for true self-unfolding is that I listen to events and situations not only in their immediacy but more basically in their relation to the all-comprehensive whole and Holy. When I am able to rest and unify myself repeatedly in this all-embracing ground, events and my reactions to them fall into place, granting me the serenity, unity, and solitude and simplicity which make the highest self-unfolding possible. Celibacy also sets me free from the myriad practical, economic and emotional preoccupations that regularly accompany the administration of a family unit and facilitates my endeavor to transcend such necessary concerns by uniting myself to their ultimate center and deepest ground.

When I consider the celibacy-obedience relationship in regard to religious life as cultural value center, I realize again that witnessing to the integration of man's listening to the immediate message of reality with his listening to the transcendent message is infinitely eased by religious celibacy. Freed from the constant care a family deserves, I am less apt to be absorbed by mere utilitarian and economic projects which affect the future of my family. Celibacy helps me to witness to openness to the sacred meaning of events and to guard this openness in myself and others without denying that we must also be present to the more immediate dimensions of life always in light of this primordial openness.

When we consider the life attitude of respectful love, symbolized by the vow of chaste love, we see again how celibacy facilitates the living of this attitude within the religious life as life form and as value center. The deepest ground of human respect is the growing awareness that the other is not merely an isolated, limited, pleasant or unpleasant appearance in my daily life situation but that somehow he emerges from the ground of the Holy and that he, like all men, is called to be a unique expression of the Sacred. Because of its necessary administrative, emotional and practical involvements, the life form of marriage may make it difficult to keep open at all times my respectful transcendent presence to the other.

Moreover, because of concerns for my own family, I may be inclined to experience others outside as mere competitors who block or abridge my efforts to gain what I need to maintain my family comfortably. Celibacy redeems me from the many involvements that would make it more difficult for me to find the other not only in his immediacy but also in his transcendent meaning. A person set free from family care and involvement can more easily witness to the value of respectful transcendent love for others, even if they may threaten his position.

In regard to the vow of poverty, celibacy facilitates considerably the attitude of a respectful and wisely modulated presence to culture and nature as gifts of the Sacred. Religious life as fundamental life form binds itself to this simplicity of spirit by the vow of poverty. This life attitude aims to facilitate the unfolding of the true self of man by preventing his fixation on culture and nature as mere means to serve utilitarian ends or external enrichment. This liberation helps man to open up continuously to the deeper meaning of things as revelations and gifts of the Sacred. He is more free to experience them as gifts to be beautified, celebrated and used as the means given man to improve the world as his home and place of worship.

Again, family involvement may necessitate focusing so much time, energy and attention to the practical and economic aspects of things that it becomes far more difficult to maintain the other style of presence to culture and nature. Religious life as a center that radiates the value of respectful presence to culture and nature is far more able to do so when its members are living the freedom of celibate life. Witnessing for transcendent presence to cultural and natural resources is infinitely facilitated when I am not at the same time badly pressed to use things for the enhancement of myself and my family and when I am not engaged in a daily competitive struggle to gain as many possessions and resources as possible.

II

Vow-ability and Call-ability

Man is a being who can experience himself as "vow-ability" and as "call-ability." Vow-ability is man's ability to vow himself; call-ability is his ability to be called and to hear this call. These abilities rest potentially in the fundamental structure of man as religious. Man would not be man if he were unable to vow himself in response to the call of the Holy. In daily life we are not usually aware of our vow-ability and call-ability because we are immersed in the anonymity of functional everydayness. And yet every man may experience that he is called to transcend this everydayness, that he is called to consecrate himself to the Transcendent at some time in his life.

This call is at once beckoning and threatening. It threatens insofar as I cannot choose my call. I experience *that* I, like others before me, am called to something in life but I cannot yet know *what* my call will be. I can accept it or reject it when it comes but I cannot choose it. And even if I come to know my call, the contents will by far exceed my grasp; they will reach beyond what I can foresee. The call is beckoning too, for I realize somehow that if I do not direct or vow my life in some meaningful way, my life is in danger of becoming meaningless, scattered, inconsistent, dispersed and imprisoned in functional everydayness.

The experience of vow-ability and call-ability is initially mysterious. The call to vow my life is a call to the whole of my being as I am related to the whole and Holy. Because I am uniquely called by the Holy to unfold my life within a fundamental life form, it is so that life takes on a hidden meaning and consistency, even though it is improbable that I shall see precisely what this consistency is at any given moment.

The mystery of my life call may gain in clarity as my life proceeds. While I do not know in advance the details of the divine articulation of my life, I do know somehow that every event, encounter and experience of my life blends together mysteriously and harmoniously. If I were asked to explain how a seemingly disparate array of happenings are expressions of a call that unifies my life, I would most likely be at a loss for words. The unfolding of my life is a mystery. I can only rest in an abiding faith that the call is always there, filtering through seemingly unrelated incidents, choices and events. I may be blessed with an occasional glimpse of the mysterious consistency of my life, but such moments are fleeting. Most often I must live in the humble awareness that I am following my life call though I cannot know in advance the full reason why I am called. This can be revealed only in the course of my life of faith. The only certitude I have is the certitude of faith that I am called.

Faith in the call and its mystery grants me the flexibility I need to respond to life, which is never totally predictable. When I live in anticipation of daily revelations of my mysterious call, I live also in quiet readiness for all possible unanticipated events and happenings. The call may call me forth in ways I never expected, ways which are original and new though still in harmony with my former modes of being and acting. The attitudes of total readiness to respond to the new and unexpected and the total willingness to harmonize my response to new situations as far as possible with my past are rooted in faith in my unique call. The abiding awareness of being called personally and continually thus implies openness to the possibility of harmonizing my response to new events as far as possible with my responses to former events and is an integral part of the dynamic attitude of flexible fidelity to my call.

Faith in my life call also grants me strength and serenity insofar as it is the deepest possible experience of being confirmed in the unique meaningfulnss of my life. Every person needs to feel worthwhile. He needs to be affirmed by himself and confirmed by others.

The need for confirmation by significant persons like parents, teachers and friends may tempt me to conform blindly to the expectations of others in order to gain their approval and adulation. But faith in the life call protects me from false conformity, for it is the experience of my unique self as infinitely confirmed by the Eternal.

The self-affirmation this experience of the Eternal instills in me is not dependent on the whimsical moods of the crowd, the fleeting enthusiasms of a cultural period, the passing success of my enterprises, or the limited insights of my friends. This self-affirmation resides in my faith in the Infinite and the Eternal, in that call which infinitely transcends all passing situations and endeavors, all incidental judgments, all praise or condemnation. I rest in the faith that I and all people are called by the Eternal to unfold our lives uniquely and meaningfully.

Call and uniqueness are intertwined. The call makes me be what no one else is. If I do not accept my unique self as called by the Eternal, I may be inclined to flee from my self and to escape in crowd or collectivity, which holds out the promise of confirmation as long as I pay the price of conformity. Once I forsake personal responsibility to my call, I close myself off from my highest possibility of self-unfolding and presence to the Sacred. The best way I can regain my sensitivity to the call which beckons me to be my best self is by distancing myself from the crowd and at times from the other, even if he tries to be my best friend.

The attitude of serene receptive presence to my call is an expression of the celibate component of my life. The mode of celibacy, which is witnessed to in a concentrated way by those who choose celibacy as their central life style, has a place in the life of every man who wants to live in obedience to his unique call. The attitude of celibacy creates the moment in which I can be alone long enough to listen to my call. Even those who have chosen celibacy as their life style may be tempted to leave the realm of solitary listening and hide in the comfort of the leveling crowd. Nonetheless celibacy as a general human attitude means the ability not to betray my first responsibility to my unique call by aligning myself wholly with the interests and judgments of crowd, collectivity or clique.

It is utterly insignificant whether or not I succeed in the actual living out of my call in a particular time and place. What matters is my willingness to listen to the voice of the Eternal in me and my honest attempt to respond with my whole self to this call. The approval of the crowd or collectivity means nothing when I answer my unique call. I rise above the approval of crowd or collectivity and view my life in the light of eternity.

Life Call and Availability

My life call reveals itself in a variety of temporal

calls which fall into place within the fundamental call
of my life. While all of these temporal calls are necessary, not all of them are equally meaningful in the
light of my life call. Only one revelation of my life
call influences me more deeply and lastingly than all
the others. This is my call to one or the other fundamental lasting life form. While a chosen life form
does not exhaust the infinite possibilities of personal
unfolding, my life form reveals to me the specific style
within which I shall have to find and live my unique
call.

Because man is essentially "vow-ability," the call
means among other things that he is called at the end
of adolescence to focus his life in a definite direction
by vowing himself to one or the other fundamental
lasting life forms. When I discover my vow-ability, I
discover also my orientation toward an implicit or explicit life vow or life consecration. The experience of
myself as vow-ability reveals my life as a complex unfolding whole to be related freely and consciously to
the Sacred within a fundamental life form. When I
choose a fundamental life form and vow myself to it,
I do so in the awareness that this is the way I shall
have to find and live the primary call which I am from
eternity and for eternity.

The fundamental life form which I choose should
be in tune with the revelations of my primary and
eternal call which I have received up to the time that
I leave adolescence before vowing my life in one or

the other definite direction. While it is true that the option for one or the other vowed life style limits my availability for certain other styles, this choice does not exclude the variety of ways within this life style by which I can unfold my uniqueness.

Faithfulness to my call to a fundamental life form always makes me unavailable for other calls incompatible with the life form to which I have vowed myself. This is not so surprising, for it is humanly impossible to be available to every call. Human availability is subtle and complex. My unique availability is determined in the first place by my life call. This call is revealed to me partly in light of my personality structure, life history, environment, temperament, talents and deficiencies. For example, Einstein, van Gogh, Ghandi, and Florence Nightingale were persons who in response to their life call made themselves available to humanity generously and effectively. However, the style and tone of their availability was quite different for each of them.

Einstein was called to make himself available to humanity as a creative theoretical scientist. Thanks to his faithfulness to his call the world of culture and science profoundly changed. Paradoxically, the unsparing availability of Einstein for science was possible only because he made himself less available as a socialite or social reformer. Florence Nightingale, on the contrary, could make herself fully available to the sick and wounded in the war only by making herself less available for science.

This illustrates briefly that every call with its subsequent availability implies a corresponding unavailability. As long as I remain an adolescent, living a prevowed life, I shall maintain my availability for many disparate enterprises. When I discover my call to a fundamental life form at the end of adolescence and begin traversing the road toward adulthood, I am forced necessarily to limit my availability but this very limiting means a deepening. For example, when I am called to be a religious, I have to be available first of all as a witness to the sacred dimension of my cultural activities, whether they are intellectual, aesthetic, social or manual. I can be deeply available for this dimension when I limit my participation in other dimensions. One way of doing so is to replenish my presence to the Holy in recollection, for this presence may have been dissipated during the working day. While recollecting myself in prayer and silence, I cannot be available at that precise moment to others. In religious life, therefore, this is one instance of the necessary unavailability which must be fostered so that I can be fully available as the unique cultural-religious participant I am called to become.

Human life as response to the primary life call and to a fundamental life form is thus a dialogue of availability and unavailability. For the religious this dialogue is restricted to the characteristic availability-unavailability structure which is his as a religious. Within this fundamental life form he is called to specific tasks, each one of which implies in turn its own availability-unavailability dialogue. If I am called to be a teacher in a university I have to make myself less available to various other social, pastoral and apostolic demands in order to be more available as a profound and scholarly teacher, who is on par with his secular counterparts. The amount of reading, reflection and preparation needed to develop a radiant cultural and intellectual availability to the world of science or art necessitates a corresponding withdrawal from other activities and encounters. On the other hand, when I am called to be available as a chaplain to all the university students, I have to make myself less available to study as a full-time occupation in order to be more available as a pastor to as many students as I can reach.

Betraying my specific availability is betraying my specific call and therewith betraying my deepest self. If many people would be seduced by some contemporary cause to betray their specific availability, society would lose its balance and sooner or later seriously damage its all-rounded cultural unfolding.

Partial Invitations and Life Call

I am a dialogue with the Eternal as calling in the variety of my life situations. In this dialogue I become my unique self. However, while I am always called, I may not always be aware of the call as call. To be sure, I may experience many invitations from institutions, situations and others to make myself available in a certain way. However, not every invitation to be or do something touches my life orientation as a whole.

For instance, if I were invited to join a card club, I could not say that this invitation is as fundamental to my life call as the invitation to marry a person or to assume the celibate religious life form. On the other hand, every partial invitation can be related to my eternal call insofar as everything in my life can and should be brought into harmony with my life call as it reveals itself to me during my personal history.

Every invitation points to my call-ability and may at certain moments reveal me to myself as a being called upon. While none of these partial invitations should be confused with the life call itself, they must be seen in relation to this call. "Call" is identified here with the call to consecrate my life in a total, final and transcendent way to the Sacred within one or the other fundamental life forms, such as in marriage, in single life or in religious life. In this invitation, my whole being is called in an ultimate way. I may even experience the eternal call itself as touching me directly in my most unique self.

The beautiful response of Mary, "Be it done unto me according to Your word," expresses a totally faithful Christian response to the life call as revealing the lasting life situation in which one is to find his salvation. Mary's response expresses the awareness of being totally called upon by the Eternal and at the same time the unawareness of how one's concrete salvation and self-unfolding will happen within this life situation. The same response signifies an attitude of total readiness to listen to the call of the Eternal, the only attitude worthy of expression when one is confronted by the call to consecrate his life.

In order to clarify the difference between the central event of the life call and my authentic response to it, on the one hand, and on the other hand, the various partial forms of invitation, it is necessary to discuss in turn seduction, request and offer, appeal and call.

Seduction

One form of invitation to be or do something is seduction. Seduction does not direct itself to my full humanity. It plays on my needs, passions, fantasies, dreams and passing excitements, which have neither filtered through the reasonable evaluation of the managing me nor through me as self or spirit. One who seduces me plays on my needs, while at the same time clouding my responsibility and freedom.

It may happen, for example, that a community sets out to attract young people for its junior seminary or for its aspirancy by vividly depicting the attractions of sports and play. This picture may influence the unconscious needs of the young and may seduce them to join a junior seminary or aspirancy for the wrong reasons.

Another example of seduction may be found in a minority group where temporarily the only outstanding and relatively educated persons happen to be priests, sisters and brothers. A family in this minority sector of society may be devoured by unconscious needs for status and position which in turn are passed on to their children. They assimilate unwittingly their parents' needs and fears. In this case, such an overwhelming need may become the ideal opening for seduction. When this need is activated by the seductive person, it may be almost impossible to resist the strong pull of desires emanating from the awakened drive. If the family or some other significant person were to entice the child to enter junior seminary or aspirancy with the unspoken implicit suggestion that this will bring status to the child and his family, as nothing else can, the family and the child may be taken in by seduction masking as call.

Seduction is responded to not with a rationally weighed promise nor with an inspired commitment or consecration but with fascination. The person is almost hypnotized by the possibility of fulfilling the needs which are gnawing at his inner life and freedom. While he may believe that seduction masking as call invites him to consecrate his whole being for always to the Sacred, in fact seduction and subsequent fascination are by nature partial, periodical and mundane.

Seduction does not direct itself to me as a whole person but only to one or a few specific partial needs that are exploited by the seducer, possibly with the best of intentions. In the latter case the seducer is as much a victim of seduction as the seduced. Seduction is periodical or time-bound in its affect insofar as no lasting life style can be maintained on basis of mere need fulfillment, for mere fascination cannot satisfy for a lifetime. Seduction as distinguished from the call is not transcendent but mundane in its basic orientation. The transcendent never speaks to isolated need or fear to the detriment of one's growth in spirit and reason. While seductive elements may accompany a truly humane and divine invitation and may even at times initiate such invitations, it must be remembered that growth in human and spiritual response to such an invitation implies a gradual purification of unenlightened fascination.

In the beginning, when I have not yet learned to distinguish the realm of the spirit, my experience of the call may be muddled and confused. All my perceptions are likely to be influenced by unelucidated needs, defenses, anxieties and fantasies. Moreover, the person who invited me to enter religious life may be one who did not purify himself of his own needs and confusions. Therefore I hear in him not only the pure voice of the call that is calling me as a unique spiritual being but also his unconscious needs for status, remuneration and the success of his religious community or of himself as the successful vocational director of that community. If my call is really a true call, my experience of it and my response to it may be gradually purified of these human accretions, which will retard my growth in spirituality.

Request and Offer

With both request answered by a promise, and offer answered by a contract, we move to a higher plane of the human personality than in the case of seduction. Request and offer address themselves to the reasonable and realistic managing me. Neither request nor offer try to trick me, to play on my weakness, or to find my soft spot. Both may be accompanied by such seductive attempts as flattery or vague tidings of the unfortunate things in store for me if I pass up this "rare" chance to better myself. However, dehumanizing attempts like these are no longer part of request and offer themselves. They are added enticements which eventually may spoil the nature of request and offer and reduce them to the realm of seduction.

My answer to a request should not be in the form of fascination which makes it more difficult for me to evaluate the request reasonably and to respond freely to what is asked of me. My answer is meant to be a promise, the fruit of quiet deliberation freed from disrespectful invasions by the other on my life of needs and fears. Similarly the contract I sign in response to an offer should be the result of a free decision, promoted by the person who makes me an offer. Instead of marring the human side of an offer by seductive suggestion and vague warnings, the person offering me a contract should promote my freedom of consent by protecting me from my own fantasies and needs, which this particular contract cannot fulfill.

While the invitation implied in request and offer is fundamentally more human than that in seduction, it is not yet the deepest invitation to my whole being that can be honored with the name call or calling and which I answer with a total and final consecration of my life. These two forms of invitation to the managing me remain partial, periodical and mundane in their orientation. Request and offer are directed toward the managing me and not toward me as true self or spirit implying the whole of my personality. Request and offer are partial insofar as they invite me to make myself available for some task or action which involves only a limited number of my potentialities, energy, time and talents.

By their very nature promise and mere contract do not ask me to bind myself for a lifetime. Not only are request and offer partial and periodical; they are also mundane or intraworldly in their scope. However, they do not exclude the possibility that I may give my promise or sign a contract with personal reference to the Transcendent. When I am living in deep faith in my life call, it is no problem for me to relate every partial invitation to this lasting call and to the Eternal who is calling. Therefore, ideally every request and offer extended to me will be seen against the horizon of my life call. Nonetheless, I can make a promise that is valid and a contract that is binding with no reference to the Transcendent. The same cannot be said of the call to a life form which I can answer fully only by consecrating the whole of my being to the Sacred.

We have seen that seduction is sometimes substituted for the call and fascination for consecration. Also request or offer may take the place of the experience of the call, and promise and contract may displace consecration. This perversion is most likely to take place in an organizational and utilitarian civilization. Under the impact of these trends, even religious communities may become well-organized service associations or public utilities. The manpower needed to assist civilian institutions to cure certain ills of society may force the leaders of religious communities turned corporation to recruit more workers by depicting the social service aspect more than the religious life form itself. The more religious communities become service corporations or public utilities, the more tempting it is to imitate the features of other service corporations, which are not rooted in the fundamental religious life form.

When superiors and spiritual directors turn into executives and board officers, employees in their religious service corporations are bound to see themselves sooner or later as corporate employees who have the right to bind themselves by only a temporary promise or contract with the corporation, which they can renew when it expires. From the corporate point of view, this arrangement would be advantageous too. The religious service corporation would not have to renew the contract with those who prove themselves less productive and effective and therefore diminish the overall effectiveness of the religious corporation.

One can say nothing against the right of people to organize service corporations which administer to those in society who are in need of education, bodily care and social service. One has to admire such service organizations even more so when they want to be inspired by religious ideals which the members promote and protect in one another by living together in accordance with a common rule. One must praise their wisdom and foresight which provides that corporation members sign up only for a certain period and be given the opportunity to renew or not to renew their contract. The only thing to be avoided at any price is that one would confuse such a service corporation with something totally different, namely, religious life as a fundamental lasting life form and as the center of religious value radiation in the culture.

Once this distinction is clear, one would hope to see numerous service corporations emerging to contain the men and women who want to become contracted employees in a service which promises at the same time to foster and protect their own religious aspiration. They can foreseeably do much good for church and society, and they would enable the few who are called to the lasting religious life form to live this life of religious self-unfolding and religious witnessing in a more free and unencumbered way.

Service corporations could take over many of the institutions in which some religious may presently overextend themselves often to such a degree that their public service interferes with their religious calling. These service corporations may also offer a place to those religious who mistakenly entered religious life thinking that it was merely a religious service corporation and were painfully surprised when they discovered that the religious life form was something to which they felt not really called.

Appeal and Commitment

A more total mode of invitation is appeal to which I can respond in one of two ways: with refusal or with a full and total commitment of my life. The kind of invitation that moves me as self or spirit is called appeal to distinguish it from invitations directed to the other dimensions of my personality and from the call which is experienced on an even higher level of my true self or spirit. While seduction directs itself to the needy me, and request and offer invite the managing me, appeal is directed to my unique and true self or to me as spirit.

Appeal is not an invitation which tries to play on my needs, passions, desires or fantasies. Neither does it attempt to convince me by means of mere conceptual argument. The invitation to me as a whole person to give myself wholly to a life task appeals to that in me which is so profound and unique that it cannot be touched by mere practical arguments or syllogistic reasoning.

The intuition that I should commit my whole life unconditionally to a cause or to people cannot be awakened by means of propaganda, persuasion or enticement. Practical considerations may prepare me for the sudden event of enlightening appeal and the subsequent total commitment of my life. However, the event of insight into the fundamental meaning of my life and by subsequent affirmation of this meaning by commitment transcends mere practical and logical considerations. No amount of logic or practical understanding can ever explain to me the mysterious reason why I can unconditionally commit my whole being to a movement or cause.

Appeal is an invitation which awakens the awareness that I am destined to find my total fulfillment in a specific commitment. An appeal usually comes to me from someone's spontaneous witnessing to his own lived and inspired commitment to people, causes or movements. Appeal is the splendor of this person as committed spirit. It is the radiance of a dedicated self which makes me aware of my own deepest possibility for commitment.

93

Seduction, request and offer are answered by partial and periodical fascination, promise or contract. Appeal invites me to commit my life totally and finally. Appeal may also lead me to the experience of my life call. In that case commitment can grow to consecration, though this does not have to happen. If commitment does become consecration, it implies a transition from one level of my true self to its highest level. The lower level of me as spirit could be called the humanizing me. As spirit I am invited to humanize or spiritualize the organizational and needy aspects of my personality. As humanizing me, I am, moreover, invited to participate in some total and final way in the process of humanization or spiritualization of mankind. Commitment means giving myself finally and totally to some form of humanization of mankind which, at the same time, becomes the ideal form for me in which to humanize myself. History reveals numerous instances of ways in which such humanistic commitment contributed to the humanization of mankind and man.

The higher level of the real me could be called the sacralizing or consecrating me. Here I find myself at that most profound mysterious point of my being where I emerge continuously in my uniqueness from the ground of the Holy and where I am continuously invited and inspired to illumine all that I am and all that I encounter in this Light. I become aware that I am called to sacralize or to consecrate myself and my personal mode of participation in the process of humanization. This call to consecration is not necessarily at odds with the appeal to commitment

On the contrary, the call to consecration illumines, perfects and deepens the appeal to commitment. It grants human commitment its sacred complement; it binds the finite to the infinite; the temporal to the eternal; and it endows the human with its sacred point of reference. While appeal and commitment are still enclosed in the mundane, call and consecration are transcendent. Both commitment and consecration are final and total, though commitment is inner-worldly while consecration is transcendent.

All human beings, as we have seen, are called ultimately to consecrate their life in some way. This is the meaning of man as vow-ability and call-ability. Consecration brings every life form to its highest perfection. Marriage, for example, can remain on the mere mundane level, regarded as a commitment to one's marriage partner and family made on basis of an appeal to find and evolve a new family unit. This marriage is already infinitely more rich than a marriage based merely on the insufficient ground of fascination or on a mere promise or contract. Marriage, however, can obtain its highest meaning only when appeal deepens itself to call and when commitment in the form of a true marriage vow becomes a consecration to the Holy, who is the source of this call. No human life can reach its fullness and splendor as long as it refuses to become a consecrated life.

The celibate religious life form declares explicitly that it desires to be infinitely more than a mere mundane humanistic commitment. The religious life form is primordially an answer to a call experienced as the Holy calling. The total and final response of the religious is explicitly one of transcendent consecration to the Lord, which response witnesses that all men should elevate their lives at least implicitly to the level of call and consecration. For the religious all enticements, requests, offers and appeals are illumined by his call. They are all experienced as possible manifestations of the Lord uniquely calling him.

Dynamics of the Life Call

The life call is very different from my call to a specific life form. My life form is only one expression of my life call, albeit a most fundamental expression insofar as it sets the scene for the revelation of my life call as I vow my life and therewith end my spiritual adolescence. My life call thus places me in a definite time and place within which I am called by the Lord to be uniquely me. To know my call to a life form does not mean that I shall know my life call completely.

The life call, as we have said, is a mystery that covers the whole unique meaning of my life and makes me surpass each finite, temporal and concrete situation in which I find myself. The meaning of my life is not made by me alone nor is it made by any one concrete event. Each temporal situation is only a manifestation of my life call as a whole. Faith reveals that everything which happens to me is somehow an expression of my life call, whether or not I am able to read this expression. Fidelity to the life call implies a humble and patient openness to its future manifestations. This is the indefinite aspect of the life call, which is not yet fully definite in time and place, at least from my human perspective. I do not know, for example, what the future expressions of my life call may be and how they will happen within the life form I have chosen.

This experience of indefiniteness can be threatening. I cannot organize and manage what I do not yet know. This uncertainty and insecurity may make me fearful and anxious. To escape this anxiety, I may falsify my call by trying to define every detail of my life in advance. I may try to manipulate my life in such a way that there will be no possibility of surprise. But I am only deluding myself, for to the degree that I organize all the details of my life to that degree I am unfaithful to the mystery of my real life call. I lose my flexibility and my sense of adventure, and I become paralyzed by the rational outline of life I have projected.

The attempt to define my call with mathematical precision is rooted in the human inclination to objectivate ourselves in a thing-like fashion. We forget, however, that to be man is also to be undefined and unpredictable to some degree. If we were inclined only to objectivate ourselves, it would be bad enough, but we also suffer the inclination to objectivate others similarly. Just as I can paralyze myself, so too can I paralyze the other by reducing him and his calling to a mere definition. When I really convince him that I know his calling and all its future manifestations, I may make it impossible for him to unfold his sensitivity for possible new revelations of the life call that will come his way. Instead I should foster in myself and in the other awareness and acceptance of the relative indefiniteness of the life call so that we may both develop patient presence to the mystery and unexpected revelations of our life call.

Life Call, Life Form and Life Limitation

The most definite aspect of my life call is that of my fundamental lasting life form. Lived knowledge of this life form is a definite horizon against which the indefinite particulars of my life call may gradually reveal themselves. As we implied earlier when discussing the availability-unavailability structure of human life, the call to a fundamental life form, when affirmed, opens me to a specific field of possibilities and closes me by the same token to other fields of life and other types of possibilities. A field of dialectics emerges from this choice. From now on there will be a constant dialogue between the definite revelations of my life call within this special life form and the aspects of my life call which are still indefinite. I can discover these indefinite aspects only in dialogue with the variety of possibilities to be met within the scope of my fundamental life form and its historical unfolding.

Every fundamental life form thus implies necessarily some limitations. No matter what my life articulation may be, by its very nature it is limited and limiting. Otherwise it would not be a life form or life articulation. Take one concrete example: A man who commits himself to the marital life cannot live up to the fullness of this life form while dating other women as he did before he was married. Loss of such freedom is not a source of disturbance for him, since he realizes that the limitations inherent in his chosen life form are at the same time the necessary conditions for the kind of deepening that marriage can give to a person. If his marriage is good, he will relate intimately for a lifetime to his wife and children and grow in a way which would be impossible in a variety of temporary dates and engagements. The intensity of his family experience will give him an experience of self-unfolding which he could not find outside marriage.

The same is true for religious life as a fundamental life form. Its specific orientation of one's energy, attention, perception, emotions and actions — which we would not find in another life form — means that the religious gains unique possibilities for prayer, reflection, self-unfolding and cultural participation.

I can only begin to enjoy to the full the specific possibilities of my life form when I am able to live its limitations not as mere boundaries to my fanciful freedom but as desirable and necessary means of deepening myself within and because of these limits. In grateful presence to the possibilities of my life form, which I would find nowhere else, I may avoid fixation on those aspects not present in this life form. If I live in exclusive concentration on what my life form *is not*, instead of being present to what it *is*, I shall literally live in nothingness. Living in the nothingness of what my life form is not, I may easily come to despair about the emptiness and meaninglessness of life.

Seeing only what my life form does not offer, I may be seriously tempted to move out of it. I may imagine that another life form offers the things I am missing in my present one. While I may be right to a degree, I must never forget that each life form has its own inherent limitations. While the choice is mine to make, I should never delude myself by thinking a mere change in life form will cure my despair and fully satisfy my desires, for what I may really be seeking is a fantasy life of boundless freedom. Though changes may be made for legitimate reasons, one can never deny in focusing on the possibilities of a life form its inevitable limitations.

Life Form and the Threefold Path

As we have seen earlier, every life form when lived in a consecrated way implies the threefold path of respectful listening to the call of the Holy in events, respectful or chaste presence to the call of the Holy in self and others, and respectful presence to the call of the Holy in culture and nature. Man is structured in such a way that he can relate to the Sacred fully only in this triad of religious attitudes. This structure is already present in me before I am aware of it and before I affirm it by vowing myself to its emerging incarnation in one or the other specific life form.

Long before I am aware of my vow-ability in light of the threefold path, I am already a prepresence or unconscious tending toward the Sacred in people, events and things. This overall unconscious threefold prepresence to the Holy that I already am is limited by my basic personality form. This means that I am born with certain inherent limitations, genetically, psychologically and spiritually. These limitations determine my concrete prepresence to the Sacred long before I become aware of this presence and long before I am able to make this radical prevowed prepresence to the Sacred an explicit, affirmed vowed presence.

While every person is called to be present to the Holy, each will discover the Sacred in events, people and things in a specific way. The gifted musician, born with a refined ear for sound, is likely to discover the

Sacred in the beauty of melody more than a person not gifted with this sensitivity. Likewise a person with a unique ability to assist others graciously in their unfolding will more easily affirm the unique call of others and be more able to experience the presence of the calling Lord in these persons. This is what is meant when we say that one's personality form limits his prevowed human life.

The life form or life articulation which I choose later in life should be in tune with the limited personality form that is already radically present in me at birth. While it is true that my vowed life form should be in harmony with my fundamental personality form, the two can never be identical. I shall find in any life form aspects and dimensions that are necessarily at odds with certain aspects of my personality. As long as there is no fundamental opposition between my personality form and my life form, there is no problem for such discrepancy is normal and unavoidable. However, if there should be an absolute opposition between my personality form and a prospective life form, then it may mean usually that I am not called to this life form.

For example, I may suffer a sexual deviation which makes it impossible for me to live the marital life form at least as long as this deviation dominates me and my relationship to others. Or I may have a temperament which makes it impossible for me to live with some peace within even the most broadminded religious community. In this case again, there is a clear indication that I may not be called to the religious life form as it is lived in the West today.

A peripheral discrepancy between personality form and life form may also arise. For instance, I may harbor a temperamental aversion for the administrative duties which necessarily accompany the marital life form as lived in contemporary civilization. Another example may be a certain aversion for food prepared in large quantities as is necessarily the case in religious communities which have large houses.

While these latter characteristics may be truly mine and perhaps unchangeable, they are not so central to my personality form that they would make it impossible for me to adapt to one or the other shared life form developed by humanity over the centuries. No shared life form can adapt itself to all minor idiosyncracies of personality and temperament. Common life would be impossible if it had to be in tune with every aspect of the personality of its members. For if a life form would try to adapt itself totally to all possible minor aspects of one member's personality, it would be impossible for the same life form to adapt itself totally to another member with his own peripheral idiosyncracies different from those of the former.

Spiritual Adolescence: Period of Transition to the Vowed Life

As I grow in awareness of what I fundamentally am, I also become familiar with the variety of life forms and life styles within which the threefold path can be lived. Still undecided about the life form that will be in tune with my unique personality form, I keep on learning, experiencing and trying things out, hoping to find with God's grace the direction in which I can vow myself.

This period of search, self-discovery, and discovery of the world is the period of spiritual adolescence. It is not a time which is over for all at exactly the same moment. Its length is dependent, among other things, on the complexity and potential richness of my personality, on the confusion or relative clarity that may have surrounded me in childhood, on the amount of courage or anxiety in regard to accepting responsibility, and last but not least on the complexity of my cultural background and education. The more I am exposed to possibilities of life, æsthetic, scholarly, scientific, and religious, the more I may have to work through before it becomes clear to me what my life can best center itself in.

The length and intensity of my spiritual adolescence is compounded by the fact that I live in a society that tends to streamline people and to foster loss of self in crowds, collective organizations and cliques. The right decision to vow myself in a specific direction depends on a deep awareness of my unique individuality. Only in the depth of my uniqueness can the call of the Lord be heard. In listening and responding to this call, I am most alone. Nobody can listen for me. Nobody can respond. Neither crowd nor clique nor collectivity can relieve me from my aloneness at that central moment in my life when I decide to make the first and fundamental move to overcome my spiritual adolescence and vow my unique personality in one or the other final direction. When at this moment my decision is deeply influenced by a clique, crowd or collectivity, it should be distrusted, for no true personal decision can be a collective thing.

The great life decision, which ends the indecisions of spiritual adolescence, places me on the road to becoming concretely and lastingly available to events, people and things as invitations of the Lord as calling. The vow is an affirmation of the dynamic orientation to the Sacred which I already am. It expresses my willingness to consecrate my life to the manifestations of reality within a lasting life form because they are sacred or holy not in themselves but in the Lord who sanctifies them or calls them to sanctification. He calls all events, people and things to reveal His divine perfection and to play a role in the unfolding of His creation and in the salvation of mankind. The decision to vow one's life implies for all believing people a consecration to the Holy. For the Christian the Holy is experienced in a very specific and personal way. For him the Holy and Sacred as a dimension of events, people, culture and nature has a special meaning which he distinguishes clearly from divine being itself.

Vowing my life is thus not merely a matter of

making myself available to respectful listening to reality as an invitation of the Holy. Rather I vow to make myself available within a concrete life form shared with others and developed over generations. I discover in this period of transition from prevowed to vowed presence that there are certain fundamental life forms which make this concretization possible. I may share such a common life form with many, all the while living it uniquely. As I awaken to my freedom and personal call, I experience the Sacred as call. The first initiative was not mine but that of Him who is calling. The only thing I can do is to cooperate with the divine initiative that is gradually revealed to me.

The call is a grace and a gift. My response to it is a grace and a gift too. It is grace which leads me to consecrate my life in one or the other life form and what I bring to this life form is God's own gift of my unique personality and self-emergence.

One of the possible life forms within which I can live my threefold orienation to God is the religious life form, which like other life forms, has unfolded in history. Participation in this life form is therefore participation in human history and in the wisdom and experience of generations. It also implies a readiness on my part to enrich, correct and deepen this expression of human unfolding so that the light of contemporary insight can complement the light of past experience. Only when I have steeped myself in the fundamentals of religious life can I risk renewal of this fundamental life form in faithfulness to the wisdom of generations.

Regarding the historical origins of religious life, I find awaiting me a life form which attempted to relate man in a special way to the Infinite and Eternal. This was its primordial purpose. In East and West the religious celibate life form emerged when the individual person felt so oppressed by other life forms and organizations that he experienced a painful separation between the longing of his heart for the Sacred and his involvement in the world. He felt alienated from the sanctuary of his inner self, from the sacred ground where he could meet the Transcendent.

Religious life began when these persons in and through a fundamental, lasting life form attempted to regain the sense of sacred uniqueness before the Holy. As religious life developed, it often happened that these persons left their families, cities, and corporate church organizations to find those solitary places where they could converse with the Divine. Holy men in the East and the hermits and desert fathers in the West shared this striving to find the Sacred in solitude. Their attempt presents us with a fundamental characteristic of religious life that distinguishes it radically from any other life form, namely that of leaving *relatively* behind my family, church, civil and social organizations in order to find some measure of solitude which complements my predisposition toward full presence to the Transcendent.

The life form chosen by these men and women proved at the same time to be a witness to the necessity of some celibate solitary presence for all men. Therefore this life form was soon recognized in East and West as a religious-cultural center of value radiation, sustaining and fostering the value of recurrent moments of solitary presence to the Sacred. At times the appreciation others had for the atmosphere of sacred solitude which these religious had created, became so intense that the solitude of the religious themselves was threatened. People eager to restore in themselves their possibility for unique solitary presence to the Sacred flocked to these first religious for enlightenment. This may have been one reason why the first religious, in an effort to protect their solitude, chose to live together in groups and establish certain rules of life and conduct which would insure a measure of privacy and promote the life of religious presence they chose to live.

Originally they had left city, church organizations, family and social relationships because they had experienced full involvement in such as contrary to their predisposition and special vocation. Later, to protect a minimum of sacred privacy and solitude in spite of visitors and disciples, they formed groups of persons with like desires and predispositions to live in religious solitude.

Later on still, this life form developed a special branch of witness for presence to the Sacred called the active or participative form of religious life. The core meaning of this life is its attempt to manifest to mankind the way in which ever-renewed presence to the Divine enables one to integrate this deepest presence within a cultural participation which may take many styles and manners from manual labor to scholarly research, according to one's ability and disposition.

The religious life form, as we have seen, originated in answer to the need for a special life opportunity to be fully present to the Holy and to listen to the Divine Call to my unique person. The original celibate religious had no corporate community whatsoever. The corporate religious community is only a secondary development in religious life. Thus the corporate community receives its sole justification and meaning from the celibate solitary meaning of religious life.

It is clear that no one should enter this life who does not have some prior ability for relaxed solitude, serene aloneness and joyful privacy. An initiate to this life form who discovers that he is totally incapable of being alone in a relaxed and joyful way may be in for a lifetime of suffering if he insists on entering a religious community. He will not only torture himself but he may also become a source of suffering for others.

The celibate solitude of religious life is not merely a question of aloneness in the physical sense. The celibate religious life form refers to a style of life sometimes spent alone, sometimes together with others in a life form that promotes the growth of the person as a unique manifestation of the Lord. Christian religious life creates the conditions in which Christ can appear in a most unique way in each religious, so that a community of religious can radiate a variety of facets of Christ whose infinite richness of virtue can never be exhausted. Celibate religious life in Christianity is an attitude of self-unfolding in and with Christ as present in me in a unique, original way.

The solitary and communal modes of celibate life are not isolated instances of personal unfolding without relation to one another. On the contrary, the celibate religious life form is a rhythm of aloneness and togetherness, both sustaining the one fundamental meaning of this life form which is the personal unfolding of the celibate. The liturgy of the Christian religious community is itself an outstanding example of this dialectical relationship between aloneness and togetherness. True liturgical togetherness is neither the togetherness of the contagious crowd nor the regimented togetherness of a well-disciplined collectivity.

Since true religious presence can take place only in a human person, in the self, liturgy is dependent for its facilitation on the personal religious presence of its participants. True liturgy in the religious community is a masterful expression of the rhythm of aloneness and togetherness in the liturgical participants. The liturgy as a whole is meant to be appropriated by each participant personally, in a way which does not destroy the common truth of its message for all but which deepens and specializes the truth to what it means for me. Not all messages of a liturgical celebration can speak to each one of the participants with the same intensity. Consequently, each participant adopts before God what he is able to adopt deeply and meaningfully at this moment of his life history. To the degree that he personalizes in celibate uniqueness liturgical meaning, to that degree true prayer and true religious experience, which are always personal, may take place.

From this moment of inspiring aloneness, the liturgical participant returns with new animation to the whole liturgy he is sharing with others. His participation now carries the deep religious presence, the profound awareness of the Divine that only a person as person can experience. Others in turn who were graced with a similar personal experience may exercise the same appeal, incarnating it in their participation in the common liturgy. As a result the living liturgy of the community becomes permeated by a strong force of appeal inviting each participant to appropriate in deepest aloneness the unique personal invitation of Christ speaking to him through the common liturgy.

The liturgy of a community, as rhythm of aloneness and togetherness in service of unique unfolding, can be seen as a paradigm of the other aspects of celibate religious life in community. The corporate community renders it unavoidable that the celibate religious share a necessary minimum of common rules and customs in regard to housing, nourishment and social-economic organization. This unavoidable togetherness may never reach the absorbing intensity of family life, otherwise it would make no sense to leave family life in order to live a more free celibate religious life.

Moreover, minimum forms of togetherness must be organized and lived in such a way that they promote the unique unfolding of each celibate religious. As in the liturgy, this will be the case only when each celibate appropriates uniquely the deepest meaning of these forms of togetherness. When he does so he is able to bring to his living of these forms a personal animation and conviction which is an appeal to others to awaken their own uniqueness while sharing the same common forms of life.

Entrance to the Consecrated Life: Transitional Experiences

We have considered in general man's vow-ability and call-ability and have attempted to describe his whole prevowed life as a preparation for the vowed life. The vowed life implies for the average human being the commitment to one or the other life form. When this commitment is related to the Sacred, and when for the Christian, it is related to Christ, we may

112

call such a vowed life a consecrated life. Having re-
flected generally on the vowed life of man, we may
move toward a more specific consideration of the consecrated life by reflection on the various experiences
which signal the period of transition between the
prevowed and vowed life.

Our analysis of the vowed and prevowed life, especially in the transitional period, entails a dynamic,
developmental approach. What we are reflecting upon
are the more or less dramatic events which occur in a
human being as he begins to realize that somehow he
must vow himself in one or the other direction if he
is to unfold personally and spiritually. This is a crisis
period in the life of every man. We are pulled by the
awareness that we have to make a decision that will
influence us for time and eternity, as no decision before or after will do. The dramatic crisis of this period
is heightened by the inescapable realization that
many other factors in childhood and early adolescence
have exerted great influence on us already. Their impact will not disappear as we move toward our life
decision.

Birth was the first event for which I could not be
responsible. No freedom of insight was involved in
this decision. The situation into which I am born is
set. By comparison, the vow signals my birth as a free
human being who himself chooses his life orientation.
It is a new birth for which I alone am responsible; its
consequences will shape my unique destiny.

The awareness that I am standing at the crossroads of life before I vow myself brings home to me again the crucial drama of this period of transition. How long does this spiritual adolescence last? When did it begin? When will it end?

In the first place, it is impossible to establish precisely the time limits of this period. Such predictability, if possible, would presuppose that the transition from a prevowed to a vowed life can be organized like a time sheet. If so, it would be only a peripheral aspect of man, but this transition is one of life itself. It is a transition of human presence, implying growth in lived awareness and self-discovery, growth in personal responsibility and presence to the Eternal, growth in faith and spiritual fortitude. Growth of spirit can never be timed. It is a gift that cannot be forced or compelled. As a young person, I can only ready myself for this gift by fostering the right conditions for its reception within myself and my environment.

Mine should be the humble and patient awareness that true light comes of its own accord and refuses to illumine those who try violently to capture it. Even the creation of the right conditions for this personal enlightment cannot be timed, for these conditions imply the emergence of certain sensitive and receptive attitudes, the development of which is highly dependent on the life situation in which I find myself.

We have mentioned before the external and internal aspects of one's life situation. These include among others the complexity of the culture within which I have to select my specific life orientation, my personality, character and temperament, and the spiritual and cultural richness of my family history and environment. All of these factors may help or hinder my growth.

Added to this general view of the life situation is for the Christian the mystery of redeeming grace. Living since baptism in the realm of the Holy Spirit, the vowing of life for the Christian is not merely a consecration of his life to the Sacred but to the Sacred revealed in Christ. The Holy Spirit speaks to the individual Christian in imponderable ways and events. This message of my Lord is more gift than any gift can be, for divine grace cannot be compelled. But before going further into the aspects of the life call for the Christian, we can look at the fundamental dynamics which manifest themselves generally in the period of transition before consecration.

Experience of my Fundamental Uniqueness

The crisis of the moment of vowing is related to the crisis I experience when I discover myself as more than the needy me and the managing me, when I discover my uniqueness as true self or spirit. Usually around late adolescence, I experience perhaps for the first time that simple need fulfillment or organization of self and environment is not sufficient for a meaningful life. At such moments I feel imprisoned by the immediacy of my situation; a hunger for deeper meanings overtakes me and I may experience an unexplainable boredom. Being a member of a clique, crowd or collectivity no longer satisfies me. I feel myself uniquely called by something that transcends my immediate preoccupations with family or group. I feel as if I belong ultimately only to the whole and Holy that unifies me and redeems me from a scattered incoherent life.

This moment of unexpected self-revelation normally evokes anxiety. I no longer feel protected by the crowd; I cannot hide behind the responses of the group in which I once felt so wholeheartedly involved. And yet what seems to be calling me is so indefinite, strange and mysterious that I long to return to the clear cut categories that used to guide the managing me in the mastery of my world. I long to return to the safety of this prior life but I cannot.

Not yet aware that the managing me can be integrated within my newly discovered self enhances my fear that I may be lost if I give in to the urge to live on the self level. I cannot yet see that the managing me is good and necessary, that it is the means by which I can structure my presence within my daily environment and incarnate my higher inspiration concretely. Therefore I may experience the tendency to regress solely to the level of the managing me. But once the self is awakened there is no turning back without feelings of guilt and dissatisfaction. I can repress or deny this experience but I can never make it disappear. Neither can I convince myself that I can find myself by mere fulfillment of my needs and passions on the level of the needy me.

These dramatic shifts from level to level represent a movement of circular self-disclosure. In each one of these shifts — from presence on the self level to presence on the level of the managing me and the needy me — I am influenced by what I experience on the other level. In light of the fleeting but unforgettable experiences of my true self, all that I do as the organizer of my life and environment and as a person who takes care of basic needs and desires is transformed. Now that I have experienced my true self, I see more clearly what life orientation I can choose on basis of what I know about my self as an organizer and as a person with a specific constellation of needs and desires.

The experience of my fundamental uniqueness also makes me aware of how different I am from others, even on the level of need and practicality. Circular self-disclosure prepares me for the insight that it is necessary to make a unique life choice. Gradually I come to accept that only in solitude am I able to move out of daily practicality and away from the group which prevents me from discovering myself on a deeper level. In the aloneness of my room, I may recap-

ture the experience that I am more than mere need
or practicality. This coming home to myself is a typical discovery of every human being, for only man
can be concerned about his life as a whole, about his
life orientation and about his ideal life form. Only man
is self-presence, self-reflection, and self-expression.

The Christian dimension also undergoes change
during this initial transitional experience. When I am
a Christian, the process of self-disclosure entails a
new discovery of Christ. As needy me, Christ may
have been the person I asked to grant me the fulfillment of certain needs and desires. On the level of the
managing me, the Lord may have been the divine
helper assisting me in the execution of my practical
plans and projects. Now on the level of the true self,
I may experience Him at the core of my uniqueness
calling me to be my most unique self, intimately
united in, with and through Him in answer to the
will of the Father. My Lord is experienced not only
as a divine friend who can fulfill my needs, or as a
divine aid who can assist me in my projects, but as
the source of my Christian uniqueness who makes me
be in a new and divine way in this world.

From what we have said, it may be clear that
when I vow or consecrate my life without the experience of self-disclosure, I am building on sand. I should
not try to escape these deeply human experiences nor
should I fear the loneliness characteristic of spiritual
adolescence. It is lonely when I discover that I am

different from everyone else, that I am totally and radically responsible for my own life. This experience may evoke such great anxiety that I instinctively try again to disappear in crowd or clique, forgetting that all I would succeed in doing is escaping the self-discovery without which I can never vow my life in a responsible way.

Experience of Transcending the Functional and Needy Me

A second experience of this transitional period leading also to temporary loneliness, is that of transcending the functional and needy me, first negatively then positively. During this experience I not only feel alienated from other people and things that fulfilled my needs but also from functions which once meant a great deal to me. Not even things I used to do with pleasure satisfy me as they did before. I experience their irrelevance, transitoriness and vanity.

This boredom is the negative phase of the discovery of my true self or spirit. It is negatively experienced because I do not yet experience what my true self is. I feel only the limitations of mere need fulfillment or of being merely a good functionary in society, somehow sensing that if my functional effectiveness is the ultimate meaning of my life, my life is not really that meaningful. But in the loneliness of this moment of self-disclosure, I discover myself as transcending the needy and functional me. This experience of my true humanity allows me to transcend mere function-

119

alism and becomes positive to the degree that I am able to anticipate and appreciate the meaning that will be mine when I am able to live on the level of the unique self, when I finally vow my life.

The restlessness of this period may veil the vowable presence that I am. However, it can become a creative restlessness when it leads me to search for a vowable life articulation. Keeping this creative restlessness alive may thus help me to come to my deepest mode of self-unfolding.

It is not so strange that in this time of crisis, when transcending the functional and needy me, a crisis of faith may also take place. Previous to this moment, my faith may have been a functional faith, merely an adherence to a practical list of do's and don'ts. I may have identified my functional faith with the total faith experience that will be mine only when I begin to live on the self level. As soon as the true self announces itself to me, a mere functional faith becomes dull and routine. Self-disclosure gives me an inkling of how much more faith and religious experience could mean to me.

The danger is that my mistaken identification of total faith with functional faith may lead me to reject faith altogether. Another danger is that the discovery of faith on the self level may so excite me that I abolish entirely the necessary functional aspect of faith on the practical level. In that case I would soon be trying in vain to live an unincarnated faith, no longer truly human or rooted in my real presence to the everyday world.

Experience of Self as Limited Presence

In our analysis thus far, we have described the period of life that prepares me for the vow as a series of dynamic experiences that influence one another in a circular movement of self-disclosure. We have also described the experience of self-discovery and the experience of transcendence of the needy me and the functional me. Another discovery, which also prepares me for the moment of vowing my life, is the experience of self as limited presence and as finiteness.

The experience of my limitations reveals to me increasingly that I cannot orient my life in all possible directions at the same time, for my life is limited in space and brief in time. Therefore at a certain moment I must begin to focus my life and its development in a limited direction.

Awareness of personal limitation is bound to my former transitional experiences. At the same time that I become aware of my self and of the needy and functional me, I experience my unique self as an openness to the whole and the Holy. Against the horizon of the whole and Holy, I experience deeply the limitation of my life. I experience my nearness to death, the minuteness of my possibilities, the finiteness and tentativeness of my own wisdom and insight. These experiences are only vaguely present to me; I cannot precisely conceptualize them but neither can I deny their presence. Initially it may be sheer torture to live within worlds which seem to tear me apart: the world of radiant openness to the whole and Holy and the world of concrete daily functional living where I seem able to do so little.

To escape living in the tension of these polarities, I may flee into a fantasy world where I can perform rare feats and live numerous lives. At other times, depending on the situation, I may be tempted to take drugs to induce a temporary feeling of expansion of consciousness and of liberation from daily limitations. At other times, again, I may decide to drop out of society in search of a freedom and liberation from daily life that exists nowhere.

The only possible solution for this tension is to live it dynamically by consecrating my finite life within a fundamental life form. Vowing bridges the gap between presence to the whole and Holy and living my finiteness in daily life. Vow or consecration binds my life, married, single or religious, to a determined orientation to the whole and Holy to which my true self can be present only in a limited way. It endows daily life with the luster of the eternal, making each movement infinitely meaningful and granting a peace and serenity that no need satisfaction in isolation can ever give.

The experience of finiteness thus has a negative and a positive phase. It is negative insofar as the discovery of my finiteness in the light of the whole and

Holy can lead to discouragement and depression and positive insofar as I discover that I can bind my finiteness to the Infinite by vowing my life to the whole and Holy.

If I am a Christian, this latter phase is facilitated by the revelation that the Holy became man and lived among us as the radical union of finiteness and the Infinite. The Lord lived a most limited life in an obscure town in a small corner of the Roman Empire. He engaged in a public life, surrounded on all sides by the most limited persons and yet at the same time every moment was of infinite value and meaning because it was vowed to the will of the Father.

Experience of Life-Responsibility, Life-Guilt and Life-Sin

In this period of transition, I also undergo the experience of self as responsibility. Related to this latter experience is the possibility of life-guilt and life-sin. In such experiences, I become aware of myself as a person who transcends need and functionality and is called to realize in a unique though limited way, human and spiritual values discovered in moments of openness.

Emerging self-awareness forces upon me the anxious realization that I must do something with my life. I become aware of a unique call in the core of my being to make my life worthwhile and valuable. At the same time I feel that I am unbelievably free in regard to this call. I am able to respond or not to respond. Never before did I realize that my life was so much in my own hands. This awesome experience of responsibiilty opens to me another new experience which could be called the experience of life-guilt, not in regard to one or the other incidental transgression but in regard to my life as a whole.

When I do not respond to what I am convinced is my call, I cannot help but feel a deep, all-pervading guilt. It is the life-guilt which surges up from the depth of my being when I realize that I am wasting my life, that I am not making the most of what it should be within the limits of my possibilities. Life-guilt, as distinct from everyday guilt about incidental failings and deficiencies, is vague and undefined. I cannot precisely say what its object is, at least not in the same sense that I can readily identify the point at which I fell away from my moral code.

Life-guilt, on the contrary, is about life as a whole and as a possibility to be realized, life as undefined and yet as uniquely definite for me. Life-guilt may lead to an overall feeling of failure or betrayal, of waste and refusal due to my unwillingness to respond to my life call and its challenge to search tirelessly for the meaning of that call. It may be even more difficult to identify the source of this guilt when I am, for example, engaged in charitable enterprises which would seem to satisfy my life call but which do not prevent the recurrent pang that maybe I am wasting my life after all.

124

A betrayal of my life call can take place before I accept one or the other fundamental life form as well as after this acceptance. For as we have seen, vowing myself to one or the other life form in response to my call determines only the fundamental style, limits and possibilities within which my call will be gradually revealed to me. But each revelation of my personal calling by the Spirit offers a new occasion for betrayal, for refusal to respond, and leads to the subsequent experiences of life-guilt and of life-sin.

Paradoxically, however, the experience of life-guilt is a grace and a gift, for it exhorts me every time to return to my call. If I were to waste my life in a steady and stubborn refusal to respond to my life call, I may open the way to a growing feeling of boredom and cynicism, meaninglessness and despair. Due to a somewhat functional emphasis on isolated identifiable sins, I may have lost that vivid sense of responsibility for my life as a whole. This tragic loss may be overcome at the moment in the period of transition when I awaken to the awareness that I harm myself more fundamentally by wasting my life than by transgressing a particular aspect of my moral code.

Along with all the other experiences we have mentioned, the experiences of life-responsibility, life-guilt and life-sin ready me for the life decision that will end the period of spiritual adolescence. If these vital experiences have not come to a head before initiation into one or the other life form, I shall inevitably suffer

125

the consequences later on. For example, during initiation to the religious life form, a well-prepared master of religious living and his assistants can help the initiate through these preparatory experiences, which will be highly beneficial in later life. For without undergoing them, the vowed life is likely not to be rooted in the experiential ground it presupposes.

Lacking these experiences, the initiate may concern himself onesidedly with isolated endeavors which do not touch the meaning of his life as a whole. When later on certain practices, occupations or secondary meanings of the religious life form are questioned, changed or rejected, the unprepared initiate may feel tempted to leave religious life, which has from the beginning been identified with incidental devotions, customs, and enterprises unenlightened by the life call.

For the Christian, Christ exemplifies most movingly fidelity to the life call. His life should be the source of lasting inspiration for all those seeking to respond wholly within a chosen life style to the variety of unpredictable revelations of the mysterious call orienting their life. Christ's whole life is pervaded by a loving concern for the will of the Father. His three temptations in the desert are temptations not to follow the will of the Father but to betray it for the fulfillment of other human needs depicted enticingly by Satan. No matter in what way the will of the Father is revealed to Him, Christ surrenders to it, even if the anxiety of its consequences leads him to cry out in the anguish of the garden. The same faithfulness of His celibate religious presence to the call of the Father leads the Lord to sacrifice the tender bonds of family, telling His beloved mother, "Do you not know that I must be about my Father's business?"

Experience of Self as Prepresence to the Sacred

A last experience typical of the period of transition is the awareness that I am already a prepresence to the Sacred. Having described previously the experiences of myself as unique, as transcendence of the needy and the functional me, as presence to the whole in a limited way, and as responsibility for my life as a whole, we have seen that all these experiences lead to the awareness that I must commit my life to one or the other fundamental lasting life form. The experience of myself as prepresence to the Sacred leads in addition to the insight that my life dedication should not be simply an intramundane commitment but that it should be related to the Sacred to which I am already oriented in the depth of my being.

When I raise my commitment to a vow, it means both that I affirm the prepresence to the Sacred that I already am and that I turn this presence into a freely willed explicit presence. Awareness of my relation to the Sacred in the best moments of adolescence may lead, on the one hand, to a feeling of dissatisfaction with events, people and things isolated from their Sacred ground and, on the other hand, to a feeling of joy and serenity that my life is lifted toward the mystery that surrounds and carries us all. This dual experience then interacts spontaneously with all the other experiences of this transitional period and instills in me the conviction that the commitment of my life as a whole should be a true consecration. I know now that I want my life commitment to be illumined by the Holy and, when I am a Christian, I want my life as married life, single life or religious life to be consecrated to the Father in, through and with the Lord, to whom I am present in the core of my being.

The experiences we have described move me necessarily in the direction of consecration. The recurrent experiences of my limits, of the possible meaninglessness of my life, of its dispersion in a variety of isolated incidents and enterprises, and of my subsequent disintegration may lead me to find my ultimate meaning in response to the whole and Holy, which alone can illumine the limited presence I am. These negative experiences threaten my life and person, forcing me to ponder the whole of my life and inviting me to listen to the call that I am in the depth of my existence.

Unfortunately there is always taking place simultaneously a process of cultural and personal repression and distortion of these experiences. Contemporary civilization partly shields me against the impact of the emergence of personal awareness of the prepresence to the Holy that I already am. People representing this aspect of my civilization exhort me to be practical, to make a good match, to get a job and to forget about all these floating ideas and feelings. In spite of cultural shielding, however, I may be able to protect the profound awareness that I must vow myself.

A fine marriage preparation or a good novitiate, for example, enables me to experience myself as vow-ability. In such favorable conditions, it is less easy to escape the responsible decision I must make in regard to the choice of a fundamental life form. This option does not guarantee, however, that I shall not be tempted again and again to shy away from the awareness that my life as a whole should be a life of fidelity to the Holy as calling. Even after vowing my life, my central purpose may be dimmed by other incidental ambitions which may seem more important to me temporarily than my presence to the Holy. Therefore I have to recall myself to my deepest authenticity in meditation, retreat and recollection.

If a vowed life desires to keep its intensity, it has to be renewed continuously. Though I may try to hide in the crowd, though the gang and the clique may silence momentarily the voice of God in my life, when I fall away I shall experience again the limits and meaninglessness of my life. Then the life-guilt that emerges may call me back to myself.

Even my best efforts may not be enough to make me wholly faithful to God as calling me in the sense of doing always what He demands of me. No matter, for then I can continue my human faithfulness by living in repentance. Repentance is a mode of reaffirmation of the call which I betray in my daily deeds. Repentance implies that I am willing to be fundamentally loyal to my call, though I cannot always live up to it in reality.

True guilt and the repentance which follows are a source of joy, for these are the means by which I can be present to the Holy in humble acknowledgment of my deficiency. I can bear the daily experiences of guilt, sorrow and repentance if I have faith in the Holy calling me and know that He who calls is infinitely good and merciful. The repentant Christian who knows that his Redeemer lives can bear guilt in the patient awareness that awaiting him always is infinite forgiveness and redemption.

Commitment and Consecration to a
Lasting Life Style

As we have seen, my life begins to center and direct itself definitely when I harmonize my plans and projects, desires and strivings with a consistent style of life shared by generations of men and women who, throughout history, have attempted to express the fullness of their humanity in specific forms of love and labor. Lonely attempts of self-integration, unsustained by these common designs, are liable to scatter like leaves in the wind. There comes a time when I feel invited to choose a common mode of life sustained by human community and history within which I can find and unfold myself.

As long as my life remains uncommitted, it remains somehow adolescent, tentative and diffuse. Many roads are open to me. My fantasy flutters with the passing breeze. While I envision far away places and fascinating feats, uprooting myself by scattered experiment, my life seems sporadic and dispersed. If I do not orient myself decisively, adolescence may never leave me. However, as soon as I decide on my life's consecration, my whole being begins to center itself in my chosen course of engagement.

When I choose to marry, for example, my thoughts, expectations, feelings, motives and comportment begin to center themselves in this project and its realization. I date so that I may discover the person whom I may love as a compatible companion for life. I dress and behave in such a way that someone still unknown may discover me as lovable too. During courtship I move away from the indefiniteness of adolescence and toward a lasting dynamic state of life. Already the preparation for the life form of marriage endows my personal existence with coherence and integrative design. The marriage commitment may or may not be the final outcome of this course. For no matter how beautiful my tentative encounter with the other may have been, it may prove still not deep enough to find and foster a lifelong togetherness. When I choose to commit myself to marriage, I choose also to sacrifice

131

the manifold dreams and designs of adolescence for the responsibilities of adulthood.

For most men some kind of personal commitment within the frame of a common life orientation ends the indefiniteness and the multiplicity of disjointed possibilities of adolescence. My commitment initiates my travel toward maturity. There is a prelude to this leap during which I hesitate and fluctuate before risking the delightful and disillusioning prospects of a binding form of life. At the moment of grace, however, my uncommitted life becomes lastingly consecrated or vowed.

Many may neither speak of their commitment nor reflect on it, but it is obvious from their very comportment that they have set their course and intend to maintain it, in spite of frustration, suffering and misunderstanding. There is about them a serenity and solidity which seems to be missing in those who did not yet vow their lives.

In any life form, the risk of disillusionment is present as profusely as the promise of fulfillment. Life form means as much finitude as openness to the infinite. If I flee my vow at the first hint of harshness, I may spend my life fleeing from one engagement to another, escaping myself and my opportunity for human growth. Instead of flourishing in the rich soil of a steady form of life, I may wither under continual transplantation from soil to soil, from life form to life form, for my roots can never reach deep enough. However, if I embrace the burden, beauty and challenge of my calling, I may attain that acceptance and transcendence which is the gift of the vowed and vowing life.

A vow may be regarded in many ways. I may view it from the outside, as a thing, and describe it as I would describe a stone or a slab of marble. I may say it means this or that in accordance with its definition by law and custom and with its outward appearance in the behavior of people who already vowed their lives.

Though worthwhile, this approach is not the only one, for as we have seen I may also explore vows and vowing from the dynamic viewpoint, from the perspective of the human person as unfolding. Then I may discover that vows are not merely a promise of conformity to custom, forms and formulæ objectivated in writings and institutions outside me. Such forms are implied and truly necessary to incarnate, express and support my commitment. The dynamic meaning of the human vow, however, is the vowing of a lasting life project, which implies the reorientation of my interiority, of my motivation, thought, imagination, expectation and emotion in tune with my new specialized presence in the world and in accordance with the necessary external shared expressions which support a specific vowed presence.

Vowing is first of all fidelity to a new style of motivation, imagining, expecting, feeling and perceiving.

133

To be sure, this fidelity needs also the appropriation and upholding of an external, common style of life. Unfortunately, the appreciation of the vowing life as a style of interiority is lessened in our behavioristic society. Many who set the tone of this civilization are experts in looking at things from the outside and measuring them merely in a detached way. The western world is permeated by a passion and compulsion for appearances and infinitely less concerned with attitudes and intentions. This climate may influence my appreciation of the life of the vows.

I may be inclined to live the vows only as something I do, or the way I behave. The vowed life may thus be experienced as merely a commitment in an outward manner to a code of behavior and appearance, neither appropriated inwardly nor renewed creatively in repeated moments of recollection. My main concern at the moment may even be to find how far outside this comportment I can go without harming vowed appearances and outward behavior. In the meantime I neglect my interiority; I neglect the personality dynamics to which I vowed myself primordially.

A religious, for example, may betray his vows inwardly long before he betrays them publicly. Merely acting outwardly as a religious is not enough to sustain one's vowed project of life. For vowing is also a matter of lived orientation and inner growth. It is appropriation of an inner life form; it is a reformation of the style of my motivation, thought, imagination, expectation, feeling, and perception in accordance with my calling. Consecration of my interiority is what really counts, especially in times of turmoil and confusion. If I see the consecrated life as mere external comportment, if I have not disciplined my expectations in accordance with an inner religious presence, I may not be able to maintain my fidelity.

Such structuring of my interiority does not mean willful, aggressive domination of my feelings and emotions. It is not an anxious, agitated questioning: Do I feel the right thing? Think the right thing? Imagine the right thing? Such compulsion destroys the art of living which implies a quiet and playful rootedness in my vowed orientation and in the sublime values which it reveals.

To vow my life is thus to vow the structure and movement of my motivation, thought, interest, expectation and perception. The center of interiority which makes such commitment possible, under the impetus of grace, is my will. My willingness to take an enduring stand commits me to a project of life which lasts as long as I maintain my initial decision.

The beginning of all willing is the movement of my interest and attention. When I allow my attention to shift and dwell beyond my life style, I am already willing in another dimension of human presence. Once my presence is totally turned toward a style of life incompatible with my original commitment, there may come a moment when I cannot immediately will otherwise.

If my vowed life is the married life, for example, I may already be unfaithful to my commitment when I begin to focus my interest and attention on another person as an eligible partner in married love. At the moment I redirect my perception and emotion in this way, a shifting of my will sets in and a gradual loss of fidelity may result. At a certain moment I may find myself so passionately absorbed in the other that no return to fidelity seems possible.

A married person commits himself to a style of motivation, thinking, perceiving, desiring, feeling and imagining that is different from that of an unmarried person. While the person before marriage can imagine many possible marriages, the married person should no longer dream like this, for it diminishes the flawless consistency of the style of interiority to which he is committed.

The person in religious life, like the married person, has to adopt gradually another way of thinking, feeling and imagining than he had before vowing his life as a celibate witness to the Holy. His vow, moreover, implies the decision to serenely guard the movement of his attention and imagination.

If I were to look longingly at a different life than that to which I committed myself and begin to center myself there, perhaps unwittingly, I would already be moving away from my calling. To look in another direction as an eligible life style for me, especially if I have already chosen one lasting form of life, is potentially fatal. This disloyal disorientation may be accompanied by a diminished attempt to truly *live* the values of my chosen life. Instead I compare my chosen values intellectually and abstractly with the values of other lives which have excited my imagination and emotion.

Flight into onesided abstraction potentially paralyzes my present style of interiority. For values as values are not revealed by abstract thinking; they are only revealed to me in the process of living. If I take a stand outside myself, merely reflecting on the values of my life orientation without really trying to live them, I am liable to lose them as the guiding stars in the firmament of my life.

Living values means that I incarnate their richness and substance concretely in accordance with a deepening commitment to my life situation. When I dream only about the life out there, and eagerly live it in my excited imagination, the life I am called to live may lose its flavor, not because it is no longer meaningful, but because I no longer live it. Thus once I have made my commitment, it is destructive to begin imagining another life style as one of possible central value for me. If I neglect the steady rediscovery of the values of my calling by leaving them forlorn as mere abstractions, like castles in the air, I shall soon be unable to sense them.

When I perceive the vows from the dynamic viewpoint of the unfolding person, I find thus that vowing my life is my entrance to potential maturity after the indecision and dispersion of adolescence. While vowing my life in a certain direction does not in and by itself guarantee human maturity, it is the beginning of the road.

Vowing is not merely a matter of thinking but of willing myself to a lasting form of life with all its limitations and possibilities. Such commitment implies a creative configuration of my whole style of thinking, perceiving, desiring, feeling, expecting and imagining into a rich, consistent interiority which deepens and intensifies with the passing of time.

This tuning of my interiority to the tone of the evolving form of religious life, passed on to me by generations of former religious, may be more relevant than ever before. Increasingly today, the person who has committed himself to religious life as a participant in the culture may be on his own in many situations. His surroundings may not always furnish the regularity of community living in regard to prayer and recollected presence to the Holy. In his unique cultural participation, the religious may be more than ever dependent on a well-tuned interiority.

If inner transformation does not take place early in religious life, if religious life becomes only a matter of meeting external expectations, then there may be no means of ultimately distinguishing the life of the vows from the professional life I am pursuing. They may seem one and the same until only the external element of my religious life remains. When this distinction is no longer lived, external customs are not enough to bind me to a way of life. Only when the life form I live is the incarnation of what I really am, can it become a lasting life of recollection and participation rooted in presence to the Holy.

III

Religious Life as Life Style
and Life Symbol

We have seen already that the human person and that humanity as such are called to be an openness to reality. Man can be open to reality on two levels. One level is the level of the immediate manipulation, dominance, and organization of reality and can be called the level of the managing me. It is as manager that man inscribes himself concretely in the world.

The other level is the level where I am present to reality not in its immediate, practical, incidental, temporal manifestations but to the deeper underlying ground of reality in its transcendent meaning, to the whole of reality that in religious experience is known as the Holy. This level of presence that enriches and deepens me as a human being is the level of the human self.

Two levels are thus identified: the self level of presence to reality that reaches its transcendent meaning and the managing level of presence to reality where we are dealing with the immediate aspects of reality. For our purposes here, it is sufficient to discuss these two levels of presence without dealing with a third level of presence, that of the needy me.

Ideally, self and managing me are integrated in the harmonious personality. However, this ideal harmony is never totally reached; we are always on the way toward this integration, toward this reconciliation of self and managing me. In order to be efficient the managing me, on the practical level of reality, needs three things. It needs to secure power or influence to a certain degree; secondly, it needs to attain a certain pleasure in whatever one does; and thirdly, it needs to secure possessions, for certain things are needed to do other things. So power, pleasure, possession are three main conditions for man as managing if he wants to inscribe himself concretely in the everyday world.

Unfortunately, it is always possible that these conditions, after which I have to strive, do not remain mere conditions for me, but become ends in themselves. I may become totally oriented toward power, pleasure or possession isolated from their function to serve the incarnation of my true self emerging from the Holy and moving toward the Holy. The more I come to know myself, however, the more I realize that I am always tempted to become overinvolved in the striving for power, pleasure, and possession.

Like every human person, I am basically living in conflict and in opposition. On the one hand, I must strive repeatedly to emerge from my preoccupation with power, pleasure and possession, in order to keep my deepest self free for the deeper meaning of reality. On the other hand, I must use my position of power, pleasure and possession to incarnate in my daily life the true values that are disclosed to me in my self-openness.

On the level of openness of the self, I find in all human beings another triad of fundamental attitudes. We experienced the triad of power, pleasure and possession on the level of the managing me. On the level of the self, we discovered already the triad of openness to the deepest meaning of my historical situation (obedience), a loving respectful openness to self and others (respectful or chaste love), and thirdly the attitude of respectful celebration and use of things (poverty). These two triads of attitudes form the basic structure of the human being as a being in opposition and in progress, in conflict and on the road.

At every moment of life, I experience the polarity of these two triads. One pole is the triad of power in which I try to master the situation, pleasure in which I try to find a certain peripheral fulfillment which helps me to continue my work, and finally possession in which I need certain things in order to manage my situation effectively. The other pole is the triad of obedience, respectful love, and respectful presence to things. These attitudes help me to be present to reality on a higher level and to permeate the three atti-

143

tudes of the managing me with their light, radiance and meaning.

The polarity of the two triads is found not only in individuals but also in human cultures. Cultures are *human* cultures to the degree that the *self* of the people of the cultures has predominance over their *managing* orientation. A culture can deteriorate under pressure of an unbridled lust for power, pleasure, or possession. When these forces begin to take over, it is evident how much religious life is needed to radiate those values which foster cultural unfolding.

Religious celibates vow themselves to live the healing attitudes of obedience, respectful presence to others, and respectful presence to things which help people and culture transcend the triad of forces on the level of the managing me. This is not to imply that the three managing attitudes are unnecessary. The celibate religious, like all others, needs to a degree the three orientations of the managing me.

To be effective in religious life, I have to find my place in an implicit power structure of the community. When I speak in my community, there are certain things which I can and cannot say without diminishing my possible good influence. Also pleasure is necessary for material success. In the community things must be available and arranged in such a way that life becomes pleasurable in varying degrees. Otherwise, it would be difficult to function smoothly and pleasantly as a community. Also certain possessions are necessary. I may give up many possessions, but I need such things as decent living quarters and books or tools for my professional task in order to function effectively in daily life. However, as a religious celibate, I do not stop there. Along with celibates in all religions, I vow to foster, develop, and unfold in a special way the triad of attitudes of the real self, which are the basis of true culture.

This is not to identify religious life simply with a vowed threefold openness that makes true culture possible, but to stress one aspect of its uniqueness. We must add that in religious life, one vows also to strive after the deepest meaning of history, of the other, and of things as well as of God Himself. In other words, the religious vows not only to dedicate himself in a special and explicit way to the triad of self-unfolding, but he vows also that he will do so in presence to the Holy as the ground of all historical, human, and natural reality.

Added to this is the fact that the person takes another special vow, the vow of celibacy. By celibacy he chooses a certain freedom from social establishment, sustained and symbolized by the establishment of the family. Celibacy sets the religious distinctly apart from every other person outside religious life. The religious who vows celibacy does so with the implicit intention to live his life in a certain style. His intention is to live celibacy in communion or in community in order to better pursue a threefold fundamental presence to the Holy as manifested in cultural life. He affirms that there is a certain coherence between him and others who lived the same life in the past, live it now and will continue to live it in the future. Therefore, the communion of religious celibates to which he belongs spreads itself over time and space. The religious celibate, unlike the diocesan priest, wants to live the threefold path toward culture as a manifestation of the Holy in a special style — a style which makes him more free for this witnessing.

The diocesan priests, for example, who vow to live together in a corporate community and at the same time remain diocesan priests, have as their aim not primordially to manifest the presence of the Holy in the culture. Their primordial aim is far more to bind and commit themselves to certain dioceses or certain missions in order to take care of the regular needs of the faithful. Their primordial style is not to participate in a variety of cultural enterprises but to bind themselves to daily care of the faithful in that diocese. Secondly, they are not aiming at witnessing in a *special way* and in a *special style* of obedience, respectful love, and respectful use of things. The latter element, that of life style, is one we would like to stress particularly in the observations to follow.

Religious life is not a life of celibacy in community in the way diocesan priests may establish a community. The celibate religious adopts a certain style of living that has proven over the millennia to make people more effective and free from the danger of over-involvement in power, pleasure, and possession. The same life style has also enhanced the symbolic power of witnessing to the threefold path of human and spiritual unfolding. In other words, when the religious celibate vows to live the threefold path, by the same token he adopts a certain style of life which makes him less open to temptations of power, pleasure, and possession.

A simple example would be the vow of poverty. Negatively this is a vow of not owning or at least not collecting things without permission and not having to take care of my own possessions in various ways that can be disturbing and that can lead to overinvolvement. Positively, poverty is the lived attitude of being more open on the self level to the right and beautiful use and celebration of things in presence to the Holy.

In other words a certain style of life that is embodied by tradition in different religions is adopted because this style has proven to be effective in overcoming and transcending overinvolvement in the triad of power, pleasure, and possession. This style of life has also enabled persons throughout history to be more present on the self level in true obedience to their historical situation, in respectful love for others, and in respectful presence to things.

A style of living obedience, respectful love, poverty, celibacy, and community is usually expressed concretely when I take vows in accordance with the rules and constitutions of the order I am entering. The rules and constitutions give not only the fundamental religious style of the threefold attitudes; they also communicate this style insofar as it is worked out, redefined and explicated in a specific religious order. In this book, however, our concern is for fundamental structures, and therefore we shall be speaking about a style fundamental to all religious life which is implicit in the various elaborations of the rules and constitutions in religious congregations and orders. Let us now dwell more explicitly on the idea of a fundamental life style.

First of all, it may be clear already that this concrete style encompasses that which strikes us as typical of religious life when we consider the taking of religious vows. When we think about religious life, we may not reflect on the fundamental openness as differentiated in this threefold attitude. We are far more impressed immediately by the very specific style in which the vows are lived by religious. However, it is most important to stress the fundamental human attitudes symbolized by the vows, attitudes which are necessary to all human beings who try to unfold themselves and to live in presence to the Holy.

I can only understand a specific religious style of life in its deepest meaning if I know how that specific style is related to this threefold attitude on the self level. Only then can I understand what this style

148

means. If I know this specific style of religious life in the strict sense alone, and never refer to the fundamental attitudes that are styled by that specific way of living, then the life style itself may become something external, something no longer rooted in self-unfolding in presence to God, something no longer serving the unfolding of these three fundamental attitudes for all men. Vowing may become somewhat empty and meaningless. It becomes difficult for humanity to understand how this special style is linked to the three fundamental attitudes that all people need and how therefore this specific style of living symbolizes for the population as a whole that which all should live, even if they live these attitudes in a different style or form of life.

When we think about style, the danger arises that style will mean for us an external thing that is not rooted in the core of human life. However, life style deeply affects the whole way of orienting my inner life, perception, emotionality, motivation and feeling. All this is implied in the life style that I accept and personally appropriate. The religious celibate accepts a style of life that should predominantly be a styling of his interiority, perception, and emotionality, a style that gradually unfolds his personality. Only secondarily does this style find its incarnation in certain external customs, buildings, rules and regulations. These are also necessary because we are beings who are incarnated. We have to embody our interiority in bodily and external signs, symbols, movements, customs and so on. But to understand how the specific *religious* life style came about, we have to probe deeper into the fundamental pre-Christian expression of religious life, for it came about long before Christian revelation. To do so we need to employ the concept of "creative religious imagination."

Man is potentially religious. Man has at the same time a creative imagination, and he wants to express his religious experience, feelings, ideals, hopes, dreams and ambitions in certain forms. This may be illustrated by a consideration of the spiritual writer. What is typical of the spiritual writer and what distinguishes him clearly from the theologian is that his speaking is the fruit of his creative religious imagination. While rational theology is strong in formal logic, conceptualized expression, and objectivating thought, the spiritual writer best expresses himself in a language that springs from his creative religious imagination. His language is, so to speak, a symbolic expression of what he experiences. The spiritual writer in all religions writes about the Sacred in relation to man and world, and he speaks about himself and other men in living relation to the Sacred.

The spiritual writer has a different language than the theologian. Sometimes it is very marked as, for example, in the poetry of St. John of the Cross; but one also finds it in a less marked way than in poetry as, for example, in the *Imitation of Christ*. These writings are not abstract conceptualized treatises about different theological notions but expressions of religious experience. They are living expressions, and therefore the best ones among them have withstood the centuries and will probably survive for centuries to come. Religious imagination leads gifted people of all centuries and of all cultures to creative expressions that are both revealing and touching. They are found in the Bible and Psalms, in the old mystical prayers of the Babylonians, Assyrians and Egyptians, in Indian and other cultures. Everywhere we discover religious expressions that spring from the creative religious imagination.

Other fruits of the religious imagination are religious ceremonies or the liturgies that develop in various religions. Take, for example, a custom such as the selection of a special object, like a chalice, that is set free from other vessels to be used only for worship of the Holy. Here the creative religious imagination creates a symbolic object that is experienced in relation to the Sacred. It is important to realize that it expresses this relation in a way that could not be substituted by a mere conceptualized expression. In other words, in the very ceremony or in the very taking care of a chalice, there is something expressed about our relationship to the Sacred that could be expressed in no other way as well.

Another fruit of the religious imagination that we can observe over the centuries in different cultures is the creation of a specific life style for certain people within the culture — a life style that has the power to disclose and heighten their religious experiences as no other style could do. The religious life style as lived by celibate religious has the power to disclose to those who live it, and to others as well, certain human and spiritual experiences. Notice we do not say it discloses them; we say only that it has the power to disclose them. Some people may not be ready for this disclosure, or they may close themselves off from it. But the power is there; and it is fascinating to see ways in which the creative religious imagination in different cultures created a specific style of living that expressed in a special way to all people that they too should live in presence to the Holy by means of the threefold path.

The creative religious imagination creates a life style which at the same time has a symbolic value insofar as it can disclose to people who are ready and open for it certain experiences that they themselves potentially or actually have. Secondly, this life style helps the people who are living it to be more personally present to the Holy.

When we speak about the power to live more effectively in presence to the Holy because of a certain life style, then we speak also about a life style which is formative. An effective formative life style has to be experienced, tried out, and found to be effective. Before it can be tried out, there must have been people who imagined *what* they should try out and then, in trying it out, *how* they could correct and improve it. One thing that is typical of religious life is its formative dimension by which we mean a disciplined limiting of life in such a way that it can be lived intensely in a specific style and orientation. In this wide sense, a formative influence is typical of any life style. For example, the married man, as soon as he is married, does not have the same freedom to date other girls. In other words, there is a free limiting inherent in his new life style — a limiting not sought for its own sake but because it helps one to unfold himself within a chosen style of life.

The life style of celibate obedience, celibate poverty, and celibate love has thus developed over the centuries in different cultures as a way of being more present to the Holy. At the same time, the function of this life style is to symbolize for all men that which they already experience in their best moments. We have seen already that the structure of man is such that he has to transcend constantly the managing dimension of his personality where he is involved in the striving for power, pleasure, and possession. We have seen how difficult this transcendence is because man easily becomes overinvolved. However, even when man becomes overinvolved in this way, there are moments when he experiences a kind of nostalgia for the Holy and its manifestations in culture and reality.

While he experiences this longing dimly, he may

not be aware of this experience. At such moments when he meets people living the religious life in the true sense, then their very life and living has the power to disclose to him the truth of his own experience: "Yes, I experience the nostalgia to live life less involved in blind striving for power, pleasure and possession. Yes, I want something more meaningful than that."

In various great religious cultures, there is always a movement in which certain people are set apart to be this needed symbol and invitation. The religious imagination created both the formative life style that we now call the religious life style, and the symbolic value of this life style. We have seen that the human being who is religious, or a human culture or subculture that is religious, not only experiences religion but also possesses a creative religious imagination enabling it to express fundamental religious attitudes in symbolic forms and also to uncover specific and concrete ways of living religion which have symbolic value. The creative imagination is present in all cultures; religious experience in its fundamental aspects is at the basis of culture; and ultimately the fundamental human structure we have described is basic to all men. Therefore it is by no means surprising that in completely different cultures and religions, a religious symbolic style of living emerged spontaneously.

Many people say religious life is community or communion; others say that the essence of this life is celibacy; others say it is celibacy in community; others say that basically its adherents are living some form of obedience, poverty, and chastity. Others again stress the life style in which the vows are lived or emphasize the living dialogue with tradition. Only when we take these fundamentals into account can we reach a comprehensive integrative understanding of the religious life in light of its fundamental structures and dynamics.

Having spoken about the general structures of all religious life, we may now apply this insight to the Christian religious life where the Holy is incarnated in Christ. The truths Christ revealed to us could never have been discovered by means of any human structure or striving alone. Living the Christian religious life is in itself a special grace that one could never obtain by asceticism alone, by theologizing alone, or even by spiritual striving without revelation and without special grace. But this grace and revelation ties in with something that is already there in the religious structure of man, some potentiality for being graced. And it is that which we first tried to discover in order to derive a fundamental insight into religious life. Also, as we mentioned in the beginning, our interest in this is deep because we are sensitive to the contemporary interest in religious life itself and to the religious stands and practices that tie in with humanity and the world.

Our intention is to show that religious life is not

alien to humanity, to the world, to the human personality, or to the human race. The only way to indicate on the deepest level how religious life is in the world, how it ties in with humanity, how there is a unity between humanity and the celibate religious, is to go to that point where grace finds, unfolds and develops what is already truly human in us.

Christian Religious Life

Until now we have spoken mainly about religious life in general and only incidentally about the specific meaning of religious life as lived in Christianity. Therefore, we would like to be somewhat more specific about Christian religious life and Christian living of the threefold path.

The most distinguishable dimension of Christian religious life is its person orientation. The Holy, searched for by the great religious of all times, revealed itself in Christ as person. Divine personhood is articulated in no religion so compellingly as in Christianity. Not only is God revealed as person; He is eternally engaged in profound personal relationships. The Holy Trinity has been made known to us as One God in three Persons, each being toward the other. This revelation is a startling disclosure of the most exemplary and intense living of personhood within the realm of personal relations. And, as if this were not enough, one of the Divine Persons came to share our human nature without losing His eternal personal re-

156

lationship with the other Divine Persons of the Trinity. Sharing human nature, Christ invites each one of us as human person to share personally and uniquely in His divine nature and to relate in and through Him personally to the Father and the Holy Spirit.

Christian religious life without destroying or minimizing the fundamental structures of all religious life permeates these structures with the unique awareness of the personal calling of each one of its celibates to be present to the Father and the Spirit in and through Jesus and to participate with the Lord in the humanization, spiritualization and redemption of the culture.

Christian Vow of Obedience

Having discussed the threefold path to human and spiritual unfolding for all men, we may ask ourselves what these three attitudes signify specifically in Christian religious life. The meaning of obedience is intimately related to the fact that the celibate religious in Christianity experiences his life essentially as a life in communion with fellow religious and with cultural participants in and among whom the Risen Lord is present.

Obedience as lived by the celibate religious in pre-Christian religions is a listening to the Holy as revealing itself in all manifestations of reality. In the Christian experience of listening, the Holy obtains a specific personal meaning. As a Christian religious, I hope to share in the obedient listening of Christ to all

157

manifestations of the will of His Father in people, events and things. This obedience implies my readiness with Christ to say, "Yes, Father," at every moment that it becomes clear to me what His will is for me.

In order to listen to the Father's will for me as hidden in all that I encounter in my daily life situation, I need the grace of enlightenment which helps me to transcend the needs and compulsions of the needy me and the managing me. This grace is given to me by the spirit of my Lord who is always with me ready to purify my modes of sensing and knowing by means of the gifts of the Holy Spirit.

As a member of a participative religious community, I may find fulfillment in some personal form of effective participation in contemporary humanity and culture. Obedience in this life setting implies that I keep in tune with the ever-changing society of man by being thoroughly engaged in the struggle to listen to all the revelations of reality in accordance with my unique possibilities and limitations. The will of the Father for me and for my participative endeavors is revealed not "out there" but in this situation in which I labor and listen.

While my cultural task may be different from that of any other celibate religious in my community, I still share with him to some degree the same culture within which all specific tasks are performed. The Spirit of Jesus speaks not only to me but potentially to my fellow religious. In each one of us the Spirit speaks in a limited way, adapting Himself to the limited abilities and limited human perspectivity of each individual religious. Therefore, each celibate will see the situation of the culture from a different perspective, for each is blessed with his own task, character, temperament, education and affinity. Accordingly, each one receives his own inspiration to the degree that he allows the Holy Spirit to illumine and deepen his limited perspectivity.

The original and sometimes divinely illuminated perspectivity of each celibate religious leads to the fortuitous fact that different aspects of the cultural situation will be revealed to different members of the community. This revelation will occur when they are truly open and listening to reality in and through Jesus who is present in each one in a unique way. The humble awareness that the Lord is not the exclusive partner of any one celibate but that He is present in all enables each person to listen respectfully to the other. Faith in Christ's presence in all may lead at the right time to a respectful dialogue between members of a Christian community. This dialogue may be about the community itself as the home sustaining personal religious unfolding or about the overall cultural situation where each individual religious participant has to be fully present in his own way when he leaves the community for his personal task and witness to the Lord.

Respectful listening to one another in the religious home is always cautious not to interfere unnecessarily with the more specialized listening that should take place within the specific task situation of each religious participant himself. Within his specific life situation outside the community, the celibate finds himself together with other specialized cultural participants. Within this group of specialists, Christ speaks in a way that could not easily be understood in detail by all members of the religious community if they themselves are not engaged in this particular cultural enterprise.

The will of the Father in regard to a task is revealed in *concrete* people, events and things. A person not engaged concretely and daily in such a situation could not easily hear in detail the will of the Father in this daily endeavor, for he is not present to the people, events and things that comprise that situation. Because of this, religious celibates in Christian community should humbly restrict their listening in regard to their fellow religious to matters pertaining to community life itself and to religious presence to the culture in general. The celibate religious who is also a specialist in such a mode of cultural participation should himself remain open to advice of a more general nature that does not presuppose a specialized knowledge of his field. He may, for example, discuss with others the human relationships he faces in his daily task and welcome respectful reminders that he seems to be getting overinvolved in his specialty to the detriment of his religious and spiritual life.

Obedience in religious community implies thus a listening to each person and to the community as a whole. It may be desirable for such a community to have a "master listener" who binds all practical views together in a unifying insight in those matters which pertain to the concrete situation of the community as promoter of each individual in that community. Listening to and with the master listener may help to foster in all members true presence to the culture without diminishing their rootedness in the religious life form which protects their specific intimacy with Christ. In other words, obedience to the will of the Father in regard to the religious home implies obedience to one another and to a master listener in case that a community has decided to appoint such a person.

From all this it should be clear that wholesome obedience does not repress personal attention to reality and openness to the voice of the Spirit. On the contrary, true listening presupposes and fosters personal inspired presence to reality as a revelation of the will of the Father to the faithful. The necessary condition for meeting Christ in the mystery of the religious community is respectful reflective listening to the voice of the community as long as its members are meaningfully speaking about the fundamental structures of religious life as lived in the religious

home and as incarnated in religious-cultural participation in general.

Respectful listening and dialogue are impossible
unless I can give up my self-preoccupation and self-
centeredness. If I hear only my own voice, I am not
ready for full participation in the life of my community. My vow of obedience is a promise to develop a
sensitivity for the voice of the community as potentially the voice of the Holy Spirit. Life in community
is consequently most rich when every member is able
to listen to the voice of every other member as a possible unique manifestation of the voice of the Lord. A
truly obedient community will therefore foster the
possibility of respectful dialogue among its members
in regard to those matters that belong radically and
fundamentally to the essence of the religious life form
itself as lived in the concrete situation of a specific
community. In respectful dialogue the voice of the
Lord may reveal itself.

In regard to the living of the fundamental structures of religious life, the listening of all to all is the
basis of true solidarity in the religious community.
Community life reaches its optimal beauty and effic-
acy in Christ when everyone at times can contribute
to the relaxed living of individual religious life and to
the personal unfolding of each celibate. To be sure,
the expression of personal insight and feeling may result in a variety of opinions, some of which will be
incompatible with others. Moreover, outspoken per-

sonalities may be tempted to drown out the voice of the Holy Spirit as possibly speaking in more quiet fellow religious. This is another reason why a religious community may find it desirable to have a master listener who is open to all the expressions of the members, the loud as well as the less vocal ones.

The more every member is ready to listen to the word of the master listener within the limits freely set by the community as a whole, the greater may be the opportunity for free expression of insights, feelings and inclinations. The certitude that everyone within the limits set by the community will abide by the word of the master listener spoken in dialogue with others guarantees that the unity, peace and serenity of the community will be maintained without detracting from the possibility of candid disclosure of opposed feelings and ideas. An atmosphere of mutual respect may then prevail in which every member can feel at home and in communion with Christ, who is the source and inspiration of the abiding respect for individual personality which characterizes an authentice Christian religious community.

The vow of obedience in a community that has freely appointed or elected master listeners presupposes not only a sensitive listening to one another but also a readiness to listen to the master listener within the limits set by the community even if his insight is not totally identical with mine. I can only do so in the faith that the Holy Spirit will somehow make the best of every situation even if His Spirit is misunderstood temporarily by myself, by my fellow religious, or by the master listener.

Compliance with the master listener does not mean that I have to deny to myself that I see and feel somewhat differently, for this would amount to an unwholesome repression which would be a barrier to full obedience. Repressed feelings, views and inclinations tend to influence my behavior unconsciously. They are by the same token withdrawn from the possibility of a direct illumination by the Holy Spirit. An obedience built on repression of my own feelings and insights is only partial. It is not the obedience of the whole me, enlightened by the Holy Spirit. Repression of my real feelings and insights may even lead to an uneasy, forced relationship between the master listener and myself or between me and my fellow religious.

The origin of these strained feelings may escape me because I have repressed the awareness of my own views and feelings, when I discovered that they were divergent from those of my community or my friends, or from those of the crowd or clique in which I have immersed myself. It is thus virtually impossible to work through these feelings and insights in a Christian way. As a Christian religious, I should be so deeply permeated by a living faith in the redeeming presence of my Lord that I dare to face and admit to myself all my thoughts and feelings, even when I realize that they may be erroneous and possibly an expression of self-centeredness.

Faith that the Holy Spirit is with me and my fellow religious makes me aware that the spirit of Jesus may use my divergent insights as an occasion of illumination in regard to the will of the Father for me, my community and my friends. Recollection before the Lord Jesus and before His Spirit creates an atmosphere of serenity, humility and distancing which may enable me with His grace to purify my insights and desires from self-centeredness, exaggeration and agitation. The peace of the Spirit may then help me to present my views and feelings to fellow religious or to the master listener in words which are less recalcitrant or cynical.

Suggestions endowed with the serenity that is the gift of the Holy Spirit may predispose fellow religious to transcend their own unenlightened impulses and compulsions so that they, too, may gather themselves in presence to the Lord Jesus and His Spirit. In His presence they may accept or reject my insights, but they will do so with grace and compassion. Their respectful presence may in turn deepen my serenity and enable me to live with their divergent response to me without denying that I still cherish and acknowledge as mine the insights and feelings they cannot yet accept.

However, if I do not work through my feelings and insights, I may be obedient on the conscious level and still experience a strain and artificiality in my relations with my fellow religious or with the master listener. This may be due to a misunderstanding of Christian obedience as a repression of those insights and feelings which do not coincide with the momentary dispositions of my fellow religious. Obedience in this sense is misconstrued. It misses the redemptive meaning of obedience in Christ, which is meant to liberate me from the anxiety evoked by the presence of evil in myself, in others and in the world. Christian obedience is an obedience graced and elevated by Christ, illuminated by the Holy Spirit and thus uniting me to the obedience of Christ to His Father. If I do not pursue this movement of grace in freedom and openness, I may remain infantile and immature instead of growing to the relaxed and unrepressed openness of the child, which Jesus identified as the outstanding trait of those who live in the liberating awareness of His redemption.

If my obedience is not yet Christian, I may become alienated from my self as graced and redeemed by Christ. Once estranged from my unique self, the locus of intimate self-revelation in Jesus, it may be difficult for the Lord to shine forth through me to those I encounter in my life of cultural participation. The Christian religious is called to witness to this world not for an impersonal Holy but for the Holy who has revealed himself as person in Christ. The specific witness of the Christian religious is best given to the degree that he is united to his true self in Christ so that he can be a personal occasion for His revelation.

The vow of Christian obedience thus asks me, because of Christ's obedience to His Father, to accept the possible sacrifice I may have to make of the execution of some of my ideas. While I can escape the sacrifice by repressing my awareness of views and feelings which differ from those of master listeners or fellow religious, true Christian obedience makes me ready to abide by the execution of the insights of others when their views prevail in my community. At the same time I allow myself to experience clearly that I personally feel differently. I do not give up the insight I believe to be best, but because of Christ's presence in the community I can say with Christ, "Yes, Father." I can sacrifice freely and joyfully the actual realization in the community of my personal feeling, interest or insight. I see that unity in Christ and respectful togetherness as celibate religious would be impossible if everyone would consider his personal insights and desires as the ultimate voice of the Holy Spirit for the community, and if everyone would force his ideas upon all others against their best insights and intentions.

The decisions about which we are speaking are those affecting the fundamental structures of religious life as lived concretely within the religious home. These differ from decisions made in Christian obedience in my unique situation of cultural participation outside the community. As we said earlier, Christian obedience in my field of cultural participation implies listening together with my cultural participants to the Holy Spirit as speaking in our concrete task-oriented situation. It is obvious that my fellow religious at home can listen to the concrete unique home situation but not to what the Spirit is saying in the situation of my cultural task insofar as it differs from theirs.

If it is a question of the inner dynamics of religious life within the religious home, then the peace, unity and atmosphere of respect within my community is more precious to me than the mere realization of every one of my desires. Peace, unity and respect foster the presence of each member to the Holy Spirit and therewith an increase in the possibility of renewing oneself daily in Christ before leaving the religious home to engage in independent participation in the culture.

The same concern for Christ's presence in the religious home imposes on the master listener and every religious the obligation to listen to the insights and desires of one another as long as they are expressed humanly and reasonably. Moreover, respect for the presence of Christ in each religious imposes the duty never to deny the possibility of concretely realizing such individual desires if they can be combined reasonably with the fundamental interests of the community.

168

Christian obedience thus prevents narrow fixation on my own onesided views under the pretense that they come directly from the Holy Spirit. The awareness that the Holy Spirit may speak in others as well as myself makes me listen all the more to fellow religious and cultural participants and keeps me free, flexible and detached in my opinions. While Christian obedience encourages me to grow in initiative, it also protects me from a onesided fanatical insistence that only my insights should be actualized in reality.

Christian Vow of Respectful Love

As we have tried to demonstrate repeatedly, the orientation of the vows point to fundamental attitudes which underlie the movement of mankind toward the humanization and spiritualization of basic needs and drives. The vow of respectful love also symbolizes this movement. It expresses explicitly and strikingly that man is called to grow beyond the mentality of crowd, collectivity and clique into true human encounter and community. This vow symbolizes that man has to open up increasingly to the other as other by overcoming his anxious self-centeredness.

Human and spiritual encounter began to evolve in various cultures when an enlightened few were able to take a stand toward their fellowman which transcended mere gregariousness in function of survival. In many cultures one finds such pockets of illuminated people. Some of these people chose to live apart from the social structures to which most others bound their lives. They imposed upon themselves a discipline rooted in experience which they hoped would free them for human and spiritual transformation of the drive toward gregariousness.

The human transformation of this drive led to a spirit of togetherness, a spirit which promotes altruistic respect for the unique dignity of self and others. Instead of merely using the other for my own needs or organizational projects, for example, I respect his integrity as well as my own. In this movement toward the affirmation of his uniqueness, I directly and indirectly help the unfolding of all mankind, which is dependent on respect for the unique goodness and ability each individual can bring to humanity.

Religious presence to self and others of the best members of pre-Christian culture was not yet enlightened by the presence of Christ in the midst of humanity. Nevertheless their experience pointed already to the sacredness of self and others, which gave the most profound motivation for the reverence due to self and others. The coming of Christ represents a striking confirmation of the religious intuition of pre-Christians in regard to the presence of the Sacred in each person.

The incarnation of the Sacred in Christ personalizes the experience of the Holy in Christian awareness as no other event could ever do. His coming is described beautifully in the Introduction to the Gospel of St. John. The Holy or the Light that silently illuminated all religious seekers since the beginning became man, inserted Himself as a true person into the process of the spiritualization of mankind, and redeemed mankind from an original sin of impurity staining man's effort to spiritualize himself.

The presence of Christ in mankind grants each human self a dignity undreamt of in generations of pre-Christian religious. They groped for this astonishing insight, and some, for example, tentatively expressed it in their growing belief that Buddha was somehow the deepest self of every human being. All of this was but a dim shadow of the revelation to come, that of the Light that came into the world and gave to as many as received Him the power of becoming sons of God. The awareness that the Word was made Flesh and is dwelling among us gave a whole new and unsuspected divine dimension to the vow of respectful love for self and others. Jesus Himself told us that whatever we do to the least estimated persons on earth, we do to Him. He described how at the end of time people will ask Him in surprise when did we clothe you, give you to drink or visit you in prison, and the answer was that anything done to the least of His brethren has also been done to Him.

The Christian vow of respectful love is the vow to respect myself and the other because of the redeeming love of Christ for each one of us. The coming of the Light into the world in the person of Christ means that the growth from crowd and collectivity to true human communion and community has been infinitely fostered.

Growth toward human communion implies a two-fold development of human love, that of love of self and of love for others. Jesus stressed the interrelation of the two by telling us to love our neighbors as we love ourselves. The Christian must live the polarity between these two attitudes, for real communion with others in Christ presupposes that he has faced and purified his personality in the aloneness and solitude which is necessary for personal growth in respectful loving presence to himself.

In solitude with Him, Christ makes me aware of the worst and the best I can be. This humble awareness of self illumines my meeting with others. Solitude fosters my deeper communion with others, and my communion with others can foster self-unfolding. True Christian love of self leads to true Christian love of others and true love of others leads to true love of self. For communion with others makes me aware when and in what way I allow Christ to be the inspiration of my encounter only in my fantasy, while in reality my needs and ambitions have taken over. The Holy Spirit may speak to me both in solitude and in my encounter with others, in self love and love of others. Each one of these revelations of the Spirit reveals to me another aspect of my Christian life.

The polarity between respectful love for self and

others is basic in the life of every Christian. The life of Jesus that each one of us has to relive in his own way exemplifies this tension. The Gospel is permeated with references to the polarity of self love and love for others in Christ's everyday life. It speaks again and again about His respectful presence to many people and of His repeated withdrawal in solitude to be alone before the Father to replenish the core of His being.

As a follower of Christ, I struggle to find harmony between these two dynamic inclinations of human love. Frequently I am inclined to give an exaggerated weight to one or the other of these two poles of the vital attitude of respectful love to which I have vowed myself. Sadly, I realize that I may not live long enough to experience like Jesus the perfect harmony between both orientations of my life of love and respect. No matter, for at the same moment I joyfully acknowledge that He alone reached that perfection, that He alone is Holy, that He alone is the most high. I can only try with His grace and His light to grow to a more harmonious embodiment of both tendencies of respectful love in the core of my personal life.

These deeply human attitudes were already operative in me long before I became conscious of them. Before becoming aware of them, I could not strive after their balanced development in a free and insightful way in the light of the message of Jesus to me. In reality, already in infancy unconscious structures of ways of being with and for myself in solitude and of relating to others were already active in me. Therefore, developing better and more sublime modes of being alone and being with others in the way of Jesus means always learning to cope with my past reactions in regard to love of self and love of others.

Living a sound and balanced attitude of a respectful love in Christ is a life-long assignment. It begins when I can be respectfully present to myself at that sacred point where I hear my most unique call. I am invited to be a personal expression of the life of Jesus. In fidelity to this invitation I need to find and foster my Christian identity in respectful love for myself as uniquely called by Him. Discovery of my Christian identity is made within the many perspectives of self God allows to emerge in me as a result of an increasing variety of life situations which I experience as expressions of the will of the Father for me.

Each new life situation, especially each new relationship with people, reveals and unfolds a new aspect of the mystery of my Christian identity, of the way in which Jesus wants me to express Himself in me. It is for this reason that respectful love for self has to be permeated by respectful Christian love for others. The mode of respectful self-love helps me to unfold myself as the uniquely Christian me. The mode of respectful love for others makes it possible for me to gain insight in my Christian uniqueness. No awareness of self is granted to man outside his awareness of others. It is precisely in my respectful Christian presence to the other that I discover myself as a unique call of the Lord. In other words, respectful presence to others and of others to me always leaves room for respectful love of self. Respectful presence to self, in turn, creates space for a mode of communion with others which is truly chaste or respectful in a Christian sense, insofar as it in no way violates the fidelity of the other to his unique calling by Christ.

Respectful Christian love for self and others promotes the experience of my uniqueness in Christ and therewith heightens my Christian sensitivity for the mystery of the uniqueness of others called by the same Holy Spirit who is calling me forth as an original and irrepeatable revelation of the life of Jesus. The commitment of the Christian religious to a chaste or respectful love thus concerns itself with the most profound human attitude, the balanced development of which determines the harmony, peace and effectiveness of human and Christian life. The vow of chaste love is a commitment to witness for a highest possible integration of the attitudes of self-love and love for others in human life in the light of Christian grace and revelation.

The Christian religious celibate chooses freely a wide and difficult field in which to demonstrate or witness to the effective integration of both modes of human love. He relinquishes his right to establish a family of his own and tries to unfold his love life in regard to persons whom he does not select in advance, neither in his religious home nor in his field of cultural participation. The participative religious agrees in advance that he will try to maintain respect for the privacy and uniqueness of any person that may enter or has already entered the same community and for any person that may appear in his field of cultural participation. No matter how deeply and spontaneously he dislikes a certain person because of difference in temperament, previous education or personal history, the Christian celibate is committed to respect him as redeemed and called by Jesus. The same vow obliges him to insist on like reverence from others, no matter if they may dislike him because of divergent interests and perhaps totally different temperaments. To maintain respectful love for one another because of Jesus is a most striking witness to the possibilities of Christian love among men despite possible antipathies on the natural personal level.

Christian Vow of Poverty

Religious poverty as a dynamic attitude of the human personality creatively modifies my relation to nature and culture. Things in my life space are revealed as gifts of the Holy to be perfected and used in a way which respects their inner meaning and beauty and which respects the people for whom things are utilized. With his needs, fantasies, ambitions, and fixations on the immediate and material, man is able to

176

abide in such respectful presence only when he distances himself repeatedly from the surface dimension of things. This spirit of distancing is called simply poverty. Unfortunately contemporary man has lost contact with himself as spirit, and for him poverty assumed mainly a material meaning.

As soon as one hears the word "poverty," he is inclined to think about squalor and misery and it is difficult for him to understand how a person could make this state of affairs the ideal of life. Nonetheless, the spirit of poverty does express a fundamental orientation of the human self or spirit. A loss of distancing from immediate gains leads easily to a disrespectful desecration of culture and nature and has harmful consequences for the human beings who have to live in culture and nature.

For example, if managers of mills and factories are not enlightened by poverty of spirit, they may allow streams and lakes to become polluted with waste material. Not only does this lead to an unnecessary loss of beauty; it is also a potential health hazard. In this case, fixation on immediate material gain may cause one to lose sight of potentially greater gain on the level of spirit and body, if people strive to keep their country beautiful and preserve its natural resources for the health and relaxation of all.

The spirit of poverty enables me to distance myself momentarily from preoccupation with mere profit and gain. Such temporary distancing creates room for the emergence of my true self or spirit, which frees my vision for the perception of deeper meanings and of possibilities to be realized in the respectful use of culture and nature, even if this does not benefit me immediately in a merely material way.

For man as religious the main explicit reference point of this right attitude toward nature and culture is the Sacred to which, as a primary point of reference, all other merely human, cultural and natural points of reference are oriented. What happens when this reference point of the Sacred reveals itself as a Divine Person in Christ? This is the question of *Christian* poverty.

As always, the Incarnation does not destroy the natural human structures developed before this event by the best religious men who honestly sought to perfect their lives in the light of the Sacred. The Sacred was not as fully known to them as it is to us, not because of our merits but because of the self-revelation of God Himself. Christianity and Christian religious life uphold the wisdom that man's reverential presence extends itself to reality as manifested not only in people and events but also in nature and culture. Therefore, the spirit of poverty as a necessary dimension of man's respectful presence to all that is, is not abolished by Christianity but redeemed, graced, and elevated to sublime heights.

Our Lord Himself was filled with tender respect for nature as the gift of His Father. His religious sensitivity vibrates in His words when He speaks in parables about lilies of the field, dressed so beautifully by the Father, and about little sparrows cared for so deeply by the Father that not one falls without His knowing it. Jesus asks men to base their trust in the Father at least partly on the fact that He manifests such great care for all other things in nature. In numerous ways He shows how the gifts of nature and culture should be used respectfully and lovingly by man.

Visiting a wedding party, He makes available in a wondrous way the finest wine so that the guests may be joyful and make merry. He multiplies the loaves and the fishes so that the crowds following Him can still their hunger and regain their vigor. When His apostles are not able to fill their nets with fish, Jesus is there to fill them to the breaking point. When Mary Magdalene, in a beautiful gesture of respectful presence to Him, pours fragrant and expensive oils over His feet He appreciates it deeply and tells the other guests that she did the right thing. He reprimands them when they murmur that this precious oil should have been sold and the money given to the poor, for their complaint reflects a onesided and materialistic view of poverty.

This respectful attitude toward the gifts of culture and nature became such a hallmark of Jesus' life that one of the main attacks on His personality was that He was a drinker of wine, a man without asceticism, who allowed His disciples to eat the corn of the field on the Sabbath. On the other hand, it was clear that His presence to the gifts of the Father was only possible because of His ability to distance Himself from the mere material meaning of things. He never became enslaved to them, but strove always to discover and celebrate their deeper meanings and possibilities in accordance with the life situation.

Poverty is thus the free and liberated use of things. Jesus was so free from things that He could honestly say that He did not possess a stone on which to lay His head. This does not mean that He never found a place to sleep, for He often stayed in the homes of his friends like Mary and Martha. It only emphasizes that He kept Himself free from onesided concern for such things. He could do so because He led a celibate religious life.

His example did not mean that the people who consecrated their life to God within the fundamental life form of marriage, for example, should not care about their food, shelter and clothing. It only meant that they should do so in His spirit of poverty so that they would not be absorbed by these preoccupations. Because it is difficult not to become absorbed by the immediate material aspects of things which are needed daily, man can profit from the visible example of people who are free from this concern, as was the celibate Jesus.

The Christian vow of poverty sets some people free to manifest this aspect of Jesus' life in their common life. These *carefree* people are called to demonstrate in their celibate religious lives the ways by which one can be open to the deeper possibilities and meanings of matter if, like Jesus, he is not individually too preoccupied with the immediate material aspect of things.

One of these deeper meanings is the æsthetic meaning of things. It is not mere coincidence that Christian monasteries at their most sublime heights — like pre-Christian monasteries — were centers of art and beauty. No profound art is possible without the spirit of poverty or of detachment from the peripheral meaning of things in culture and nature. To be sure, the main reference of Christian poverty is not the æsthetic meaning of things in isolation. These human reference points are in turn themselves related to the Father and His will and to the work of redemption and liberation that Jesus wants to pursue in and through me.

In certain forms of pre-Christian religious life, poverty had as its ultimate reference point an impersonal whole and Holy with which man, through the exercise of poverty, was to be totally identified. This conception of the meaning of poverty led in some instances to a rejection of culture and nature as such. They were seen merely as empty and deceptive appearances taking man away from the whole and Holy.

The Christian vow of poverty promotes an orientation which is the opposite of a condemnation of the good things in life. The Incarnation of the Holy in Christ makes us aware of the basic goodness of all things. The gifts of culture and nature are not bad in themselves. What can be bad is their disrespectful use by man.

Pre-Christian religious life, having such a venerable tradition and historical power, necessarily influenced the beginnings of Christian religious life. Christianity and Christian religious life are relatively young and are still in the process of finding themselves. This influence was especially felt in regard to the vow and the practice of poverty. Time and time again, in many diverse ways, Christian religious are unconsciously tempted to forego the poverty of Christ for the poverty preached and lived in pre-Christian religious life.

We see in the history of Christian religious life, the reemergence of movements which glorify the rejection of the good things of life as something holy and meritorious in itself. This pre-Christian attitude tends to reassert itself under a variety of pretexts that tie in with contemporary needs and enthusiasms. However, since Christian religious life is finding itself more and more, it becomes difficult to propose bluntly a return to pre-Christian forms of religious poverty. Only within the context of a certain mode of cultural participation may it be necessary to abdicate temporarily the use of certain gifts of the culture in respect for the sensitivity of the materially poor for whom I work. My renunciation is then a manifestation of my attitude of respectful use of things in accordance with my respect for people within this specific situation of cultural participation.

However, it is crucial for the purity of the Christian concept of poverty that I keep clearly in mind that this temporal incidental renunciation is not because the enjoyment of the good things in life is evil, but because this incidental situation makes it undesirable to hurt others by the ostentatious enjoyment of things they cannot yet possess and enjoy themselves. Such ostentation might cut off my possibility of reaching them with the redeeming love of Christ.

As soon as I confuse the essence of the Christian attitude of poverty of spirit with a temporary, incidental, culture-bound manifestation, I may unwittingly promote in religious life a return to the deficient understanding of pre-Christian poverty. I may even try to define all rules and customs of all celibate religious, in all the houses of my community, in all parts of the country, and for all times to come in terms of this one temporary excellent manifestation of the spirit of poverty in this limited situation.

The relaxed joyful and respectful use and celebration of things varies from situation to situation. A religious celibate, who is called to work in the slums, may have to use a different dress and means of transportation and living than a religious celibate who is called to incarnate Christ in an affluent suburb or a university. It is precisely the Christian attitude of poverty which guides each religious in his respectful adaptation to the sensitivity of the people he tries to reach.

The actual material expression of the spirit of poverty will vary not only in relation to the people one tries to reach but also according to the material circumstances of one's community. Moreover, the style of expression will be influenced by the style and tradition of the order or congregation to which one belongs. This traditional expression in turn may have to be adapted to the changing cultural situation.

Another characteristic of Christian poverty is that it is person-oriented. We have seen that pre-Christian religious life in its orientation toward an impersonal Holy or Sacred was inclined to see as its ideal the absorption of the individual into the whole of all that is. The Christian religious is oriented in and through the person of Christ to the person of the Father and the person of the Holy Spirit. In this light the Christian religious becomes respectfully aware of himself as a unique person called personally by Christ. Accordingly every Christian attitude takes into account the individuality of the person who maintains and develops his life orientation.

This is also true of Christian poverty. The wise use of things in respect for persons and in the context of events and their meaning implies also a respect for the uniqueness of one's own personality. In that sense the practice of poverty should be somewhat different for each religious because each religious is unique. Each one differs in physical health and strength, in sensitivity, insight and interest, in need for a certain amount and kind of recreation, and in background, preparation and task. True Christian poverty takes all of these factors respectfully into account. What is the wise and respectful use of things for one religious may prove to be an unwise and disrespectful use of things for another.

For example, a religious who is a scholar can be totally in tune with his Christian poverty when the walls of his room are covered with books which he needs for his specific mode of cultural participation. Another religious who is engaged in manual labor may be unfaithful to poverty when he fills his room with books which he never reads but which are only collected and shelved to show off his supposed intellectuality. A religious who has an occupation which compels him to travel often may be wise to insist on good travel accommodations to protect his health against the wear and tear of constant transportation. Another religious who only travels incidentally may be unwise in spending extra money to attain better accommodations.

In short, there is an infinite variety in the individual practice of religious poverty. It varies from person to person and even from one period of life to another in the same person. For the person changes and grows and the practice of poverty has to change accordingly. Most important are not the details of this practice but the spirit of Christ in which this practice is lived.

The practice of poverty should never become rigid and inflexible, isolated from the growth of the Christian personality as a whole. True Christian wisdom in regard to the wise and respectful use of things is always an openness to all the changes in one's own personality and in the situation in which one has to use things for the best interest of people.

Christian Celibacy

Speaking about religious life in general and as life style and life symbol, we realized that one's commitment to celibacy is not a commitment to celibacy as if it were a thing in itself. Christian celibacy is the consecration of my life to Christ within a specific life form which makes me available to Him and His redeemed humanity in a special way. We can compare Christian celibacy with Christian marriage. The true Christian is not committed to marriage as such, to husband, wife and children as such, but to marriage as a calling of Christ and to his family members as persons called by Christ to unfold themselves uniquely. Both Christian marriage and Christian celibacy are life forms which consecrate the humanity of the marriage partners or of the celibate to the Lord who binds our humanity to His divinity by sharing in it.

If I forget that Christian religious celibacy is only a means to make me free for a special kind of intimacy with my Redeemer and for a special kind of participation in the redemption of humanity and culture, celibacy may become a meaningless burden. What is worse, if Christian religious celibacy does not lead to the gift of myself to Jesus so that He, in and through me, may make Himself present in my situation of cultural participation, it becomes a means of self-preoccupation and self-indulgence.

Both Christian marriage and Christian celibacy are forms of consecration in and through which Christ is present in His Church and in the world. Both forms of life presuppose a special call and grace. Both have their own joys and sorrows. Both Christian marriage and Christian celibacy concern the whole of our lives. This means that we can live these Christian life forms only when we consecrate ourselves within them totally and wholeheartedly. In other words, we should not allow ourselves to drift halfheartedly into marriage or celibacy without personally thinking through what we are doing and making a deeply personal decision.

In certain Eastern religions, marriage and religious celibacy, like obedience, are less person-oriented. Structured around the experience of a prepersonal Holy, the experience of being summoned to marriage or celibate religious life was not so much that of a personal call to be responded to in a personal way. This invitation to a life form was more the experience of a configuration of circumstances which almost automatically made one's life flow into a specific marriage or into a specific type of religious life. By contrast, both *Christian* marriage and *Christian* celibacy are highly personalized expressions and articulations of our personal love for the Risen Lord and His redeemed humanity.

Deciding on a Christian married life or on a Christian celibate life means that I decide to incarnate my love for God and man within one of these fundamental forms of consecrated life. These two consecrated modes of Christian life bind our lives with Christ in God. In this binding we receive grace to love the people whom we meet within these life forms with a love that is not self-centered, possessive or conditional.

Christian religious celibacy can be a striking sign for humanity that the love of Christ enables people to renounce their right to establish and administer a family unit of their own in order to be more available to other dimensions of the religious-cultural unfolding of mankind under the inspiration of the Risen Lord. However, as a Christian celibate, I can be this sign only if the way in which I live my celibacy is not an extinction of human care but rather a source of deep respect and concern for human persons as redeemed by my Lord and for the culture as already marked by grace and redemption.

Therefore, I should avoid pride about my call to celibacy. Pride does not lead to respectful human encounter but to disrespect, condescension and the attempt to impose my own ideas upon the lives of others, seducing them into submission by manifestations of care and understanding.

Pride of celibacy makes my celibacy worthless. It destroys the fundamental meaning of Christian celibacy which is to make me more free to incarnate in the culture the infinite respect of Christ for all men. True celibacy leads to a deep and abiding respect for every human being redeemed by Christ's blood. Thus my celibacy cannot be indifferent, for it calls me to transform and expand my natural respect for a few people into a total Christian respect for those who will be entrusted to me in the course of my celibate life. The heart of the Christian celibate should overflow with an immense respect for man and culture, enabling him to engage dynamically in various enterprises. Otherwise celibacy may become a burden instead of a source of youthful dynamism.

Celibacy will not free me from suffering but this suffering is not so much a matter of what I give up as it is a matter of what I take on. The respectful presence to humanity and culture to which I commit myself by following the call to celibacy means exposing myself to possible hurt and pain. When I try in light of the Holy Spirit to make the best of my cultural situation, I become vulnerable. I may be hurt deeply by those who do not want me to succeed, who fear the pursuit of excellence, who want the cultural situation to stay as it is because of their own established interests.

When I strive for excellence because of Christ, I may be a threat for those in whom I awaken guilt feelings, envy and jealousy because of their own lack of dynamic religious-cultural presence. Knowing this, I may often be tempted to forget the implications of my consecration, to retire from others and from my cultural situation in order not to risk being hurt again. When I find myself thus alone, misunderstood, and isolated from a cultural situation that does not welcome my efforts, I may experience a desire to have a family of my own. Why should I not give myself primarily to a small group of persons lastingly bound to me by trusting family ties? Why did Christ call me to be available to always new people in new situations? At such moments the desire to find peace, simplicity and solidity of life in a family of one's own can be very strong. Intellectually, I may realize that I am idealizing marriage but emotionally I cannot deny its deep momentary attraction.

At moments like these, the religious home where the celibate lives assumes a new importance. Religious celibates in Christian community should help one another to live the gift of celibacy by creating an atmosphere of mutual respect, kindness and cordiality, which reflects the compassion Jesus revealed to all those he met and loved. Love for the celibate life is difficult to maintain in a religious home where the atmosphere is cool, dreary and stifling. When I consecrate my life as a religious celibate, I also commit myself to uphold the celibacy of others who share my religious home. In a certain way I bear responsibility for them as Christ bore responsibility for me. Thus I should contribute as best I can to the creation of a climate of respect, companionship and relaxation. Such a climate may prevent or diminish the desire for a family of my own.

In order to avoid the penchant to dramatize my celibacy as an unusual heroic sacrifice, I should understand that a Christian marriage which is exclusive and indissoluble also involves a real sacrifice. My brothers and sisters who accept Christian marriage are called to symbolize in their lasting life union the union of Christ and the Church. They, too, follow a true vocation which involves fidelity to a primordial concern for the family, regardless of the pain and suffering this may include. Just as I receive the call to the non-exclusiveness of celibate love, they too are called to a primordial marital and parental love in Christ. The only thing that matters is that I follow Christ in the mode of life He has destined for me from all eternity.

Both Christian forms of life bring their own renunciations and sufferings as well as joys and pleasures. Both are modes of true self-fulfillment in service of Christ, His Church, and redeemed humanity and culture. Each vocation is a gift and grace from

God. The crucial thing is not that I am married or live the life of celibacy, but that I choose *my* calling, the calling in which I can reach true self-realization in Christ. The important thing is not the life form of marriage or of celibacy but that I live marriage or celibacy in Christian love for those entrusted to my care.

The life of Christian celibacy is a special way of living in and with Christ, who relinquished His human right to establish a family of His own. This does not mean that Christ was less human; it means that He gave up one fundamental form of human life and realized the fullness of His humanity in religious celibacy as another form of human life to which He was called by the Father. So when God calls me to live this life form in and with Christ, it does not mean that I give up my call to be a full and vital human being. Rather I strive to incarnate Christ in this world in and through my full human presence in daily cultural participation. What counts ultimately is that my consecration with Christ in the celibate life form is a consecraion of my heart, an inner orientation of my being, a basic attitude. This is what matters most of all.

When I realize that it is the particular will of God that I marry or choose the celibate life, I should choose one of these two possibilities of Christian life in the awareness that each is a vocation and a gift of God. My choice of Christian celibacy or Christian marriage is my response to a divine call. I should not expect that celibacy or marriage will make my Christian life easier. Each one of these fundamental life forms has its own graces and limitations. However, it is true that the celibate life, when sustained by a religious home, does make me more free for presence to my Lord and for care of my neighbor.

When I share the solitude of celibacy with my Lord, I am in special communion with Him and more able to relive that special aspect of His life. This advantage, however, may be destroyed by my pride or by my lack of charity. Nonetheless, when I really live the freedom of celibacy, it stands to reason that I shall be less divided than my fellow Christians, who live the exclusive priority of marital and parental care and love. Marriage necessarily takes away a certain availability for Christ and for redeemed humanity. Because I am celibate, I can make myself more available in my religious-cultural participation. When I do not use my freedom for this fuller gift of myself, it is then that my life becomes false and inferior to that of the married Christian.

A Christian husband and wife who truly love and respect one another and their children may do far more for Christ and redeemed humanity than the religious who has lost his love for Christ as present in the region of the world entrusted to his care. Loss of religious-cultural presence may occur when I allow myself to become overinvolved in the care of my own position in my religious home and my welfare in the field of cultural participation I have chosen outside my religious home. If this continues, I am likely to lose the fruit of my celibacy, that relaxed detachment which keeps me free for my Lord and His task for me. Living celibacy in a halfhearted manner may put me far below the married Christian who lives his consecrated life form authentically.

Celibacy is a gift which far from making me proud should make me humbly aware that I can never live up to the fullness of the demands of this vocation. If I live only the negative meaning of this consecration, namely not to establish a family of my own, celibacy may become deadening to me. Far more enlivening is my attempt to live its positive meaning, which is to grow daily in union with Christ and in respect and care for all those around me within the limits of my possibilities and my specialized task.

Christian celibacy, like Christian marriage, can be lived most fully only as a result of special graces which are granted to me by the Lord. Therefore, the Christian consecration of life within an indissoluble marriage or a permanent celibacy is an act of trust in God. It is more a gift of God to me than a gift from me to God. I can only dare to assume this gift in such an irrevocable manner because I have received from Him the knowledge that He is faithful and does not repent of having called me to this fundamental Christian form of life. Therefore, whenever I am tempted to

194

doubt my calling, I should turn to the Lord and renew my faith that He does not regret His gift to me even if I have been unfaithful to Him.

The same is true for my brothers and sisters called to the sometimes joyful, sometimes painful burden of an indissoluble Christian marriage. Perhaps I can at times sacrifice for them the doubts and difficulties I may suffer in celibacy. They may find less occasion for prayer than I do and yet they need His grace just as much in order to be faithful to the exclusive priority of their marital and parental love as I must be faithful to the freedom of celibacy.

As a celibate I may experience freedom from the constant worries and cares they have to live through for the sake of their family. I am less distracted by the host of problems they face every day, more available for the life of prayer and able to respond more easily and freely to certain needs of redeemed humanity. This is not to say that my celibacy should lead me to indulge in a careless life without anxiety or pressure. It is just that celibacy commits me to real involvement in my task in the world, which my Lord imposes on me. I do not have to care for a husband, wife or children, but I have to care, as St. Paul says, for the things of the Lord. I am celibate like Jesus not to achieve an easy life without suffering but in order to be like my Lord in His efforts to redeem humanity.

Celibacy makes me more available to the radiating

power of the Risen Lord in the culture. Freedom from family life offers me more time to listen to the voice of the Lord which calls to me in my daily life situation. The freedom of celibacy removes all kinds of preoccupations which would make it more difficult for me to hear the Lord in my daily surroundings. Deep involvement in the needs and problems of the family unit may tune me out to the needs and demands of others outside this exclusive relationship. I was called by the Lord to the celibate life form so that I would not be bound by familial responsibility. I deprive myself of the exclusive priority of marital love in order to devote myself more completely to mankind and man sustained by my community in my specific mode of religious-cultural participation. Celibacy means also that I should be present to my Lord in prayer and not overwhelmed by the concerns of this world. Ultimately, only He can fill my need for lasting security and intimacy. Prayer will thus always take a foremost place in my celibate life.

The participative life of the Christian religious celibate is thus a rhythm of participation and recollected presence to the Lord. My participation is religious to the degree that I am open to the deepest ground of that in which I am participating.

As soon as concern for power, pleasure, and possession prevails, I am living mainly in the world of management and manipulation to the neglect of my best self. My participation is then no longer a response to my concern for the unfolding of my deepest self, the other and our culture in light of the Lord.

As a Christian religious celibate, I willingly choose to vow my life in a manner which lessens the possibilities that are open to other persons for overinvolvement in strivings for power, pleasure and possession. My three vows not only imply a commitment to the threefold life orientation symbolized by these vows and necessary for each man who strives after religious maturity; they are also a commitment to a specific form of life which freely diminishes the occasions and possibilities to make power, pleasure and possession the last meaning of life. One who lives the vowed and vowing life thus fosters the unfolding of culture and history by witnessing for its sacred ground.

If I attempt to insert myself in the world of power, pleasure and possession without a corresponding deepening of my recollected presence to Christ, I may sooner or later fail to serve Him in and through my cultural participation. Overwhelmed by the need to master the immediate situation, I may neglect to center myself in recollected presence to the Lord. Participation becomes anxious agitation. Concern becomes preoccupation with recognition. Such tension destroys the rhythm of recollection and participation, a fundamental rhythm of every human life. Every person who strives for emotional and spiritual maturity must live its ebb and flow. It is not a question of how much time should be spent in recollection or how much in participation. This is a problem to be solved in light of the personality of each celibate in accordance with his task-orientation and the rule of his community.

The meaning of this dynamic of the life call may be seen if we again distance ourselves momentarily from celibate religious life and speak of this rhythmic living of recollection and action in another life form, that of marriage and the family. When a man marries, he commits himself to his wife and children in an indissoluble bond of love and support. This loving care and concern is incarnated throughout his life. If marital love is true, it will deepen over the years, granting meaning and substance to all things a man and wife do together, from paying bills and changing diapers, to dining by candlelight and spending an evening at the theater. The more functional aspects of married life then become means of incarnating their love, care and concern.

However, many husbands and wives find it difficult to maintain the transcendent aspect of their love. After a few years of marriage, the love they seemed to have begins to diminish and may even disappear. The functions of daily life are no longer a delightful incarnation of their affection for one another and for the children. They are a drudgery. Life for them becomes automatic, empty, meaningless and dreary. The beautiful intentionality of love that should be inspiring all these little tasks and elevating them above the mundane level — the love that should make their togetherness radiant and joyful — fades and dies. Life together is difficult to live. The house is a dungeon and they are prisoners of their own bitterness.

What is the meaning of this death of love, this death of inspiration? Men and women caught in this dilemma are no longer able to be faithful to the rhythm of marital life — that of a recollected celebration of love and the overflowing of this celebration in the unfolding of their daily lives. They may become so preoccupied with necessary family functions that they are unable to find special moments of recollection when their life together may be seen in its true light, when values and ideals may once again shine through the drudgery of routine. In treasured moments of mere togetherness, they may celebrate their love, distancing themselves from daily pressure and routine.

Married life without times of transcendence is hard to bear, for it is then that man and wife may find their way back to the fullness of their love. This fullness should spill over into daily duties. They return to routine responsibilities radiant and renewed. Their life together is no longer a collection of isolated events without meaning. In recollection all moments are interwoven in the splendor of their love.

Celibate religious life that strives to incarnate itself in daily living participates in the same rhythm of recollection and participation as married life. No life can be lived deeply without some recollection. In participative religious life, I am present to the Lord and to the field of incarnation of this presence, whether my chosen labor is that of a nurse, teacher, administrator, cook, artist or author. Every field, these included, implies some routine aspects which in and by themselves may seem meaningless and isolated. However, if I live in the ebb and flow of recollection and action, if I gather myself together from time to time to celebrate in silence my love for the Lord, I may gradually be filled with the grace of presence to transcend the inevitable unpleasant aspects of cultural participation.

Transcendence does not imply an escape from my concrete situation. Rather it is an intense deepening. I feel inclined to move more fully into my field of incarnation, to really meet the children in my classroom, the patients under my care, to compose, paint, write, study or design better than before, to be more respectful, generous and gracious for the guests of my convent or community. Each thing I do takes on a glow which radiates the light of the Lord whom I meet in my recollection. Without this ebb and flow, my religious life may become as meaningless as the life of that married person who is unable to celebrate his love, who never recollects the meaning of his marriage in light of the mutual trust to which two persons originally assented.

Recollection to celebrate my highest values is something to be strived after, so that I may gain profound insight into the true meaning of my religious-cultural participation. Recollected presence to Christ changes the things in daily life from isolated entities to meaningful aspects of an harmonious totality. As in a circular movement, I may find in my field of incarnation manifold revelations of the mystery of the Lord which nourish my religious life and help transform my world.

My call to religious life is also an invitation to unfold the culture in light of the religious perspective. Some may lose themselves in the immediacy of persons, things and events, but I must be the one to point toward their transcendent value. This is the meaning my life style symbolizes to the beholder of religious life. To cherish this perspective, I may have to distance myself at times from the mere mastery of things in order to experience culture and civilization as a movement to be redeemed and purified by Christ. Without recurrent recollection, I may lose this perspective which alone gives full meaning to my life. When I resurrect this attitude within myself, I discover in all things traces of the manifold presence of the Lord. I recognize that recollection and incarnation both feed and nourish the life of the spirit that elevates my doing beyond the level of routine, custom and habit.

Presence to the Lord is not a matter of logical

thinking, nor is it something I can reason myself into experiencing. It cannot be compelled, for this presence is a gift and a grace. Its most basic attitude is not activity but receptivity. Its most fundamental orientation is not force but relaxation, not the way of willfulness but of a certain passivity.

In order to live this religious attitude and to foster the living of the rhythm of recollection and participation in himself and others, the religious celibate chooses freely to bind himself to a certain style of life symbolized by a respectful obedience to the dynamics of the life situation as a temporal and local manifestation of the Lord; a chaste or respectful love for self and others as uniquely called and graced by the Sacred; and a respectful use, transformation and celebration of things natural and cultural as gifts of God.

These three fundamental dynamics of the evolving religious personality — obedience, chastity and poverty — lead to religious maturity when personally appropriated. The vowed religious lives the threefold path in a concentrated way by his commitment to celibacy and community. The beholder of this life, the religious layman or woman, living these attitudes in a less concentrated, less explicit style, looks to the vowed religious for inspiration and insight into the structure of recollection and participation that lies at the root of religious unfolding for man.

Already in the life of a small child, there is a noticeable reconciliation of recollection and action. Something flashes before the child, perhaps a silver spoon or a brightly shining cup. He sees it and, after a moment's hesitation, moves toward it, at first groping helplessly and gradually becoming more sure and sensitive.

This rhythm of perception, hesitation and motion, however primitive in childhood, is a foreshadowing of the integration of profound recollection and meaningful participation fostered by religious living. In dealing with the union of recollection and action, we are therefore touching upon some of the most fundamental structures of human life.

Muscular action and sense perception, unified in childhood, develop a far deeper unity and refinement as life goes on. The child no longer explores his surroundings merely by means of his senses, which see a flashing toy or hear a tapping noise and move toward them. As he matures, both perception and motion become attuned to the world around him. He masters his muscles and motions in accordance with the situation as a whole. Where before action was prompted by the need for immediate satisfaction, now his perception needs to be attuned to many perspectives of the situation. The moment of stillness before action must thus be correspondingly increased.

When a man was but a child, food and drink appeared and with just a moment's hesitation, he ate heartily. However, now that he is grown, the situation and its surroundings have to be considered too. Let us say he is invited for the first time to his girl friend's home for dinner. He sits patiently, observing what the rest of the family does, not daring to make the first move. He is unusually recollected. Even before he went there, he pondered over what he would do. His desire to dine is undiminished. However, to find the right mode of response and make a favorable impression on her parents, he knows he has to be aware of more than merely the dinner he is dying to eat.

Mature participation goes hand in hand with a growing need to recollect myself in presence to all aspects of a situation. Recollection thus belongs to the essence of human action as distinguished from mere motion. The two are no more separable than the unified rhythm of perception, hesitation and motion in early childhood. Moments of standing still are preludes to profound human action. The more prolonged the recollection, the more profound the action may be.

The great pianist is not one who concentrates only on technique; his soul is in his playing. He was gifted with a certain sensitivity, but he never takes this gift for granted. He knows that practice alone will not bring to light his creative response to magnificent musical compositions. He has to pore over the music, listen to others' playing for long hours and feel the expectation of his audience, if he is to nurture his gift and bring it to full and lasting flowering.

The more meaningful the action, the more deep and prolonged recollection has to be. The two are interwoven. If the pianist were to neglect his need for recollection and play constantly for money or fame without quiet preparation, he would soon appear superficial to an audience of taste and discrimination.

True human action is recognizable by this standing back to resource myself in the meaning of my endeavor in all its manifestations — functional, social, æsthetic and transcendent. For every human action and situation has also a transcendent meaning insofar as it is rooted in the Sacred. The vowed religious, like the religious layman or woman, perceives the manifold meanings of a situation, but he is one called mainly to center upon the Holy as revealed in that situation.

To be receptive to the revelation of the Holy in persons, things and events, I as a religious have to stand still and recollect this presence in all I do. As one who has vowed my life in obedience, respectful love and respectful use and celebration of things as gifts of the Lord, I incur the responsibility to keep religious presence alive among mankind and man. My life is living witness that one or the other perspective alone — only the functional or only the social — is not enough. Unlike others who are not called to this life orientation, I as a vowed religious should stress by my very life style the unbreakable bond between participation in which I am present to culture and civilization as manifestations of the Holy and recollection which allows me to see my life of action in its truest light.

205

Religious represent in a special style and intensity the receptivity of all men to the transcendent dimension of life and culture. While all men are called to unite action and recollection in their own lives not all are called to spend the same time and effort in lively witness to this unity. It cannot be denied that this unity is deeply embedded in human life; however, it stands in danger of neglect in a civilization where the sense of accomplishment for pure ego satisfaction may supersede the ultimate sense of human endeavor as the unfolding of self and others by growth in action in light of the Sacred. More than ever, persons are needed who by their very lives unite participation and religious presence in tune with man's need for passing beyond mere motion and agitation into the realm of transcendent human action.

IV

Obstacles to Religious Living

in Western Culture

As the former explorations disclose, the style of thinking characteristic of Religion and Personality or Fundamental Spirituality differs from the linear kind of reflection typical of most other disciplines. The approach of spirituality is concentric or spiral. It is not passing from one point of information to another but concentrating on, for example, one life attitude and delving deeper into its meaning and structure as well as its actual or possible relationship to other life attitudes or situations. The student of spirituality stands still to ask: What does this mean? What is its structure? What does it say to my life? What does it say to the life of my community, and how does it affect my culture?

After this brief methodological consideration, we may turn to an explication of the difficulties occasioned by the rise of certain trends in the movement of human history in the western world and about ways in which they may affect humane and religious living.

Utilitarianism

Many problems of contemporary religious life are problems plaguing my civilization. While some may leave the consecrated life due to personal difficulties, others may depart never seeing that ills which seem peculiar to this life form are common to all life forms in the western world. Certain ailments prevailed in my culture before I entered my community, and these will not be dissolved when I go. One obstacle to humane and religious living in the West is that of utilitarianism, which should not be confused with enlightened usefulness.

Utilitarianism maintains that the main value in life is to be measurably successful. The effectiveness, not the goodness, truth and beauty of things, persons, deeds and encounters, is what counts. Is it productive, profitable, practically relevant? These are for many the guidelines of life and living.

Initiates to religious life are persons who may have grown up in a pragmatic environment. They entered communities of participative religious, which not uncommonly, were organized tightly around certain works. To keep these enterprises functioning seemed in some cases to be the ultimate and exclusive meaning of the community and its members. This emphasis and, at times, inflexible fixation may have taken over unwittingly in religious life.

In former ages which marked the beginning of religious life, men or women came together to spend their lives in labor and contemplation under the guidance of a master of interiority. They chose to live together in mutual support and encouragement, vowing to live in full presence to the Lord, and, through their prayer and witnessing, to lead others to grace and salvation.

Religious presence was their primary purpose. Social enterprises may or may not have occupied them, depending on their situation. Some groups desired to serve others in specific ways, so they began to care for the sick, teach children, and aid the poor and disadvantaged. Cultural participation expressed in service became a secondary purpose organically and continuously flowing from their life of presence to the Holy.

In some instances religious life became wholly service-oriented. Heads of congregations, directors of formation, members of councils were influenced by this trend. Empty places in highly organized community enterprises had to be filled by competent professionals. Staffing the intricate organizational complexes they supervised became a central preoccupation. Some religious seemed imbued with the principle that their first obligation was to uphold the external organizational effectiveness of the community.

Often to be a good religious meant mainly spending myself in service of whatever functional endeavors my community was committed to support. So long as I readied myself to be inserted into any empty place within the system, I would seem to be fulfilling my deepest unique call to witness to the Holy in community and culture. Thus my efficiency and productivity became the dominating norm in the implicit silent evaluation of my religious life. When utilitarianism takes over to such an extent, some religious may have the sincere conviction that the only meaning of their lives is to serve society. However pertinent this may be, service can never be the exclusive meaning of the consecrated life form.

Choosing to commit myself to the threefold path of human and spiritual unfolding frees me to explore and to live the fullness of humane and religious living and to communicate this fullness to others. The life of the vows involves a special call to those who are drawn to live before the Lord in obedience to the deepest reality of the historical situation, in respectful love for self and others, and in respectful presence to the transcendent message of nature and culture. As a religious, I am sustained in this quest by my community. If, together with others, I reach a fullness of personal and spiritual growth — from this depth — I may reach out and be of unique service to the culture. Ideally I stand among men as one of the religious-cultural participants who have traditionally led the search for holiness and wholeness. Participative religious life is thus not primordially a life of isolated utilitarian service but of service emerging from a vowed presence to the Holy as appearing in natural and cultural situations, in people and in things.

The trend toward utilitarian take-over of human and spiritual life dominates western culture as a whole. All of us feel pushed and pulled to perform efficiently and effectively. We feel guilty when we are not doing something. Religious are not necessarily an exception to this rule. They too feel guilty when not being recognizably useful, when, for instance, engaged in play, æsthetic pursuits, or prayer.

While people outside religious life may have like guilt feelings, they are more easily inclined to say, "Forget about it; I've enough on my mind already." It is not unusual, however, to hear generous religious, who already labor excessively, express the desire to take on more responsibility than they can physically or emotionally bear. Such excessive availability harms religious life which is meant to be a radiant center of human and spiritual values, sustained by relaxation, play, contemplation, and appreciation of æsthetic beauty.

Though utilitarianism affects society at large, it has a particularly pernicious affect on the living of the threefold path of religious presence. Living the religious attitudes of obedience, respectful love and respectful presence to things natural and cultural is distinct from the mere development of practical habits which facilitate effective teamwork. Such habits of efficiency may be developed by following without question the team leaders' organizational pointers, by fostering camaraderie and cooperation among the team members, and by instilling a sense of parsimony and frugality. Though the three religious attitudes are in themselves boundaries to a merely utilitarian approach, they may still be perverted precisely because they also tend to make the religious more useful, cooperative and efficient. Perversion sets in when this latter secondary result is experienced not as a gratifying side effect but as *the* value and meaning of the threefold path. Perversion like this may also occur because those who enter religious life come to it from a society already inclined to overestimate the value of the pragmatic.

Utilitarianism and Obedience

Obedience, or listening to the call of God in the dynamism of daily events, implies openness to the whole of my historical situation. In this context listening to history means not only attention to data collected from the past, but also a dynamic listening to the unfolding of my life in an emerging time and place. Full listening to reality guides my wise response to all dimensions of my life situation. The revelations of reality are experienced as invitations to me from the Lord to make the best of every happening. I do so in a rhythm of changing what can and should be changed, upholding respectfully what seems already good, and patiently bearing with what is not yet changeable at this moment.

However, to the utilitarian mind there should be only openness to one aspect of life and life situation, namely, that of usefulness. Once this becomes the foundation of change and adaptation, fundamental listening to the deepest possibilities of human and spiritual unfolding is often confused with listening to the details of the practical productive life alone. Because my listening is attuned mainly to the organizational aspect of reality, to my capacity to perform or direct a variety of tasks, pseudo-religious pragmatism may become a substitute for concentrated religious presence. If I am a religious who is also a teacher, the effectiveness of my total personal and religious life may in some respects be judged by the way in which I plan my classes, keep the schoolroom quiet, and get my grades to the office on time. The worth of my personal and religious life is thus measured by the success of my professional life. It becomes more and more difficult to be peacefully present to the unique beauty and value of my life form when the dynamic living of this attitude is leveled by a onesided utilitarian view.

Utilitarianism and Chaste Celibate Love

The vow of celibacy and of chaste or respectful love guides my relation to self and others. In the deepest sense chastity or non-violating love means that I respect my own and the other's integrity not only physically but also psychologically and spiritually. This presupposes an attitude of profound respect for the mystery of his being and for his inalienable human right to privacy.

Directly contrary to this is the mere pragmatic approach, for then I see the other and myself mainly in terms of our potential productivity. The life of consecrated commitment to the unfolding of self, others and surroundings may be stifled in situations where production and profitableness are the highest wisdom. The attitude of chaste, celibate love, which in a sense is a vow of *useless* love, is transformed under the impact of this trend into a vow of increased usefulness. It becomes merely a practical means of being most effectively available for the performance of needed functions in society without being encumbered by an exclusive familial relationship.

This is not to say that my celibate life should not promote practical endeavors which may benefit others. It is simply a reminder that none of these modes of service can be equated with the ultimate meaning of respectful love. Ideally service and respect complement one another, but in a culture which overvalues the pragmatic, it is easy to violate the integrity of others by forcing my projects on those who do not see the wisdom of my particular practical solution to their problems. This is only one symptom of utilitarianism's pernicious effect on celibate and non-violating love.

Utilitarianism and Poverty

Poverty of spirit opens me to the wise enjoyment and use of things not only in their immediacy but in their capacity to reveal the hidden, transcendent meaning of human life and culture. Poverty nourishes my quiet appreciation of the silent companions of my daily life as gifts of God. These gifts include my clothes and furniture, my house and room, my food and drink, my books and tools. Poverty of spirit lets me taste the goodness of the small and simple things of life waiting patiently for my appreciation of them.

Once these things become dear to me, once I can handle them delicately with grace and care, I may be able to use them wisely and devoutly to foster God's work and the welfare of self and others. I also live this attitude when I listen to music, bring my eyes to rest in the beauty of art, enjoy the graciousness of my bodily movements and quiet my soul in the silent stillness of prayer. Poverty thus implies the willingness to re-create myself and to develop a taste for the wise and respectful use of things.

Without such an approach, the spirit of poverty may become a Spartan form of pragmatism. Mere practical involvement seems to be an adequate substitute for human and religious experience. Those who live in less attractive houses — serviceable but not beautiful — may be lauded as "holier" than those who occupy houses which reflect æsthetic appreciation.

The sense of beauty, which is also useless, is replaced by a sense of service which is always useful.

However, I cannot readily experience a life of prayerful presence to the Holy, illumined by deep religious experience, if my mode of presence to reality is merely utilitarian. The guideline that only the serviceable is worthwhile does not help to deepen my life of æsthetic appreciation, prayer, and human encounter. Equal emphasis should be given to the enjoyment of beauty and the readiness for relaxation. Without this, when I begin to relax — to do nothing in the deepest sense — I feel immediately guilty because somehow I am betraying implicit standards of conduct which do not include "wasting time." Even if I play, I feel that I should somehow be useful in play. So play is more and more a matter of meeting a definite schedule. Also I find myself making excuses for why I am sitting still, enjoying nature, reading or listening to music. I feel compelled to explain what I am doing. Poverty of spirit should free me for recollection and relaxation which is the beginning of any possibility of play, true human encounter, prayer or religious experience.

Thus when we consider obstacles to religious living and to religious life in western culture, it is necessary to go to the roots of western culture where this life is situated, as well as to examine certain fashionable trends which may have encroached upon it. How does utilitarianism affect the religious life form and

216

the thinking, willing, perceiving, feeling person who enters religious life?

Such questioning implies investigation of the impact utilitarianism has had on my personal life and on the lives of others. If task orientation has taken over in my religious community, persons may be appointed to leading positions solely on basis of their effectiveness as administrators. Fellow religious may fail to report sickness for fear that their work will suffer. Having been indoctrinated in the myth of service, any thought of self is branded as selfish. Even though I may suffer, the work goes on. Such is the perversion of common sense in a community that glorifies mere practicality to the detriment of human self-unfolding in presence to the Lord.

One crucial responsibility of those who initiate the young into religious life is to make these early years more than a mere period of utilitarian training. The person entering religious life may be already infected by the bent toward utilitarianism. The unconscious predisposition to build his life on motives of measurable achievement should be faced directly by each candidate. Otherwise it is conceivable that this orientation will win out. When he enters the culture in a professional capacity, he may gradually become unfaithful to his call to be a religious-cultural participant.

Thus before finally committing himself to the religious life form, the initiate should recognize tendencies to idolize the pragmatic in isolation from humane and religious witnessing. Even his question, "What is the purpose of religious life?", may initially be a utilitarian question, especially if he enters a congregation which has made massive attempts to serve the functional society. Consequently, fundamental spirituality, which is inseparable from the original religious life form in eastern and western religions, may never be his.

Hopefully, a renewed atmosphere will be fostered by persons in formation, who, together with others, recognize that utilitarianism as such can become an obstacle to full human and religious living, both inside and outside the community. Again, religious themselves should point the way for all men toward a lessening of this influence by living also human and spiritual instead of mere utilitarian values.

Rationalism and Behaviorism

As we have seen, certain tendencies in western culture seem detrimental to the full development of the consecrated life and to religious living for man in general. In addition to utilitarianism, two of these trends, involving the culture as a whole, could be labeled "behaviorism" and "rationalism." These terms are used to identify neither psychological nor philosophical systems of thought. In this case they merely point toward predominant modes of living in western culture.

Rationalism as a life style is the rigorous attempt to base all my life and every human encounter only on insight that can be obtained by means of logic. Consequently, I neglect all the light steadily shed on my life by other powers of reason and reflection; by faith, common sense and tradition; by observation and perception; and by experience, emotion and sensitivity.

In this onesided analytical approach to reality, various dimensions are lifted from my life situation as a whole and juggled in a dance of abstract ideas. While logic should be regarded as one excellent aid to wise living, logic alone may cause me to lose touch with everyday reality. Ideas, concepts, rationales, and systems of thought, have a way of becoming blindly closed in upon themselves. Thought should not be divorced from life. Neither should it repress life. Logic is only one side of self-unfolding. It does not necessarily make me a whole person able to find and live human and spiritual values in world and culture.

As man became more subservient to the processes of production and consumption, rationalism invaded the day to day organization of human life. Affection, emotion, religious experience, æsthetic perception — all came to be regarded as interruptions, as pleasant breaks — to prepare one for even greater effectiveness in the process of production. Rationalism welding human life to technique was not only peculiar to industry; it also became the guiding principle for many social institutions, like schools, hospitals, churches, and religious congregations, which were seen as places to prepare people to assume their place in a task-oriented society.

Technical rationality, which is a great blessing, can become a curse when applied indiscriminately to all areas of life and living. Yet this is what happened in western civilization. Man became an arm of the machine. He began to live almost wholly out of his mind on the plateau of pure rationality.

A similar trend, closely related to technical rationalism, is the life style of behaviorism. No one would deny the human need to develop proper and effecfective patterns of external behavior. Conditioned learning or training is a necessary step toward personal growth. If I had to rely on my own insight to discover modes of accepted behavior, I would probably be regarded as an unbearable nuisance. Long before I am able to challenge or change certain common codes of conduct and comportment, I need first to adopt them without totally understanding their importance and then to experience personally their value and meaning.

However, behaviorism as a life style is the exaltation of conditioned learning as the main principle of personality formation. My life becomes a computation of rules, customs, and codes which I never appropriate personally. Technical rationalism supports this tendency by training people to adhere inflexibly to their precisioned planning of life and living in spite of changes in their situation. The less one bothers about personal appropriation and meaningfulness, the more smoothly can he be wedded to the machinery of a certain system.

Participative religious communities emerge from the tumultuous seas of cultural movements. Members are drawn from this society and return to it as persons prepared to assume their place as religious-cultural participants. Religious, like their fellowmen, are aware of the value and necessity of technical rationality as well as the need for a certain amount of behavioristic training. This appreciation is understandable. One who has failed to foster his capacity for logical thought and right patterns of comportment can make only a limited contribution to the unfolding of community and culture. However rationalism and behaviorism, when blown out of proportion in religious life, take on peculiar forms. What may develop within this life form is a onesided trend toward theological rationalism or religious behaviorism — both of which stifle lived spirituality.

Theology becomes theological rationalism when religious are led to believe that formation in theological conceptualization, traditional or progressive, is an adequate preparation for the art of living one's chosen life form. I can be an excellent theologian and at the same time remain naive in the art of religious living. Though highly trained in theological abstraction, I may be totally out of touch with my inner self and my life situation. I may be oblivious to my unconscious envy, jealousy and need for status and popularity. I may be filled with a hidden pride which closes me off from the Spirit and prevents me from truly caring for anyone but myself.

To educate religious initiates in rational theology alone, no matter how traditional or progressive it may be, does not guarantee that they will gain insight in the concrete problems of living and unfolding their celibate lives in community. The consecrated life can be lived to the full when I learn not only the science of rational theology but also the gracious art of religious living. When the praiseworthy development of theological rationalism is not complemented by a well-formed interiority, many will be inclined to substitute theological principles for true presence to self and others. However, abstract principles alone cannot always help me to cope with the unexpected problems and pleasures of life. Alienated from my deepest self, I may turn the beauty and freedom of religious life into an outline of cerebral do's and don'ts. Meanwhile, desires and passions may grow unchecked in the depths of my personal life.

The triumphant march of rationalism in the West led to an increasing veneration of theological systems and a decrease in appreciation of any discipline that occupied itself with the art of religious living. Consequently spirituality died as a central concern in many religious communities. In the past, theological formation was complemented by formation in the spiritual life. Spirituality, as expounded by the great spiritual writers, is another term for the art and discipline of religious living. As time went on, however, the contemporary adaptation and development of the manifold insights spiritual writers gathered from their own experience and that of others whom they guided was neglected. Therefore, the probings, recommendations and language of spirituality seem to many today obsolete and out of touch with later reflections on the psychological and social conditions of man.

Understandably, spirituality not updated in content and expression became somewhat irrelevant in the eyes of contemporary young men and women entering religious life. Often all that was left of the treasures of spirituality were outlines of some of its main points, accompanied by explanations of the ways in which these insights paralleled certain traditional or contemporary theological systems. In the meantime one real task of spirituality, that of the integration of religious experience and insight with the passions, needs, emotions and desires of man and with his life situation, became secondary to training in rational explanations of belief — systems of thought which by themselves do not necessarily foster lived spirituality.

The art of religious living or fundamental spirituality has not only been supplanted by rational outlines of certain abstract principles of spirituality; it has also been weakened by a trend toward religious behaviorism. When I try to live the consecrated life in the style of religious behaviorism, I am likely to reduce its richness to an exact execution of external codes of conduct — codes which seem to promise a perfect incarnation of holiness. Behavioristic training, as opposed to personal and spiritual formation, proposes a long list of rules and regulations which, if followed faithfully, will supposedly lead me to perfection.

To be sure, a certain amount of conditioned learning is necessary for human development in any direction. Such learning is as much a part of the religious life form as of any other lasting life form. Behaviorism becomes onesided when training in externals is not continuously complemented by growth in presence to myself and others as called by God, accompanied by an awareness of my own motives, desires, passions, needs and feelings.

I should experience not only the general meaning of the behavior patterns in which I am being initiated but also what they mean concretely for my unique personality with its individual inheritance and history. Only in this way can I come to know why and how I welcome spontaneously or resist unconsciously a certain custom or rule, why and how I tend unwittingly to abuse a prescribed pattern in order to enhance my self-image or the image others have of me.

A related tendency, which may displace authentic spirituality, is that of pietism. Pietism is the attempt to substitute for the authentic affective dimension of spirituality a collection of shallow sentiments, which may be unrelated to the inner reality of a person. Pious feelings are harmful or propitious only in relation to what they mean for the person: how authentically are they rooted in his emerging self, how well or how little have they been appropriated? Pietism becomes disintegrative when a desired collection of pious feelings are superimposed on my personality. These unassimilated feelings may be at odds with my hidden strivings and emotions. They may even be used as an escape from the painful task of really facing myself, as a defense against real religious transformation of my deeper personality.

True spirituality, on the contrary, cultivates a profound but peaceful self-confrontation before the Lord. Deepening self-presence before God will prevent the pretense that I possess religious feelings described by others when in reality I do not or not yet experience them in depth. If I deceive myself about this, devotional feelings may belong to me like so many items isolated from my personality and added to an already amassed collection of rational systems and behavioristic techniques, all of which may lessen day by day the possibility of growth in the spiritual life. For my deepest self may never come to terms with a superimposed piety.

When personal and spiritual formation is replaced by rationalistic, behavioristic and pietistic training in postulancy, novitiate, juniorate or seminary, the initiate may seek and seemingly find desirable thoughts, feelings, and patterns of behavior without growing in presence to his true feelings, thoughts and motivations. An initial orientation like this will affect his later attempts to unfold his religious life — attempts which often fail.

Alienation from my real feelings, thoughts and motivations prevents me from participating in the culture as a radiant witness to the Lord. I cannot easily grow in respectful love, care and concern for God, man and world if I have never found the way to dialogue with my personal and prepersonal likes and dislikes. Pious feelings, unsustained by inner affirmation, are likely to fail me in a crisis situation.

From this it may be clear how crucial it is for the future of religious life that those who enter this lasting life form are guided by well-prepared masters of interiority, who can help them grow in presence to their true selves before God. Initiates to religious life are called to develop a personal, concrete spirituality, rooted in realistic dialogue with themselves and their situation. It must not be forgotten that these candidates, like their cultural counterparts, are influenced by rationalism and behaviorism, peculiar to western technological civilization. Such trends may incline them to move away from the whole, to reduce or expand reality out of proportion according to their isolated scheme of things.

For instance, some initiates are tempted early in

religious life to build an idealized picture of self and community that can never be reached. In the meantime they neglect to center their thinking, willing, imagining, perceiving, feeling selves in this life form as it is and as, with time, compassion, patience and ongoing efforts to improve, it may become. Consequently, later on they fail ultimately to reach those who are searching for real persons, not agitated dreamers.

Accepting the limitations of my life situation is always an entrance to grace. Under the impact of rationalism and behaviorism, however, it becomes rather easy to will my attention in the opposite direction, away from my real need for redemption, away from the spiritual experience of the Lord's love for me. The tragedy is, if this experience is not central at the beginning of religious life, I may be taken in totally by these and like obstacles to religious living in the culture, while my fellow cultural participants may already be looking for ways to pass beyond these barriers.

Specialization

Specialization can be identified as another possible obstacle to religious living in contemporary western society. I am known in this society for the position I hold, not necessarily for the human qualities I unfold. In the West, positional titles are highly valued for they convey status and may result in elaborate offices, bigger houses, and expensive cars. We no longer recognize one another by our inner dimensions but by our outward appearances. As a result, there may be an identification of my personal, real value with my special status and position. This may lead potentially to a falsification of self. I may have a very important job and still be a poor person; I may also have a very poor job and be gifted with a fine personality. But in western civilization, where specialization is an ultimate goal for many, we tend to identify human life with specialized labor, inner value with positional title.

People come to religious life from a culture in which they too were evaluated according to their capacity for production and success by means of specialized knowledge and skills. Unfortunately, they may find that the same trend has crept into religious life. If I identify my total worthwhileness with professional specialization, academic degree or administrative position, I may be inclined to put all my security in status. Consequently, as soon as someone else is called to a more distinguished specialty of rank, task or profession, I may feel a pang of jealousy. Because the other is getting ahead of me, he becomes a threat to me. In short, I am entangled in the throes of anxious competition based not on inner values but on outer position and specialized attainment.

That this is harmful to the whole atmosphere of religious life is undeniable. Unconscious competition for special positions may lead to tension in the community. Moreover, it may harm schools and hospitals staffed by religious, for some may want to be assigned to specialties not suited to them. It seems a vicious circle, for without such a position they may lose their self-confidence. The same could be said of some superiors who feel lost when they have to leave this position. Being a superior gave them a sense of value and losing a leading place may make them feel anxious and insecure.

Unconscious striving for distinction tends to make religious life less relevant in the world. If specialty and position are the only criteria of value, one whose talents do not fit the prescribed positional niches may never be able to find himself and offer the unique gift of religious witnessing to the culture. If the community attempts to streamline everyone in order to fit them into a certain specialty, it may breed professional mediocrity, not because the members themselves are mediocre but because they may be discouraged in the pursuit of their unique contribution to religious-cultural unfolding. To engage in other areas of cultural participation where one is truly at home may be looked upon as an unwillingness to serve. These situations did not occur so readily in the founding years of religious life, for then specialization or professionalism was not as pervasive a part of the culture. What would be called "lesser" occupations now had their own dignity then.

In our society the idea of personal value is tied intimately to the profession one specializes in and not to the person he is. The evaluation of the specialized occupation is linked unconsciously in turn to the Greek mind-body split which may still influence our power of estimation.

For example, today it may be difficult to find someone to prepare the meals creatively and graciously for community and guests. Some may like this service and have the refined taste and creative talent for it. Their personality may stand to grow through it, but because meal preparation does not convey status in a civilization which suffers from the split between mind and body, this person may decide that she should be a teacher or nurse. Even her family may step in and protest that their daughter did not enter the religious life to involve herself in care of bodily nourishment, a work that may seem to some western minds far removed from pure spirit. The family believes she should be in a school or hospital. A religious college or high school teacher, who must incidentally serve a visitor to the community, may astonish him by her lack of graciousness, of refinement and care for every detail of the meal and every need of the guest. He may sense behind her prim, austere behavior, repugnance for the "lowly" things of the body as compared with the "higher" things of the classroom, the textbook, the group discussion.

Even though it is not possible to overcome this tendency to overestimate distinguished specialization at once, we should try to do something about it. The impact of specialization is too grave to be brushed aside. One way to cope with it at present is to make clear from the first day of initiation that unconscious positional ambition and subsequent positional envy does exist and that this kind of ambition and envy may be due, among other things, to a wrong identification of my value with my successful specialization.

There are other implications of the influence of western specialization on religious life. Before the age of specialized positions, religious understood that religious life was a total way of life, a life form. They would define religious life as a life style and not as a specialization. Later on when participative congregations emerged, it became difficult for some members to think about religious life as a life form. They began to think about it as a specialization. This is not strange because it was the main way in which western man thought at the time. He was inclined to define everything by specialization.

If someone asked a religious what he did, he would hardly respond, "I am a person set free to be a witness to the Lord in the culture." Rather he would identify his life with his profession, as most non-religious would do if asked the same question. One would not be likely to say, "I am a man whose life style is to love my family." Rather he would be a carpenter or a stock broker. Life style has thus been reduced to a matter of defining what I do.

Sometimes congregations seem to take a similar line. To the question, "What is your congregation?", the response may be, "We are a congregation especially dedicated to education or to nursing, or we are founded to serve the underdeveloped nations or to do social work." Instead of defining religious life primarily as a mode of being in the world involving the whole person, it was defined in terms of a certain specialization. We are still caught in this dilemma.

Regarding a religious community, people ask sometimes, "What is its special purpose? What do they specialize in?" As soon as the specialized purpose disappears, they may think this specific religious community will disappear too. This is not true. Religious life is not a specialization; it is not a function but a fundamental life form, a mode of presence to the Lord. So, if, in the course of history, specialized enterprises like schools, hospitals or missions have to be closed, religious life will not necessarily die. Those who believe that this life is only a matter of, for example, teaching, may rightly conclude that they can teach just as well outside of the religious community. But teaching is only one specialization which helps to express religious life culturally in a special moment of history. There will still be religious devoted to this life form even if they find themselves doing something else at another moment in history.

Even more seriously, specialization, in one of its notable forms like professionalism, may have begun to define my daily psychological life more than the fundamental form of religious life itself. My feelings, emotions and thoughts revolve around my profession which may have been equated implicitly and unconsciously with the whole of religious life. If I am a specialist in chemistry, for example, I may teach high school chemistry, go to the university for further course work, and center my reading around books, magazines and articles devoted to chemistry. This means that my ideas and perceptions are organized around my specialization. As a result I may do less reading in other fields. Poetry and fiction are squeezed into my routine and only then in small doses. Chemistry centers my attention and begins to direct my whole psychological life. Such a decisive orientation is even more possible when my specialization is in some area of the human sciences. The latter sciences bring a degree of self-awareness and are not as easily distinguishable from my personal life as the physical sciences are.

Religious thus have to be cautious when it comes to organizing their lives around a particular specialization. Outside religious life, people who contract for a job may find that it does not fit them and proceed to change to another. But this may not be so easy in a religious congregation which has schools or hospitals to staff and automatically places aspirants in that frame.

Conflict between person and profession can lead to a breakdown. It may happen that a religious gifted with a poetic nature is placed as a mathematics teacher, a specialization which may force him constantly to repress his poetic nature. At some moment he may express a zealous desire to become involved in work in the inner city. In this case it may be questionable how much this decision reflects true zeal and how much it may arise from an unconscious feeling of unfulfillment in the classroom. The sudden burst of at last "finding myself" may sometimes be a symptom of an unconscious desire to escape onesided specialization.

Instead of stressing specialization as the end of religious life, I should begin to reemphasize this life as a mode of being before the Lord which is lived out in different kinds of cultural participation. However, the present situation cannot be changed overnight. Many communities today are bound to highly specialized common endeavors. There may be no clear distinction between living space and labor space in community. The same people I work and compete with in the school and in the hospital may be those I meet in my community. This means that there may never be a lessening of unconscious competition between various religious.

The same competition exists outside religious life but the difference is that men and women competing in a labor space do not always come home to the same living space. When they go home they can let down their guard and relax in order to face the competition of the following day. In religious life, however, tension may mount because there is no separation between living space (community life) and the space of positional competition (labor space). Though this division is not possible at once because of the historical situation, it is possible for the time being to foster a shift from isolated specialization to the whole person. Total formation in the dimension of wisdom, of humane attitudes and of prayerful presence to the Lord cannot come through specialization. A shift in attitude must precede a return to humane and religious living.

If religious life becomes the road by which I deepen myself as a prayerful wise person of refined sensitivity, I can bring to my specialization a radiant religious personality. As a religious who is a teacher, poet, painter, nurse, architect or manual laborer, I may be able to inspire others who may not live in an atmosphere which cultivates personal and spiritual formation. Religious life makes me free for these values. It gives me time to relax so that I can be available in a special way to many others. If I had a family, I would probably have less time and opportunity to go beyond my function and grow toward becoming a deep, rich person with a great deal to give.

The specialist attitude can unfold only a narrow niche of my life. On the other hand, when I listen to music and engage in dialogue, when I enjoy nature and pray silently, I am becoming a source of richness for those whom I shall meet in cultural participation. The fact that I am truly living the radiance of my faith will make me a better specialist insofar as my profession will be integrated within the whole of my personality. I shall be myself, not just the work I do.

However, as long as religious life is identified with professional specialization, defections may increase. Religious may decide to leave because they can be good, sometimes even better, specialists outside religious life than inside. Only when I clarify for myself and others that the consecrated life of presence to the Lord is far more than a specialization — that it is the road toward developing as a whole person in a beautifully relaxed way — shall I begin to experience and live the unique richness of my chosen life form.

As we have seen, religious life in the West is influenced by a functional society which values the usefulness rather than the goodness, truth and beauty of persons, events and things. Caught in the current of this trend, some communities may have extended themselves so far that professionalism dominates the atmosphere of community living. The religious life form is consequently given secondary place. The value of specialization assumes a prominent position, for this is the road by which one produces good educators, nurses and administrators who may or may not have evolved a deep interiority in presence to the Lord.

Specialization of labor or study is frequently isolated from the formation of the whole religious person. As a religious I may become a master or doctor in a certain field. This is a noteworthy accomplishment, provided I have at the same time evolved a deep human wisdom and experienced a true self-emergence which enables me to see my specialization as only one side of life. I need to resist the tendency to mistake my specialized limited insight for an in-depth knowledge of every dimension of my life situation. I can be a learned psychologist and a child in religious living, a professor of English and freshman in human relationships, a doctor of medicine and a failure in the wisdom of love. This is not to deny the need for specialization but only to remind me of its dangers. It may lead to the closed belief that because I am good in one field I am automatically good in all others.

Unfortunately, specialization and professional training may have taken over formation in the deeper living of humane and religious attitudes. The main bent of initiation into religious life may not be formation in the wisdom and beauty of human and spiritual values but in preparation for a future position. Not all directors of formation are well prepared to give formation in the art of religious living. As a consequence, in some places the original meaning and purpose of novitiate has been disbanded so that new candidates will have more time to prepare for their profession already during the canonical year.

Moreover, specialization is often the guiding light in the choice and the appointment of a novice master or directress of novices. While specialized knowledge in theology, counseling or psychology may solve a given problem, it may not give initiates the formation they need in the art of religious living and fundamental spirituality.

Although participative religious sooner or later enter the specialized world, they can become aware of its onesidedness by gaining the proper formation in religious living at home. Stressing specialization early in religious life may result in its eventual domination of the community. The central questions about religious life cannot be answered by mere specialization. As a religious, I am called to unfold myself in Christ as a whole person before God. I must be able to contemplate and pray, to enjoy æsthetic beauty and radiate its essence, to unfold wisdom, understanding and dignity. With wisdom I can discover the true values of life; with understanding I can relate to others in a deeply reverent manner; with dignity, I can distance myself from the moment and strive to perceive the deepest reality of my life situation. All these dimensions of living must be initiated early in religious life. Only then can I become a specialist with a minimum of risk of dehumanization.

If specialization is onesidedly fostered in religious communities, it may endanger future religious-cultural participation. The culture of the West is at the moment undergoing vast changes from a mechanized specialized culture to one where the most important emphasis will be on the whole person. The age of specialization is giving way to an age of wholeness. People will have more time for living religion, enjoying beauty and play, and deepening wisdom in general.

How dramatic it will be if religious are mainly specialists in one field and not deeply involved religious persons who can answer the needs of this new population. How dramatic it will be if many seeking persons have to resort to other sources for formation in the art of humane and religious living. Many already express the need for humanization and spiritualization, but when they talk to religious the latter often cannot really communicate the secrets of presence to self, others and the Sacred. They talk about education and organization, about technical renewal and adaptation, but not about religious experience and wisdom. In other words, there is already a crying out among the population for human and religious experience and yet some religious seem more able to compete professionally than to radiate the joy and peace of a humane and religious presence.

Thus in formation, religious must foster the fullness of their life form. This does not mean that specialization must be forsaken, only that it should be placed in its proper perspective. My preparation for full human and religious living must begin in postulancy, novitiate, and juniorate. Then I need a lifetime to deepen the insights of my initiation. Reflective participation in my life form begins when I learn, among other things, to reflect on the pernicious effect specialization may have on the life of the vows.

Specialization and Obedience

The vow of obedience is a commitment under the authority and tradition of my community and in dialogue with others to listen to the whole of reality in order to read God's invitation and to answer it wisely and courageously. Obedience is by its very nature a commitment to a comprehensive religious presence to *all* dimensions of reality within the limits of my possibilities. Only in the light of the fullest possible understanding of our situation can I, together with my fellow religious, find the best answers to support and renew my community and my culture at this moment of history.

However, over-specialization has made this listening extremely difficult. Isolated specialization may tempt a specialist to think that his insight covers the whole of reality. However, the answer of the psychologist, sociologist, or theologian is only one inroad to reality. Full comprehensive listening is virtually impossible if I have not been formed thoroughly in the art of knowing how to relate to reality as a whole.

Specialization and Chaste Celibate Love

The vow of respectful love means that I am committed to my self-unfolding and to the unfolding of the other as called by the Sacred. This respectful presence enables me to accept myself and others as they are, to see their potentialities for balance and wisdom as well as for onesided exaggeration. Respect for the other always involves an opening of myself to him and to his unique world, to his full reality.

However, when I am centered primarily in my profession, respect for the other may be diminished insofar as I see him in terms of my specialization. For example, a mathematician may tend to judge the whole child in light of his competency in the field of algebra. A testing psychologist may categorize a person merely in terms of a measurable cluster of personality traits. Superiors specialized in administration may not know what to do with less efficient people.

Every specialization throws only one kind of light on the person and, if I let it, may blind me to all other dimensions of his personality. I should always be able to transcend my specialty in growing respect for the sacred core of the other which specialized knowledge alone cannot penetrate.

Specialization and Poverty

Poverty is the vow which opens me to the things that matter in my situation and helps me to use things natural and cultural in a wise and balanced way. Here again, I can only handle things wisely if I am open to the whole of nature and culture which contains them.

For example, if I am a monetary specialist and only view things economically I may be tempted to say: "Why make this house beautiful? It costs money and we can use money for other purposes. Less æsthetic furnishings will do." But a beautiful house expresses and fosters our common humanity and brings out the spiritual essence of things. When I sense this beauty, it may help me to use things religiously. To do so I have to live in the spirit of poverty which enables me to distance myself from the mere immediate, course, material and practical meaning of things.

Specialization has affected the practical living of the vow of poverty in other ways. The practice of poverty in regard to the religious community and its members implies among other things the wise expenditure of our resources in accordance with the right hierarchy of values. The highest value or aim of the religious community is the human and spiritual unfolding of each religious as a whole person. In some communities increasing the library with books on general human and religious formation seems less important than buying books which tie in with the specialization being pursued. Many are willing to spend money for specialized education but when it comes to freeing a religious for preparation in formation of the whole person, it seems less necessary. In most congregations persons in primary formation programs are not prepared for just that specific task. While the directress of novices, juniors, or postulants must form the whole person in the art of religious living, she may have no preparation in human and spiritual formation to meet the demands of the candidates she encounters.

Functional Homogeneity

Another obstacle to a balanced unfolding of religious life in the West is the dominance of functional homogeneity. We are children of a civilization entrenched in a gigantic process of mechanization and technical growth. We have found ways of minutely systematizing not only the process of manufacturing but also the effective use of time. To keep the machine of mass production running smoothly, manufacturers must divide their products into homogeneous pieces. For example, goods are packaged in the same wrapper, houses are modeled after standard plans, cars are made on an assembly line. This principle of homogeneity — of conquering reality by dividing it into equal parts — enables producers to provide the goods society needs to sustain an expanding, affluent population.

When man initiates a certain process as central in his civilization, it tends to affect his total perception of himself and his world. Lately we have been inclined to apply the principle of functional homogeneity not only to organization of time and production but also to human life. This attempt may hinder true self-unfolding.

Because religious communities are emerging in this cultural climate, they may be tempted to insert into the process of human and spiritual unfolding the same homogeneity that has proven so successful in the manufacturing of goods and services. The same principles that guide the organization of staff units in hos-

pitals or of grading in schools may be applied ram-
pantly to personal and spiritual formation and to the
initiation of young religious with no thought of the
perils inherent in this trend toward technical-func-
tional homogeneity.

The use of homogeneous productive units implies
that all individuals are tailored in accordance with the
demands of the production process. While I may cut a
tree into homogeneous pieces of wood to make a floor,.
I cannot so easily trim a human being to malleable
size. For example, I may try to feed seminarians and
novices into a hypothetical formation machine. While
these initiates may be trained to execute a series of
effective routines, they may come out rather uncre-
ative members of a religious collectivity unable to become involved as unique self-reliant persons in the
unfolding of history and culture.

The pernicious consequences of this approach may
not be felt until there is general questioning by religious of the homogeneity dominating their lives. In
the past a director of formation may have trained
novices to be homogeneous persons capable of thinking, feeling and doing relatively the same thing. Now,
however, young men and women who enter religious
life must be prepared to live their unique commitment among people who express all kinds of opinions,
some of which are wise and some of which lack wisdom. Where before personal responsibility could be
absorbed by the group, now responsibility is thrown

back on the lonely religious witness in the culture.

Initiates who did not find themselves *as religious*, who did not learn to think, feel and pray *as persons*, may be unable to distinguish between what is fundamental to the living of their life form and what is merely transitory. As recipients of only homogeneous information, they may lose sight of the uniqueness of their personal call to witness for the Sacred in community and culture.

Initiates also have to be prepared to accept the painful fact that not everyone who has consecrated his life to God is automatically a person of deep insight and prophetic vision. Early in religious life, I have to prepare myself to see all sides of the situation and not to hold as necessarily true all that is spoken or written by a religious speaker or writer.

Ideally, the young person who dedicates his life to the religious-cultural unfolding of self and world desires to witness for presence to the Lord in every walk of life, in every task, in every position, which is in tune with his background and personality. His life should radiate wisdom, which is not simply the end product of specialization. To hold a certain position, I need to train for that special field. But to be a radiant witness to the Lord is not attained through specialized procedure and practice. That is why the period of initiation is not meant to be a time of learning but a time of growth in wisdom and self-discovery.

I am asked for this short period to come home to

my own experience, to discover what I can and cannot do, what I can and cannot bear, to find my own limited pace of achievement, to bless adversity as a road to true human and spiritual growth. Thus persons in charge of formation can no longer simply place their initiates in homogeneous boxes; they have to stimulate their critical and prayerful thinking. Initiates must be able, for instance, to read a book or article and see in what way it is no longer an objective rendering of a balanced view of their life situation but rather an expression of the unconscious anger of the writer, of his repressed guilt feelings or unsolved sexual problems. They should be able to disinguish the immature, emotional utterance from the truly wise, creative, prophetic insight which grows out of patient presence to the Lord in a limited life situation.

Many who leave religious life feel unconscious resentment because the ideal they have cherished is not always lived and may never be lived in their lifetime or the lifetime of many to come. Often, if they do leave, they try to assuage the pain by diminishing the life they have left, avowing that its ideal could not be lived within the confines of a religious community. If persons in the period of initiation have only been trained to follow blindly what this or that person writes, they are liable to fall victim later to a one-sided view of another author, a view which is local and temporal, and cease listening to the deepest meaning of their historical situation and their true selves. They too may be tempted to give up rather than staying to answer the appeal of fellow cultural participants who often look to them for insight in the meaning they feel missing in their lives.

To make religious initiates uncritical receivers of written or spoken opinions can be treacherous, for false attitudes formed early in religious life may prevail when they leave the novitiate. Later on they may fall in with persons who seem wise and creative on the surface but who deep down are rebellious, immature and yet clever enough to absorb others in their unconscious problems and resentments. For this period training in specialized areas is not as basic as formation in being present to my own experience. This is a condition for ongoing development of the attitude of receptive acceptance of self and quiet self-presence so needed for a rich and full religious life.

Homogeneity of consciousness, which tends to set uniform standards of thought, feeling, behavior and response, leads to a decrease in authentic spirituality. For formation of a religious personality, many may substitute a homogeneous cutting up of the mystery of their interiority. They do not perceive and accept themselves as unique persons called by the spirit and yet absorbed in conscious or unconscious social trends and plagued by their own jealousy, envy, and anxious need for achievement. Instead they divide themselves up into behavioral pieces who failed to operate properly twelve or fifteen times a week.

The radical moment by moment need for redemption is not felt deeply in one whose life is tabulated on a homogeneous list. Only when I dare to ask why am I so jealous or eager for sympathy and distinction do I dare to gain insight into the dynamic movement of my personality. True unfolding of the personality is a movement away from the complacent comfort of common consciousness. It is a movement toward a personal awareness of myself as loved by the Lord and in turn loving of Him and others.

Functional homogeneity, like specialization and utilitarianism, has its time and place. It is only necessary to recognize how absorption by the homogeneity of common consciousness can harm my personal and spiritual formation and unfolding. There was a time in which prayer was streamlined and some persons never developed a prayer life of their own. This homogeneous trend may be one reason why some religious cannot distinguish between their religious life form and their daily professional experience. More than ever a personal, intimate, intensive life of presence to God is needed to sustain religious self-unfolding. Such growth can never be piecemeal. Thus it is necessary to seek ways in which homogeneity can give way to personal, unique religious presence.

Alienation from Personal Experience

One of the reasons why I may be alienated from personal experience is that I tend to rest complacent-

ly in a common consciousness which I did not appropriate and expand personally and creatively. This is
harmful insofar as it takes me away from my own
consciousness and may halt the continual dialogue
which should take place between my personal consciousness and the common consciousness that surrounds me and from which I emerge continuously.

How do I become aware of my consciousness? First
of all, I am aware of my experiences in a naive way as
a child. The small child is aware spontaneously of
what he feels and expresses this bluntly. The insidi-
ous process of alienation from experience begins when
he is adapted to the functional society. Contemporary
adaptation is in considerable measure a training in
alienation from spontaneous awareness. The spontaneous child can hardly be recognized after ten or
twelve years of adaptation to a functional, homogeneous society. He has for the most part lost his creativity. A kind of dullness and emptiness has replaced
spontaneity. Unprepared as a rule for personal living,
he attaches himself to an "in-group" and is welded to
the common consciousness that sustains this group.

Groupism and Alienation from Self

Coming together in a group may be one source of
alienation from experience, especially if I am not
aware of certain factors which already incline me to
live outside myself. For along with groupism comes
the unfortunate situation of specialization which

249

breeds the technical theologian, the technical philosopher, the technical psychologist — necessary intellectuals whose specialties nonetheless may become substitutes for personal unfolding of the whole man in lived faith and experience. Developing myself as a whole person is a matter of first being present to my own experience, not to the method by which to deal with it or the conceptual tools to analyze and systematize it intellectually. For example, I must first experience presence to the Lord before understanding what this presence truly means.

The nature of technical specialization and the acute development of abstractionism in the West makes us masters of living outside ourselves and outside the confines of the present moment. We place ourselves abstractly in a new situation where we believe our problems may be solved. But if we have not come home to ourselves, no place outside ourselves will satisfy us. We shall always be searching for the better place, for the more understanding person, the more exciting group, and in the meantime our lives may pass us by.

Both groupism and specialism may be used as means for alienating myself from my experience. On the one hand, I am inclined to live outside myself in the comfort of the common consciousness and, on the other hand, I am inclined to believe that maturity is a matter of specialization. While these developments are not necessarily bad, they may harm personal unfolding if I make them the center of my life project.

A person coming from this culture who enters religious life may be tempted to do the same thing he has been trained to do by the culture, namely, to accept blindly certain categories of stereotyped thought without making them his own. The solution for this is not necessarily to oppose all categories of thought in which generations of both East and West have expressed the truth and beauty of religious life. Rather, the answer is to try to experience the great truths of religious living in accordance with my situation of unique commitment to this life form in this specific time and place.

Nonetheless, the difficulty of self-alienation and alienation from experience is especially real for the young person entering religious life. He has to grow beyond the group mentality he has just left and move toward centeredness in the deepest reality of his life. The only way he can do this is by meeting mature people who have not only found themselves but who have also come to understand the contemporary cultural situation and the means it has evolved for self-alienation.

A director who is not himself a master of interiority is likely to be closed to the true needs of an initiate unconsciously yearning to find himself and yet imprisoned by his yearning to be *in* with the group. An unprepared master of religious living may have absorbed a rigid style of life which cautiously keeps out the kinds of problems facing the initiate. If he himself is unprepared to face the real difficulties of religious living, he may succumb to flattery, which is only a means of feeling *in* with what he cannot understand.

The security of an unprepared master of interiority may not be built on personal presence to God but on people outside himself who tell him he is wise, visionary and able to see the truth others fail to heed. In this atmosphere of in-group flattery, weak persons become weaker and the forthright and honest may not survive. Those formed by this master may be unable to face the reality to come in their future religious life.

It is disconcerting to meet religious who frankly confess that they have never had any religious experience. They simply took over the categories in which others speak about religious life and appropriated certain pietistic devotions, which never reached deeper than sentiment.

How easily this wears off in the humdrum of daily living. Without a real confrontation in which I deeply experience these central truths, I may not be able to live them from day to day. If I do discover that life is not as smooth as I dreamed it would be, that there are imperfections in myself, in others, in my superiors, in the Church, in my western culture, I am at once amazed and embittered by it. And if I really begin looking around me I may discover that all these imperfections are not only in my religious community, but also in all religious communities, all religions, all people, and all humanity.

Furthermore, there is no amount of renewal which will ever take away the fundamental greediness, hostility, aggression, disordered sensuality, envy, and jealousy of man, whether one is a religious or a person outside of religious life. Facing this situation is a first step toward becoming aware of myself as I really am. Finally I may come eye to eye with the great truth of the Christian faith — that without the experience of redemption there is no hope of experiencing the deepest meaning of reality.

However painful this experience may be, it is a real one, and it can lead me to experience at last the necessity of a Divine Redeemer. The words "redeemer" and "redemption" are memorized as children. I have heard them spoken from the pulpit and uttered them in community prayers. But was this need a reality for me? Did I feel that without redemption I could not do it alone?

The moment I feel united in this struggle with others is the moment of grace that can lead to personal awareness of my self and of the human condition. This is the silent moment of kneeling humbly before the Lord and from my own humiliation and despair resting in the blessed wonder that I am truly loved, that I have been redeemed by another, and that He asks only that I open myself to this grace. It is also the hallowed ground from which true compassion springs.

His kindness to me invites me to participate in the world of the Divine Redeemer within the limits of the possibilities of this hour of human unfolding. This is only one example of how my life experience, the experience of what I really am in all my limitations, can become the occasion of profound religious experience.

Alienation from self-experience is always alienation from religion. It is not so surprising that contemporary western man is alienated from religious living, for, as we have seen, contemporary man is alienated from his own deepest being. He lives in the dispersion of common consciousness; he lives in the near or the far but rarely in the now. He is a stranger to his own interiority. And therefore he cannot really be in touch with life or with others. Thinned out, emptied out, he has lost the very ground from which religious living emerges.

This movement away from the experience of self-presence to the Lord is pernicious in religious life, for those who are religious by commitment have chosen a life form which reminds mankind of the experience of the Sacred which gives meaning to life. However, if as a religious, I am unable to be present to my own experience, if I am absorbed in pietistic and behavioristic practices instead of living my life in recollection and religious participation, I may never radiate the truth of faith to other people. Somehow those outside religious life, who have gone back to the deepest meaning of life experience, immediately sense something false, something missing in religious themselves. If I am not at home with the true meaning of religious living, I cannot communicate this meaning to others.

Personal and Spiritual Formation of Religious

The cardinal time of life for the religious is the period of initiation. Here is where the great shift from one way of living to an entirely new mode of presence must take place. It is a time of conversion from superficiality to depth of living, and this conversion for modern man always implies an inversion temporarily into interiority.

We experience today an increasing freedom from certain traditional structures in religious life. This movement may also mean that the burden of religious unfolding and stability will be centered in the novitiate, juniorate and the first adaptative years after the juniorate. If inner transformation did not take place in this prolonged period of initiation, the self-reliant, free religious of the future will be lost in the culture which he tries to heal.

This shift in the center of responsibility for religious unfolding reestablishes the original centrality of the master of religious living. The master of religious living stands at the heart of consecrated life and its lived continuation as religious. He is called by the Lord to inspire and safeguard the continuous rebirth and abiding presence of his community *as religious*.

255

This person at the center of religious life has been institutionalized in the West as novice master, directress of novices, of junior sisters or postulants, or as a director of a house of formation of religious seminarians. Historically his position is central and primary. The consecrated life in the East and West emerged when celibate men or women gathered around a wise and experienced master of interior life to be taught and formed in the ways of the spirit. Some of these masters became founders and superiors of communities of those who had come to them initially, not for the founding of a community, but for the communication of living spirituality. Establishment of a corporate communal life became in some cultures a secondary means of fostering the personal and spiritual growth of celibate religious. Nevertheless, even then the living contact with the master of spirituality remained initially a first means of religious development and inspiration.

The expansion and increasing institutionalization of religious life already lessened the central position of the master of religious living. This tendency was strengthened as religious communities in the West became responsible for extensive cultural and social services. The demand for professionals was pressing. Time, energy and attention had to be expended to select and prepare religious in specialized fields like nursing, social service and education. Selection of efficient task-oriented superiors became paramount.

The core person of religious life, the master of spirituality, became less central. Less time and effort was given to the choice and preparation of this crucial person who would have the responsibility of communicating the religious life form itself to initiates entering these communities.

The consequences of diminishing what should be a primary concern could be devastating. Unformed directors of formation may substitute for the cultivation of interiority a training in outward style and manner no longer rooted in true self-unfolding. Well-prepared masters, on the contrary, would be able to unveil the motivations guiding this mode of living and to evolve in the initiate means of appropriating personally and renewing creatively some of the habits, customs and devotions revered by generations. The not fully prepared master of the inner life may exert a onesided influence. Instead of unfolding patiently with each candidate unique modes of presence to God, he may unwittingly confine religious life to mere conformity with customs and devotions and thus fail to set in motion the dynamics of turning one's whole being toward the Lord.

As long as religious life escaped pervasive cultural questioning, the consequences of such deficiencies did not appear so clearly. Now that this questioning is almost universal, many are unable to experience anew the very meaning of their consecrated life, which may not have been communicated to them in a living way during the years of their formation.

Some have found on their own, or in contact with a spiritual guide, the road toward self-integration in presence to the Lord. Others, however, may leave, confused, embittered and sometimes distorted by a split between peripheral devotions, impersonal patterns of living and their hidden need for personal and spiritual unfolding which such behavior and piety alone cannot accomplish. Others again may attempt to turn religious life into something which it is not, for instance, a mere service association. Still others may develop personality disturbances, for they were not able to find and integrate themselves under wise and sensitive guidance in the vital years of initiation.

These problems will become more acute when religious celibates will be increasingly on their own in independent forms of cultural participation outside their religious home. In the past the religious community would protect their fidelity by structures which more or less isolated them from the culture they had to transform. In the future their fidelity has to originate in their transformed interiority, in their awareness of their unconscious needs and defenses, in their personal presence to the Lord, restored daily in their religious home.

The seriousness of this situation led some superiors to surmise that disturbances and difficulties could be traced to insufficient theological training. Consequently, some of them sent novice masters and directresses of novices to obtain a degree in the sacred sciences. In certain cases the master of religious living became mainly a teacher of theology.

Central as this field is for a more precise understanding of the Revelation and its implications, there is a distinction between a teacher of theology and a master of interiority. The teacher of theology researches, explains and justifies an understanding of the faith; the master of interiority communicates a living of the faith, a lived spirituality evolved over the centuries and in our time potentially enlightened by certain insights and findings of the human sciences. Both tasks are related but not identical. An exclusive substitution of theology for the art and science of religious living may further deplete a formation already impoverished by behaviorism and devotionalism.

It was found that the mere theoretical knowledge of theology did not necessarily lead to a well-integrated concrete living of all the dynamics and dimensions of personal and spiritual self-unfolding. Neither did abstract theological insights solve by necessity all practical problems, anxieties and tensions engendered in the striving for religious transformation. The expectation that theology should solve all practical problems of human and spiritual development could not be met.

This gave impetus to a search for other disciplines which might be able to solve the countless problems of formation. Some were sent for study and training to counseling centers, psychology departments and psychoanalytic institutes. At times the director of formation turned into a counselor, therapist or analyst. If this orientation were to become primary, it would be more pernicious than the former responses. Social arts and sciences do not necessarily go beyond a relatively meaningful but humanistic life orientation.

Such disciplines, when not enlightened by religious insight, may help religious to face certain personality problems without helping them to live religiously. While they may seem an attractive alternative to religious behaviorism, devotionalism or theologism, none of them can replace growth in living faith and the incarnation of this faith in all regions and dynamics of the personality.

On the basis of his limited and specialized knowledge, a director trained mainly as a psychologist, sociologist, therapist or analyst may have great difficulty integrating spirituality and those aspects of the human sciences which are secondary but valuable aids in religious formation. If he is not well versed in ways of bringing to life the humanity, faith and spirituality of the candidate, his influence as counselor, therapist or analyst could lead to a further decrease in the already impoverished spirituality of religious life in the West.

Discipline of Lived Spirituality:
The Master of Religious Living

The broken line of spirituality developed over the

centuries by outstanding masters must be taken up again and enriched by pertinent insights of the human sciences. It is the responsibility of every religious and especially of those in formation to make this tradition viable and effective for the men and women who come to religious life from contemporary culture.

The specific responsibility of the master of interiority in regard to these initiates is vastly different from that of the theology professor, psychologist, sociologist, therapist or analyst. Even theology of spirituality is not exactly the same as the art and science of concrete lived spirituality as can be seen from a superficial comparison of, for example, the treatise on the virtues in the *Summa Theologica* of St. Thomas with the spiritual writings of St. Teresa of Avila and St. John of the Cross.

We need a contemporary expression of the age-old discipline of lived spirituality. Initiation in lived spirituality is essential for those who are called to spend at least part of their lives in the personality formation of religious. They should study the principles, structures and dynamics of religious unfolding and formation in light of the specific demands and unique problems of religious life in our time and of the personal and spiritual formation of religious. The time and financial support for this study and initiation should be generously granted by the community, for these persons have to qualify as masters of religious life to whom the future and very survival of a religious community *as religious* will be entrusted.

The religious-cultural participant of the future is far more dependent on his initiation into religious life than the well-protected religious of the past. The latter could survive as a religious because of a community life that prolonged certain aspects of the novitiate. The latter has less chance for survival if postulancy, novitiate, juniorate and the first years of supervised adaptation did not enable him to develop personal depth and interior spiritual structuring. In the future the possibility of survival for a religious community may very well be in the hands of the masters of initiation.

The future director needs a fundamental initiation into the knowledge, experience, sensitivity, wisdom and art of guidance and communication necessary for effective personality formation. It would be impossible and therefore irresponsible to try within a short time to achieve the inner transformation he is in need of; to form him in familiarity with the masters and writers of spirituality; to teach him the viable contributions of various human sciences; to train him in the art and dynamics of formation, guidance and counseling; to acquaint him with the ways of prayer, its obstacles and possibilities; to make him understand and evaluate the manifold contemporary cultural and social influences, confusions and prejudices which his future initiates will have to clarify in themselves and to cope with under his guidance; to train him in pertinent research in spirituality and the human sciences; to help him to develop the difficult art of expressing himself clearly, concisely, convincingly and attractively in his lectures and conferences; to teach him theoretically and practically how to deal with personality problems and dynamics and to make him a master in spotting and evaluating symptoms of psychopathology which may interfere with the religious unfolding of the initiate.

It is for these reasons that beyond intellectual capacity and human sensitivity, directors of formation should be selected on the basis of their personal integrity, emotional maturity and commitment to religious life. They will have to meet the pressing need for the relevant integration of life and religion. The very survival of religious life *as religious* in the West is almost exclusively in their hands. Positions of such responsibility can be met only by well-balanced directors of high motivation with sincere mature concern for those religious whom they may guide in the future.

A true master of religious life is also a master of personality formation whose life and labor is sustained by his insights and findings in the field of Religion and Personality and renewed by continual research in this area. Candidates to be initiated in the life of the vows come to their director from a complex civilization. The structure of values, the clarities, confusions, consistencies and inconsistencies of this society already influence the lives of these candidates. The master of religious life is called to help them become aware of these influences and to assist them in their attempt to harmonize them with the demands of their vocation.

The contemporary religious candidates, for whose initiation he is responsible, share more or less consciously in the traditional search of mankind for the meaning of life. At present, however, these future religious are called to a life that demands a spirituality involved in everyday reality, an asceticism of cultural participation that after their initiation helps them to unfold the culture, not flee from it.

The master of religious life should be able to show them that the vows are not only a means of self-unfolding but also of an enlightened participation in the culture as a revelation of the Sacred. The director clarifies for them how the threefold path of religious development, symbolized by the vows, is a necessary path to personal growth for them and in a different way for all men who desire to live mature, meaningful lives.

For every person some implicit or explicit vow ends the indecision and multiplicity of vocational possibilities in adolescence and initiates the period of growth toward full maturity. The true commitment of a vowed life entails a threefold orientation toward the Sacred: a respectful obedience to the dynamics of my life situation as a temporal and local manifestation of God; a chaste or respectful love for self and others as uniquely called and graced by the Sacred; and a respectful use and celebration of things natural and cultural as gifts of the Holy.

These three fundamental attitudes of the evolving religious personality — obedience, chastity and poverty — lead to religious maturity when personally appropriated. The vowed religious lives the threefold path in a concentrated way by his commitment to celibacy and community. The beholder of this life, the religious layman or woman living these attitudes in a less concentrated, less explicit style, looks to the vowed religious for inspiration and awareness of this structure that lies at the root of religious unfolding of man.

The director aims primarily at developing the positive potentialities of the candidates. However, he should realize that in them, as in most healthy human beings, there are at least some disruptive tendencies that hinder the possibility of self-discovery and self-integration.

From early childhood the candidates may have developed ways of denying, escaping, resisting and evading their true calling. They are often not aware of such repressed tendencies as those to rage, hostility, compulsion, resentment of authority, religious frigidity, envy and jealousy. Such unconscious leanings make it difficult for them to be truly open to God, to themselves and to their fellow religious. A childlike search for security may make them overdependent. They will carry over some of these attitudes into their religious life unless they are brought to light and integrated into their personality in relationship with an understanding director, well-versed in the dynamics of human development.

An unprepared director may mistake such impulsive or compulsive inclinations for mature attitudes. Immature dependency may pass for religious trust; obsessive-compulsive traits may have the appearance of a sense of responsibility. Such errors are less likely in relationship with a well-prepared, experienced director who is able to recognize these disintegrative traits.

In order that the light of the vows may illumine all dimensions of life, the director should help the candidate to accept himself as he really is. In facing himself, the aspirant experiences deeply, perhaps for the first time, personal responsibility for his own life and learns to accept his limitations. Though he may suffer, it is in this suffering that he grows. Creative unrest causes him to question the complacent pattern of his past and may lead him to reach out for a deeper meaning of the religious life in which he is being initiated.

The ultimate aim of personality formation of religious has always been to bring the religious aspirants closer to an awareness and acceptance of the Divine in their lives and to bring about an increasing integration of all their attitudes and feelings in light of this awareness. The director fosters this religious presence not only by the strength of his word but also, and perhaps most of all, by a personally lived, deeply experienced spiritual life that radiates to others and inspires them to strive toward a similar depth in their own spiritual unfolding. For this integration, it is necessary that the master of religious life knows how to help candidates, among other things, to be in tune with their own feeling, willing, thinking and imagining; to discover their unique project of life; and to accept their own limitations as well as those of their cultural participants in a creative, respectful way.

Their director helps them to learn what modes of life would be in harmony with their religious vocation — which modes should perhaps be discarded — and how to respond wisely to conflicts which may result. Under the direction of a well-prepared master of religious life, the candidates may come to recognize contemporary displacements of God and to discover how all events in life may be seen in His light.

To reach these and other aims, the master or director of religious life must pursue continual research. Scholarly study clarifies the fundamental meaning and structure of the religious attitude and demonstrates the dynamics of its unfolding and interaction with the other dimensions of the human personality. Specific developmental problems of religious can be solved satisfactorily only when they are related to the meanings and implications of the far deeper and universal structures of the religious orientation common to all men and disclosed in their dynamics by the study of Religion and Personality or Fundamental Spirituality.

Guidance or imparting of information about religious and spiritual matters or even advice about appropriate action is not enough. The religious candidates are most likely searching not only for the meaning of vowed presence to God, but also for ways of integrating this meaning with their own unique personalities and life situations.

The master of religious living should also develop the art and discipline of reflective participation. He must learn how to participate in the movement of a person's life and how to participate in such a movement as expressed in the work of an artist, writer, thinker or poet. At the same time he must be able to reflect wisely on what he experiences in that participation. Both his reflection and the conceptualization and expression of this reflection should always remain in tune with his participation, even if his reflection is illuminated by his insights in the human sciences.

Reflective participation in the unique personal and spiritual unfolding of the religious entering his community presupposes that the director has gained wisdom and insight into man's religious development and, more specifically, into the dynamics of the life of the vows. The study of cultural, social and anthropological factors prepares him for a keen understanding of the multiple forces which shaped the personalities of those who look to him for enlightenment.

A precious source of insight and inspiration comes to him from the experiential and reflective communications of past and present masters of interiority, endowed with special gifts of observation and expression.

Then, too, certain aspects of the dynamics of human and religious unfolding have been highlighted by thinkers, artists, writers, psychotherapists and social scientists deeply interested in the emergence of the human person. To capture and integrate that wisdom and relevant information which is available throughout literature and throughout the records of many human sciences, the master of religious life should become a master of research.

His research, or searching again, of relevant literature has to be done in the light of reflective participation in religious living itself. Such research demands also the harmonious integration of the insights thus uncovered into a consistent theory of the aspect of religious life under study, whether it is prayer, obedience, celibacy, detachment, community relationship, friendship, or authority problems.

The trustworthy, diligent and disciplined exercise of reflective participation, meaningful selectivity, and theoretical integration demands a thorough training in a variety of research methods that assures a high probability of reliable outcomes. The director who has been well-prepared to ponder the structures and dynamics of human and spiritual unfolding may willingly continue to research this field as a source of effective religious formation of others through writing, speaking and teaching. Research training in the light of participative reflection is thus central in the preparation of directors of religious life.

The augmentation of religious available as masters of interiority may be one possible response to the need for renewal in commitment and spirit. Renewal can be achieved in most of its facets by theological instruction, committee meetings, chapter deliberations, referendum, authority reform, adaptation of activity and reformulation of rules and constitutions. However, renewal of spirit, inner transformation, reorientation and reintegration of personality dynamics cannot be secured by decree and decision alone.

Committee proposals and chapter deliberations should strive to create conditions which foster personal renewal in living faith. This will make room for the resurrection of true formation which is the communication of an inner life form by an inspiring person who knows and lives this form of interiority deeply himself.

Fundamental Dynamics of Religious Formation

During initiation into religious life, the initiate will undergo a transformation of consciousness. This transformation is the first step in a dynamic process which will involve the transfiguration of his whole life. Transformed consciousness implies transfigured feeling, imagining, thinking, anticipating, willing and perceiving. These modes and modalities of consciousness are transformed in the course of one's vowing life. The period of initiation is the beginning of this transformation. Transformation of consciousness in religious life takes place by means of the living communication of the religious life form by an enlightened and inspiring master of religious living. The initiate attempts to profoundly assimilate and appropriate this life form. This process is called religious formation. The fundamental structure of this life form has been developed over many centuries. Ideally the initiate will discover in the words and acts of his spiritual master those precious insights in religious living that have been disclosed by previous generations who have struggled to live this life style. When in answer to his call he enters a community, the initiate is confronted by a condensation of the experience of centuries, one which includes aspects of universal validity and aspects that were only useful during a certain cultural period. Fortunately, it is not for the initiate to decide which customs are fundamental and which are only temporal accretions. His primary responsibility is to enter into the deepest *why* and *how* of religious life with respect and reverence.

The life form he has chosen is laden with wisdom which a beginner cannot grasp. Critical, cynical questioning of all that he cannot understand immediately takes away the disposition of reverence, docility and experiential readiness which are all necessary for the very possibility of a true initiation into a life form. No less than a sense of wonder should fill the initiate when approaching this life form.

Transformation includes formation of consciousness, or the communication of a specific life form by which one acquires an inner form that guides his thinking, feeling, perceiving self. Introduction to outward forms is also included, but it is not primary. Formation is something that happens on the inside. Any outward form will remain empty and immovable if an initiate does not make it his own. Outer forms are revitalized and made viable only insofar as the religious can be present to them interiorly.

The master of religious living and the customs of the house of initiation are there mainly to communicate this life form to the initiates, but the master of religious living alone cannot be held responsible for the initiate's success or failure to live this life form. Both he and the initiate must live in dialectical interaction, one supporting the other. The master of religious life is helpless without the cooperation of each initiate. When this cooperation is granted, formation goes to the very core of one's being, so that he begins to personalize the life form communicated to him.

Religious initiation or formation is vastly different from other preparatory forms of training like boot camp or pre-med school. Formation is neither education nor information. If these processes were to take the place of formation, they could alienate the religious initiate from his deepest self. Technical training and information gathering are directed only toward outer, partial aspects of the personality.

The kind of preparation fostered in the period of formation affects the initiate's whole personality. If the mark of religious life were to make one or the other kind of isolated training the total basis for formation of the whole personality, it would only force initiates to flee from their deepest selves into self-estrangement. Objective information and technical training are important, but if they become the only thing, they may estrange the initiate from himself. The house of formation, however, should be the place where one is cured of self-alienation, where he comes home to himself.

Formation which is replaced by psychologism or therapism can also become a force of self-alienation. When psychology and therapy are used indiscriminately, they may become harmful substitutes for authentic religious experience. Initiation is not the time for mere psychotherapy. Real formation thus lies between the two extremes of mere technical training and information gathering, on the one hand, and psychologism and therapism on the other. To develop either style of behavior onesidedly in the period of

273

formation is to lose an opportunity to gain substance and deepen in interiority.

Some of the young men and women who enter a house of formation may have been impressed by the contemporary stress on the value of experience. They feel that they should be open to experience, that they should by no means repress it but live it in its fullness. These expressions have a certain value and meaning but they may be misunderstood. Hence the master of religious living also incurs the responsibility to direct the initiate in his confrontation with his experience. He has to communicate to him that the most important thing in life is not experience as such, but the attitude one takes toward experience. What he does with experience, the way in which he integrates it in his life is what counts. He must learn to find himself and his project of life on the basis of his *critical* and *enlightened* openness to experience.

A full human and religious being is first of all a free being with a free and liberated will. The will is that core of his being where the initiate has to take a stand, where he has to design his religious existence and to project his life within the religious life form into which he is being initiated. The initiate, like all other men, can only *become* in dialogue with his experience. Experience is, as it were, the matter out of which he builds up his personalized religious life project within the frame of the religious form. Experience is the life information on which he nourishes himself; it shows him possible ways of being himself; it shows him possible ways of being himself. On the one hand, experience precedes the taking of a stand. On the other hand, experience comes after or succeeds the taking of a stand. The initiate as an unfolding religious is always a living dialogue between his freedom and his experience. Partly he grows out of his experience and partly he directs his experience in dialogue with his master of religious living or his spiritual director.

Openness to experience thus obtains a very definite meaning for the initiate. It surely does not mean and should never mean that the director encourages him to throw himself into as many religious and human experiences as possible. An indiscriminate seeking of experiences leads to chaos, confusion, disintegration of the personality. It fosters hysterical tendencies. Authentic openness to experience is a human openness dignified by human freedom and the ability to take a human stand. It means that the experiences that come to him naturally in his daily situations during his religious exercises and readings are neither repressed nor allowed to lead him to ecstatic exaltation. The initiate should be open to them in the sense that he attempts to take a free reflective stand toward them. Since he is developing a certain life style in dialogue with the religious form, he should look reflectively at the experiences which come to him from the perspective of the person he already is and is becoming.

In this reflective look rooted in his freedom, the candidate may begin to see whether or not he can integrate this experience in his life as a dynamic formative factor which he will freely allow to shape and direct his life. When he comes to the conclusion that he should grant this experience a role in his life, it is quite possible that he will receive more and more experiences in the same vein. If he decides against a prevalent formative role of this specific experience in his life, he will probably receive less and less experiences in that line. For his receptivity and sensitivity are partly influenced by his free decision. The increase or decrease of a certain kind of experience is thus a result of the dialogue between the candidate as freedom and as experiencing.

Openness to experience does not mean that the initiate should hunt for experience or that he should consider "having experiences" as a worthwhile end in itself. Neither should he hunt for religious experience. Even the great masters in the exceptional experience called mystical always warned that this experience in and by itself was not ultimately important. What was crucial, they taught, was authentic religious living, not the religious experience in and by itself.

During his initiation the candidate should learn that from now on he should evaluate all coming experience also in light of the great religious life project in which he is being initiated. The religious life project is among other things also a project of experience. It

276

is a project of evaluating all of one's experiences in dialogue with the great masters of religious life of past and present who have lived this project effectively and have given shape to it in their living.

The ways in which one can value experiences and shape his life around this evaluation are potentially infinite. If a man would not decide on some definite life project, he would be torn apart by the inexhaustible number of meanings that experiences may have for him. When man finally does decide on some unifying life project, he has found a solid ground from which to evaluate experiences meaningfully, which otherwise would overwhelm him and tear him in countless directions.

The initiate in religious life should be led to illuminate his experiences increasingly by his new stand in life. This is true of his past and present experiences in his daily personal encounters as well as of those evoked by his readings or by the speakers he has listened to. He should realize that experiences which he allows to engulf him are destructive. He cannot build an integrated life upon them. A religious effort that aims mainly at the promotion of experience apart from the life project is a wrong effort destined to fail.

As the initiate prepares himself for the final commitment or consecration of his life, he transcends the relatively undisciplined openness of adolescence and grows to the disciplined openness of a lasting life form which he freely chooses. His mature, human, Christian openness to experience is a free, dignified and chosen openness. Prepersonal immature openness to all experience is enslaving rather than liberating, for it may leave the person helplessly awash in a flood of unvalued and unintegrated experiences which ultimately make no sense at all.

The master of religious living should be familiar with the dynamics of the life of experience. The way in which the initiate confronts the experiences that come to meet him in daily life and in the modern media of communication is decisive for his future as a religious. It is one of the tasks of the master to introduce initiates in truly religious ways of dealing with their experience.

If the candidate does not come to terms with his experience, he may eventually escape it altogether by becoming absorbed totally in his occupation. This is the religious who is a compulsive worker, who dreads being alone with the reality of his life. Keeping busy may be a defense against having to deal with experiences he cannot as easily repress in moments of silence and solitude. However, if he is able to distance himself from the immediate and gain insight into his whole situation, the meaning of his call to religious life, and the living of religious values in community and culture, he may be able to begin living in deep religious presence.

V

The Healing Power
of the Vows

Man is a manifold presence to the world, to himself, and to his fellowman, and to the Sacred as it manifests itself in them. Only when he lives and experiences this plurality of presence as a unity which harmonizes his relations to himself and to others, to things and to events, can he be at peace.

Man becomes harmonious through his integration with the whole which surrounds and surpasses him and with the Holy as its ground. Interior discord is a sign of a personal life lacking harmony. The man who is not at one with himself, who is divided and fragmented, lacks the joy, serenity and effectiveness which make life meaningful.

The forces of wholeness and harmony, both the integrating self and the integrating Holy, should complement one another. When I am fundamentally present to the whole and its source, I feel freed from fragmentation and redeemed from discord. Integration with the whole and Holy invites self-integration. The

harmony and recollection which self-integration implies silently readies me for the advent of the Holy
in my life.

The more I experience serenity of presence to myself and all that is, the more I shall be able to feel at
home in the whole of creation. Such harmonious self-
presence is possible because I experience my last-
meaning in the Holy from Whom life continually flows.

Absence of the harmonizing Holy in my life may
make it difficult for me to dispel the discord which
threatens my self-integration and integration in all
that is. Unfortunately, the urbanization of Western
society, and its subsequent functionalization and specialization of human tendencies, has contributed to
this lack of wholeness. Consequently, many feel lost
and fragmented. Fragmentation is the consequence of
inner disintegration; feeling lost is the awareness that
somehow I am not in tune with my deepest striving
for wholeness, unity and harmony.

The dividing forces of civilization seem to be
stronger than the forces of harmony and integration.
Thus there arises in us the need to be made whole.
We need to be healed, for healing restores to wholeness that which is wounded, hurt and disrupted.

The need for healing is most obvious when we are
physically ill. The physician is a person trained to restore to wholeness the disrupted bio-chemical processes of the body. He helps nature to reintegrate
the diseased organism within the harmonious func-

tioning of the body as a whole. Healing, or making whole, is also necessary for the human personality and the human community. Both the physical and social sciences demonstrate that the absence of wholeness may lead to diseases which mar the effectiveness of persons and mitigate the possibilities of strong communal functioning.

It should not be surprising that the disruptive state of the human situation has prompted certain people to dedicate themselves to a way of life which witnesses for the fundamental healing attitude of restoring man and the human community to wholeness and harmony. The three vows taken by the participative religious point toward the healing tendencies in human life.

The Healing Power of Obedience

Obedience is the willingness to listen to reality as a revelation of possibilities to be actualized by man as the creative center of his life situation. Disobedience may be regarded as man's unwillingness to listen to life unless it fosters his own selfish plans and proposals. If I reflect upon disobedience as a divisive force of isolation, fragmentation and closure, I may see more clearly why obedience is a fundamental healing attitude.

Disobedience is a force of isolation insofar as it separates me from my awareness of the Holy as unfolding in mankind and history. Being in tune with the Holy presupposes obedience to reality as unfolding. Although I cannot be open to every aspect of life and reality, I can still be present to the Holy in this special way. The inability to see everything at once neither diminishes my embeddedness in the whole nor my experience of participation in the unfolding of mankind and man. I should be present to the Holy precisely as unfolding in this world. Participation in this unfolding is only possible when I am truly present to the whole of reality and truly aware of the limitations implied by my personality and life situation.

While it is true that I am not able to be *actually* obedient to all manifestations of life, I am obedient when I do not willfully exclude any of its possible manifestations. I am obedient when I do not close myself off from the unfolding Holy by stating in advance that I shall not listen to any further revelations of reality in the successive life situations in which I may find myself.

The attitude of obedience invites participation in the unfolding of history as flowing from the Holy. Disobedience isolates me from the cultural-religious unfolding of life in which I am called to participate. Because this is so, the disobedient man experiences sooner or later isolation from history and culture, from mankind and society, and from their transcendent meaning.

As a force of closure, disobedience is the stubborn refusal to be open when I should be open to new insights and revelations of reality. It inclines me and my community to repress a more truthful insight merely for the sake of upholding our present style of life. Such disobedience may be a principle of division and fragmentation within the person and the community when one or the other refuses to admit what has been seen, perhaps in a moment of unguarded presence, and willfully blocks this experience from further consideration. Specifying what we shall and shall not experience means that my life and that of my community must become more and more compartmentalized. To be "successfully disobedient" we must develop and maintain structures of disobedience which will insure that neither my community nor I will experience that which offers itself constantly for our consideration. Tension, sometimes evidenced by psychosomatic symptoms and neurotic disorders, is evoked when we become aware of anything which threatens to break through our well-regulated, walled-off resistance to reality. The energy channeled to develop such structures of disobedient presence is at odds with the normal flow of obedience inviting man to intensify his quest for wholeness within this specific phase of history.

The healing attitude of obedience is more needed today than perhaps ever before, because modern man is more than ever tempted to be disobedient. He is inclined to organize his life around certain tasks or preoccupations that exclude any message which is not directly relevant to his single-minded project of life. This is not to deny the need for specialization. Man needs specialization, and he should even guard against distractions which limit his productivity as a specialist. However, concentration to the point of exclusion or denial of other aspects of reality, unrelated to his specialization, is a sign of divisive disobedience. This refusal to allow the unfolding Holy to reveal itself in human life and society demands the formation of structures of disobedience, isolation, closure and fragmentation which halt the emergence and growth of society as a whole.

The power that can heal this fragmentation and restore man's oneness with reality is obedience. The participative religious, together with others who desire to serve the unfolding Holy, commits himself to a life of obedience. Less obscured by concerns for status and possession, he hopes to be able to live more perfectly a life of obedient presence to the manifestations of the unfolding Holy in the culture. This healing power is an attitude he vows to live, for obedience may help man regain the balance and unity to which he is called.

The Healing Power of Respectful Love

As we have seen, obedience is a fundamental healing attitude inviting participation in the unfolding of history as it flows from the Holy. It is the willingness to listen to reality as a revelation of possibilities to be actualized by man as the creative center of his life situation. This healing power is an attitude which certain persons vow to live. As participative religious, they commit themselves to a life of obedience so that they may help man regain the balance and unity to which he is called by the whole which surrounds and surpasses him and by the Holy as its ground.

Another attitude of healing, toward which the vow of chaste love points, is that of chaste or respectful love. Chaste love of self and others to which I vow myself can also be called respectful love. The meaning of the word "chaste" is related to that of the verb "to chasten," which means "to refine," "to purify." A chaste love is a love purified from egocentric impulses which threaten to use self-love or love of others as a means of dominating self and others, or of violating the integrity of self and others spiritually, psychologically or physically. While obedience tends to restore man to unity with unfolding reality, respectful love tends to heal the break beween man and man. Disobedience, as a force of isolation, fragmentation and closure, alienates us from the cultural-religious unfolding of life. So, too, lack of respectful love is another source of disintegration, which alienates us from mankind and man. If we reflect upon lack of loving respect as a disintegrating force in person and society, we may be able to view chaste love as a fundamental healing attitude which restores man to an abiding respect for himself and others.

When I lose respect and love for myself, I also lose respect and love for the other. I am neither able to harmonize my own personality nor to live in harmony with my fellowmen. A decrease in self-respect decreases in me the possibility of self-integration and integration with society.

Chaste or respectful love means that I accept myself wholeheartedly as emerging from the Holy in dialogue with my unique life situation. The height of loving self-respect implies the deepest possible humility. True self-love and true humility go together. The most profound act of humility is that of full acceptance of the limited gift of the Holy which I am and of full surrender to the mystery of my personal unfolding within the successive limited life situations allotted to me.

The humility of self love and self-respect implies that I do not envy the unique calling of another. I do not strive falsely to keep up appearances which are alien to my deepest self. I do not try in an unchaste or violent, disrespectful manner to force myself to accept a style of thought or feeling which is at odds with my personal calling.

If I were to indulge in such forms of self-alienation, I would replace humility by pride. Pride is the impudent attempt to be what I cannot be. Such pride, instead of leading to respectful self-love, leads to disrespectful self-hate. I do not love myself as a limited but unique call of the Holy; rather I reject my self because my self-image does not correspond to the "ideal" I have envisioned. I cannot respect what I hate, and consequently I disrespectfully deform what I am in the light of a false self-project inspired by pride.

Such unchaste self-rejection is a principle of division and fragmentation in my personality. Self-negation introduces standards, styles and ideals into my life which are incompatible with all that I am.

Unfortunately, many of us have unlearned the art of respectful listening to ourselves. We are inclined to listen too exclusively to those who have received external acclaim by raising their voices over certain issues of life and to ignore the unique voice of the Spirit speaking in our own lives. The child growing up in our hyperorganized society is especially in danger of forgetting himself. We recommend that he adapt himself to streamlined customs and institutions, to standards and styles of life, which he may not be able to assimilate in his own unique way. It is almost impossible for him not to experience the dividing forces of disrespect, self-rejection and self-alienation which have been dominating our lives.

A deep and abiding self-love and self-respect is needed to heal the self-alienating forces in contemporary life. The disturbing decrease of man's love for himself makes it mandatory that certain persons oblige themselves by holy vows to become witnesses for self-love and self-respect. As participative religious, they are uged to develop an abiding respect and love for their unique selves so that they may evoke the same humble self-respect in their fellow-men.

Respect for self is only one implication of the healing power of chaste love; it also implies respectful love for others. While self-love is a necessary condition for self-healing or self-integration, respectful love for others tends to heal the relationship between man and man.

Chaste love fosters the other as other, respecting his uniqueness and privacy and thus promoting in humanity the best conditions for the unfolding of each human person. Respectful love reveals the other not only in his immediacy but also as a unique call of the Holy, as he is in his transcendent dimension. In and through my love for the other, I may enter into a personal relationship with the Holy as unfolding in and through humanity. Respectful love for others is truly a force of healing and integration — of myself as a person and of humanity as a whole.

Here again we may see how the absence of respectful love for others, like the rejection of self, implies the disintegration of mankind, the disruption of mutuality, and ultimately alienation from the Holy. Absence of respect for the other's uniqueness, and for the conditions of his personal fulfillment in response to himself as a unique call of the Holy, presupposes that we level our relationships to superficial manifestations of togetherness in a dehumanized crowd or collectivity.

Mutual respect for one another's uniqueness is the essence of human and Christian love. To escape the burden of responsibility implied by this attitude, we tend to resort to deceitful displays of pretentious love. We substitute verbal confirmation of delight in one another for sometimes silent lack of respect. I fear the solitude that is inseparable from the dignity of being an individual man. I would rather hide in crowds that thrive on emotional slogans, neither created nor assimilated by each person individually. Such crowds may even idealize disrespectful love by calling it "brotherhood," "social justice," or "true community."

Impersonal, self-destructive togetherness, no matter how convincing its idealization, is a divisive, disintegrative force in man as man. It halts the task of healing mankind, for making whole begins only at the moment I affirm the uniqueness of the other and our mutual need to rise above the crowd and collectivity. Once I am submerged in the anxious strivings of the crowd, I tend to feel at one with all others in the pursuit of profane or sacred purposes, even though I may not have appropriated these ambitions personally.

However, so long as I continually sacrifice my true self to the whims of the crowd, my repressed personality will cry out for true community which respects the uniqueness of the person. Deep down I desire that others allow me to be who I am and stop overpower-

ing me with their seductive opinions, ideals and enthusiasms. In the core of my being, I feel apart from
the crowd of clever manipulators, the power-strivings
of disrespectful opinion makers, the profane enthusi-
asts for so-called holy causes who would rob me of my
personal inspiration and threaten to dismiss me from
their company if I do not conform blindly to their
ideas and ideals.

This cry against disrespectful distortion of the human personality will be heard to the degree that a
community encourages its members to transcend tribal collectivity. The possibility of transcending the
disrespectful crowd and emerging as unique persons
dedicated to serving the unfolding of community and
culture implies the affirmation of our uniqueness and
personal responsibility. Crowds and collectivities
threaten the emergence of true human community,
where persons respect one another and do not try to
trick one another into conformity by holding out the
promise of in-group prestige.

In the crowd, the call for the unique dignity of the
person is replaced by a glorification of the unique dignity of the in-group. This is a displacement of the
vow of respectful love which implies a commitment to
resist the egoistic impulse to merge myself with an
exclusive in-group at the expense of openness toward
others.

Only true self-love and respect for the uniqueness
of the other can heal the human divisiveness engen-

dered by various in-groups and out-groups in my community. I can be faithful to the healing power of
respectful love only if I recognize the crowd compulsion in myself. The tendency to hide in a crowd or
clique is so much a part of me that I am vulnerable to
it at every moment when I am not consciously aware
that I, as all men at this stage of human evolvement,
am inclined to fall back on the less human level of
submerging my individuality in the will of the crowd.
I must strive to transcend the level of prepersonal and
precommunity togetherness so that together we may
grow to personal respect and mutual esteem within
our communities.

It thus becomes clear that the vow of chaste or respectful love implies at the same time a constant
growth in self-love and self-respect and in love and
respect for my fellowman. Respect for the uniqueness
of the other implies the ability to see him as I see myself — as a unique manifestation and call of the Holy.
All healing respect is rooted in the growing awareness
of this sacred ground. It enables me also to love those
whom I cannot like but whom I can still respect as
persons called by the Holy to be a unique possibility
of goodness as long as they live.

Loving esteem for one another can heal the disrespectful distortion of man by man, which takes place
on the level of crowds, collectivities and cliques. Only
when we transcend this level and discover our human
dignity, can we experience a newly found presence to

ourselves and to the other. We no longer disrespect-fully subject his uniqueness to ours. We respect the other as he is in his own uniqueness, thus creating an atmosphere in which both of us can feel relaxed and unthreatened. The more those living the vow of chaste love create an atmosphere of mutual love, respect and esteem, the more its healing power will radiate to all mankind, permeating society and hastening the moment in human history when personal love and true community are valued and lived by increasing numbers of people for longer periods of time.

The Healing Power of Celibate Love

The vow of celibate love contributes to the heal-ing power of my religious consecration insofar as it frees me from the care for a family and from insertion in the many social systems and establishments which this care demands. True love for a family implies the constant incarnation of this love in concerned func-tional care. Such care for the family as the funda-mental unit of society entails participation in the many systems and establishments necessary to pro-mote the welfare of the family members for whom one is responsible. Responsibility and commitment to wife and children make it difficult for the average man to resist conformity to the standards of society. His fight for economic survival and improvement often implies a prudent compromise in the practical imple-mentation of his ideals for the sake of achieving position and promotion. It is difficult to maintain one's wholeness in everyday practice, once intimidated by envy, jealously, rivalry and unfair competition. In this atmosphere it is understandable that a man may become somewhat defensive, suspicious, or aggressive and thus fail to manifest the healing power of respectful love in daily life.

The vow of celibate love sets the religious free, at least to some degree, from total dependence on the competitive social situation. Especially when this vow is sustained by the vow of poverty, which implies freedom from economic care for extensive personal possessions, the religious who lives this vow will be more independent from the economic pressures of society, and therefore more free to develop the healing power of relaxed respect for himself and others.

The vow of celibate love also heals in another sense. Celibate love is a respectful love for the other which, however, never becomes exclusive in the sense of the exclusiveness of marital love or of an exclusive friendship. We do not mean, of course, that marital love excludes love for those who do not belong to the family. The exclusiveness to which we refer is one of primacy or priority. By its very nature, marital love implies that no love for another human being can become more compelling than the love for my marriage partner. I may be a married man or woman who deeply loves a poor family in a neglected neighborhood. I may even take the time to care for them. However, as soon as I discover that my involvement with them overrides care for my own wife and children, I am compelled to give up loving involvement with the other family. In other words, my vow of exclusive love always obliges me to limit my loving involvement with others, if this would be detrimental to the priority of my love for my partner and family, to whom I have primarily dedicated myself.

Undoubtedly many couples have found a mutually satisfactory solution to this problem by allowing one another to engage in works of love to a moderate degree, which does not interfere with their primary love and concern for one another and for their children. Nevertheless, theoretically and practically, the average man or woman who has vowed his life unconditionally to an exclusive primacy of love is less free for concrete loving involvement with others than the person who has not made such a vow.

The mere fact of physical presence to one another and to their children is not enough. The married couple must foster relaxed, warm and continual presence in loving interest, care and concern to one another and to the family. As soon as serious and playful living *for* one another and *with* one another is threatened by absorption in outside interests and external loving involvements, the marriage partners are obliged to retire from outside involvement so that they may replenish their loving presence to one another and to their children.

Modern society, with its highly competitive and rationalized procedures in school and office, offers no sanctuary for the married couple to retire quietly and concentrate on developing this relaxed openness to one another. They must usually be content with a few evening hours of respectful togetherness with their children. If these few free hours are then spent in loving involvement in other causes and persons, it is little wonder that the primacy of their loving presence to one another and to their children is threatened. Whenever possible the diminution of family presence should be recognized and avoided, if the family is to remain the central point for the possibility of the emergence of new, healthy generations which may safeguard the continuity and renewal of society.

The vow of celibate love commits the religious to a way of life which gives up the right to establish a bond of exclusive, primary love and thus removes the temptation to turn this love into one which excludes care and concern for other persons and enterprises in need of this healing attitude. The vow of celibate love is meant to insure a free flow of respectful concern for man and world as called by the Holy, which an exclusive marital love is not always able to serve in the same way and to the same degree.

Even when marital love does not prevent but fosters love for mankind as manifested in social and cultural service, it is nonetheless true that the solemn marital vow of primacy of love should limit all extra-marital concern which threatens intra-marital interest and attention. Experience teaches us that such limitations can cut drastically into the availability of the married person for people and cultural enterprises in need of his full and loving devotion.

Thus we see how useful it can be for the culture to have certain persons who commit themselves, as religious participants, to the unfolding of culture. Their vow of celibate love discloses the healing presence of the respectful attitude to the culture as a whole.

The dedication implied by such non-exclusive love seems especially needed at present. In the beginning of human history, one of mankind's primary concerns was for survival and biological expansion. It was understandable that marital love, as a basis for procreation and education of the human race within family units, would be highly promoted. At present, however, the further unfolding of the human race is no longer a problem of exclusively biological proportions, that is, of procreation in order to offset the onslaughts of sickness, famine and natural disaster. Increasingly the urge to expand the human race is being complemented by the urge to deepen its spiritualization and humanization by means of cultural endeavors which incarnate man's love for himself and others as called by the Holy to sublime heights of the spirit.

It is less necessary now, than in former ages, to exhort everyone to the founding of a family. Thus persons so disposed should feel freer than ever to follow their call to celibate love, a call which frees them from the obligations of marital love and its consequent organization and maintenance of a new restricted social unit for the propagation of the race.

The healing power of celibate love in the culture should not be understood in a narrow way. A narrow attitude toward this vow would mean restricting the presence of such freeing love to its most ostentatious expressions, such as the immediate relief of certain concrete needs of my fellowman, by giving him food, nursing his wounds, and building his house. While these are praiseworthy manifestations of my celibate love, there are others, perhaps less spectacular incarnations of this vow, which may be even more beneficial to my fellowman.

When I am called as a religious participant to incarnate my healing love for mankind and its unfolding by serving scholarship, artistic creation or scientific experimentation, I, together with my colleagues, may accomplish more for mankind than by feeding a certain number of hungry people or teaching a small number of children a certain amount of practical knowledge. By means of my contribution to such scholarly fields, I may hasten the moment in which a new insight is born. This birth of new knowledge will not only benefit one small class of school children or one small group of poor people. Untold millions may profit from it.

Possibly a certain technical and scientific development may remove the very causes of poverty for an entire population. It may also be that the emergence of a new expression in art may bring many to the threshold of a deeper humanization. Mine may be a talent and ability to incarnate my celibate love effectively in a contribution that would sustain indirectly common cultural efforts to relieve the needs of all mankind. In that case it would be foolish, perhaps even sinful, to spend my time solely relieving the concrete immediate needs of a small group of children in my community, even if I enjoy doing so and deeply love those who need my care.

I may dread the thought of embodying my vow of celibate love in the tedious service of mankind by means of study and research. There are no immediate rewards, no grateful voices and warm sympathy awaiting me; there may be no experience of concrete success. I may die long before the cultural enterprise in which I am participating as an expert grows to a moment of sudden victory over human needs — a victory which will be possible only because numerous gifted men and women have spent years of quiet dedication, experimentation and research in this unique field of service to mankind. I may be called to become one of these persons. If so, my vow of celibate love for mankind will help to free me totally for this loving contribution.

The Healing Power of Poverty

In considering the healing power of the vows, we have seen that obedience and respectful celibate love help to heal the culture. Obedience integrates man with reality as he listens with humble openness to its revelations and participates readily in its unfolding. Respectful love for himself and others heals man's inner discord and decreases his separation from his fellowman, while the vow of celibate love, by his choice, frees him for fuller commitment to the Holy in unique presence to humanity.

Presence to things can be a divisive or a healing force in my personality. My attitude is divisive when I perceive things and possessions merely for their own sake, for then I isolate them from the whole of nature, history and culture in which they gain true human meaningfulness for me.

Onesided concentration on things elevates them disproportionately in my life of imagination, expectation and striving. Such fascination with matter and its possession limits the richness of reality. It becomes difficult for the full truth of persons and situations to reveal itself to me. I impose on my environment my estimation of what is most valuable and meaningful. I can no longer approach things with a balanced view, for I see them only as materials to be used, possessed, or manipulated to serve my ambition.

Besides distorting true appreciation of things, a

299

onesided view of the importance of possession may lead to forgetfulness of other aspirations in my personality. To silence these higher needs, I must deafen myself to the outcries of my deepest being for more meaningful wholeness.

When my view of the world is clouded by greed and possessiveness, by anxious clinging to material wealth and security, I become alienated from myself. I am unable to see myself as the *person* I am, for I cannot see *things* as they really are. It is the spirit of poverty which encourages growth in true appreciation, and in wise, joyful participation in the manifold richness of my world.

While man always needs the spirit of poverty, for man in the affluent society the healing power of poverty is crucial. Without poverty of spirit, man in affluence may become a broken, fragmented man, a shattered, besieged person.

The affluent society tends to overwhelm me with an abundant variety of possibilities for satisfaction. Delectable ways of fullfilling my needs for nourishment, clothing, shelter, information and entertainment are thrust upon me by the media of communication. If I were not aware of this massive effort, I might be reduced to a mere consumer of goods. However, I can survive as an original, creative human being if I am able to resist the ubiquitous pressure to consume all that is presented to me as attractive and worthwhile.

Indiscriminate consumption is the mark of a mindless personality who lives mainly for fragmented moments of satisfaction. This person is not centered in himself as a unique expression of the Holy. His life is dispersed by the wind of fashionable possessions; his true self is lost in over-concern for convenience and commodity.

Poverty of spirit is a profound invitation to regain my self-presence and respect. It protects the center of my being from disrespectful intrusion by the propagandists of affluence. The gift of poverty enables me to rise above the compulsion for consumption and to emerge as a whole person, one who views life serenely in the affluent society instead of being utilized by its forces of promotion and production.

Modern man has to gear himself to resist commercial pressure and imposition. Poverty of spirit enables me to distance myself sufficiently from commercialism so that I can find myself and my unique style of life. In poverty, I may select that which fosters my unique call in this world and detach myself from all that can obscure and destroy my fidelity.

As we have seen, the mass media of a productive society invite all men to become indiscriminate consumers who, by their very consumption, will sustain the productive enterprises which foster the economy. Such a society tends to be not person-centered but economy-centered. Production is not in service of the growth of the human person but in service of the expansion of the economy.

It is not difficult to see that this may lead to a dehumanized, fragmented society where only consumers are respected — a society of dissatisfied persons who feel that their deepest self is neglected. Those who attain the spirit of poverty, however, may be able to distance themselves from blind production and consumption and bring to this emerging affluent civilization human purpose and meaning.

We may perceive from this how important it is culturally that the Lord calls certain persons to witness for inner freedom from the possible tyranny of possession and collection by a vow of poverty. The participative religious is called to immerse himself fully in the affluent society. At the same time he is called to manifest how one may use the treasures and resources of this civilization in tune with one's own call to be a unique cultural-religious participant.

The spirit of poverty demands distancing from the surface aspect of things to a degree unknown by former generations. Never before was there such affluence. Today our senses are bombarded by billboards, loud-speakers, television and newsprint promising us comfort, status, promotion and well-being if only we give in to them blindly and thus give up our best selves.

To maintain poverty of spirit as a necessary condition for faithfulness to myself and my call to serve

the unfolding Holy in the culture, I shall have to discipline my senses. I shall have to control my need for
status and my desire to be "in" with various establishments. Only by distancing, implied by the vow of
poverty, shall I be able to show my cultural partners
how to be faithful to their task and to themselves by
a similar effort. They too must strive to prevent the
fragmentation which may result by giving in to the
needs, desires and interests indiscriminately evoked
by their environment.

Perhaps never before in history has the spirit of
poverty been so clearly a condition for the salvation
of the human person, so necessary for the survival
of human culture. The spirit of poverty heals or makes
whole not only because it enables man to transcend
matter, but also because it *transforms* matter by
bringing out its transcendent meaning, by pointing to
values which are hidden in the heart of matter. True
artists are those who, in a spirit of poverty, are able
to go beyond the immediate appearance of matter and
unveil its deeper mystery. The seventeenth century
Dutch painter Nicholas Maes and the contemporary
American Andrew Wyeth paint simple objects that
are a part of our daily lives — a table setting, a four-
poster bed, a basket of clothing—and people we often
see — laborers, fishermen, sailors. We have seen these
things and these people numerous times. We may
deal with them regularly and yet, until we see them
like this, we never suspect their mystery. We never

experience the silent meaning and beauty which they contain and evoke until we are able to share in the poverty of spirit which is the painter's.

A poverty like this is able to detach itself from surface appearances and commune with the transcendent meaning of persons and things. They participate in the life of human values and in the mystery of the whole and Holy as unfolding in community and culture.

Aesthetic vision is possible when its ground is the spirit of poverty. During the great ages of the flowering of monastic life, a true spirit of poverty was present. A sense of beauty and graciousness prevailed. Medieval monasteries are visited today as monuments of æsthetic sensitivity. Modern man is awed by the architecture of the buildings, the gracious rooms planned by the monks to maintain peace and solitude, the hand-written and illustrated books which are the fruit of their æsthetic distance conditioned by the spirit of poverty.

Beauty and graciousness are the triumph of true humanity over mere usefulness. I may create and enjoy beauty when I am able to transcend the tyranny of useful time, useful production and indiscriminate consumption. Poverty of spirit introduces me to contemplation, prayer and recollection, to the richness of of life which lies beneath the surface waiting to be revealed.

The vow of poverty implies a wholehearted readiness for the kind of detachment that enables my æsthetic sense to grow. Living this vow in this sense creates room for the unfolding of beauty both in my home and in the community where I live as a cultural participant. This is not to say that the experience of beauty promoted by the spirit of poverty can be identified with religious experience. The experience of beauty is by itself on a different plane than that of the experience of the Divine Transcendent. However, true æsthetic experience makes me whole and recollected in presence to the beautiful, for this experience points to that which surpasses the pragmatic and utilitarian. Thus æsthetic experience, conditioned by poverty of spirit, creates a favorable atmosphere for religious presence. Thus æsthetic presence, as fruit of the spirit of poverty, shares in the healing power of this attitude. Presence to the Holy in poverty enables me to see how things and possessions are in harmony with the deeper meaning from which they emerge. My awareness of this harmonious participation redeems the things in my environment from isolation. They appear in a new light, emerging from the ground which enfolds them. They speak to me in a new way. I feel at home with them and in union with the whole in which they and I participate.

In a spirit of poverty it becomes more and more possible for me to be aware of the presence of the Holy in all things. It is this presence that sustains the life of the spirit, the life of prayerful presence or the spiritual life. The participative religious, who is called to witness for the sacred dimension of reality, should find in the spirit of poverty a rich source of personal unfolding. His life of worship and witness should be an inspiration to all those who are likewise striving to find the deepest meaning of persons, things and events in this world.

Active and Passive Strength

Whether my life is vowed in the direction of living religious values in celibacy and community, establishing and maintaining a family, or fostering my humane or political ideals, my vowed life always implies a twofold strength: active and passive.

Active strength is recognized most readily. As a religious, it is mine when I incarnate in concrete projects specific dimensions of obedience, respectful love and respectful presence to things natural and cultural. As a teacher, it is mine when I extert the effort to prepare stimulating, creative lectures. As a mother, active strength is mine when I manifest in my activities care and concern for husband and children.

In all these life styles, I need active strength to embody concretely the ideals and values to which I have committed myself. However, the vowed life style must also be lived under adverse conditions, not immediately changeable by action. Then I need the support and wisdom which can be mine if I have developed my capacity for passive strength.

To endure whatever frustration, suffering or misunderstanding comes into my vowed life, to bear with my own faults and limitations, to accept peacefully the painful reality that I may never live to see the results of my most valiant endeavors are manifestations of passive strength. Unlike active strength, passive strength is not directed against outside resistances, which challenge me to inscribe myself in a particular situation by exercising my efficiency in decision-making, organization and initiation of new projects.

Passive strength is neither building something up, nor tearing something down, nor bringing something out. The obstacles to gaining and growing in passive strength are inward, challenging my presence to the Holy and tempting me to place all my dignity and value as a human being in what seems to be outward success in the eyes of others.

I, like all men, have ambitions and dreams of achievement. Voices beckoning me to be someone and do something clamor inside me and may claim my attention most of my waking hours. Listening to these voices is only harmful when they become the dominant force in my personality. True mastery resides in my ability to quiet these clamorings for accomplishment when they beg for my full, exclusive and constant attention.

Relaxation does not mean leaving my responsibilities behind me. Rather it is the road which leads to the discovery of my unique availability as called and graced by the Lord, who alone can measure my victory or failure. Such restfulness, which takes advance as well as decline in stride, is possible only if I am related in the core of my being to the Holy.

The person who desires to remain faithful to his vow has to be open to the ground of reality in its transcendent dimension. If I think that the whole meaning of my life rests on my ability to surmount the obstacles of an unpleasant superior, colleagues who misunderstand me and crushing blows of unexpected sickness, I may fail to unfold my vowed life in relation to the Sacred.

Understandably, then, my powerlessness to control the uncontrollable may frustrate and embitter me. Lost is the vision of my local and temporal situation against the horizon of the Holy. Only in this light can I accept my incapacity to overcome unpleasantness and pain in effective action.

In my vowed life, passive strength is thus the endurance of unavoidable misconceptions surrounding both my life style and me as a person. It includes the patience to bear with a superior who seems unable to listen to the currents of thought and emotion circulating in the community, to suffer little dismay over the fact that others may never understand me, to be ready for sickness and death when they come. All of these are experiences that I cannot dominate, manipulate or control.

Living awareness and acceptance of the deepest realities of life is not a question of overcoming an external resistance, but a matter of learning to live life in whatever form it reveals itself to me. The source of my passive strength is my receptive presence to the Sacred. If the Lord is truly found at the beginning of my vowed and vowing life, I may rest in faith that somehow this disturbance has been allowed by Him. No matter how limited and limiting my situation may seem, I shall find its meaning in the whole which transcends me in time and space and in the Holy who allows everything in this world to be in a certain way.

Dialogue between Passive and Active Strength

Passive strength and presence to the Holy are not unrelated to active strength, especially in the religious life. My cultural participation as a religious, my task in the world, my personal unfolding and the unfolding of those under my care remain faithful to my religious commitment when I myself consent to the unavoidable reality of every human situation: the unpleasant community, the poor pastor, the indifferent parishioners, the demanding parents.

Growth in passive strength enables me to say to myself: "Within this painful, limited situation, I cannot do this. But perhaps I can do that." I can be gracious and tactful and gradually I may begin to exert my active strength in a way that will make a difference.

If, on the other hand, I indulge only in the exercise of active strength unilluminated and uninformed by that passive strength which acknowledges, estimates and accepts serenely the unchangeable aspects of a certain situation — I may sooner or later be blinded to possibilities for true human action guided by the Spirit. I may begin frantically to execute plans and projects that are remarkable, proper and just in my imagination, neglecting to consider that for all their seeming rightness, history may not be ready to accept such solutions. For the time being I may have to abandon these answers, but my willingness to change a chosen course of action may reveal what actually should be done to enrich this moment of history.

True and lasting accomplishment is always a manifestation of active strength sustained and supported by my capacity to distance myself from activity for its own sake. Passive strength in this sense implies a quiet, receptive evaluation of the immediate and transcendent dimensions of every life situation. The dispassionate insight thus gained is the best vantage point for adequate action the moment that history discloses that it is time for my active strength to exert itself.

The danger of seeing active strength as the only means of mastery may arise when I am, as it were, cursed with success all the time. If I am always prosperous, always undefeated, never plagued by illness or unpleasantness, I may disregard the necessity of receptivity and acceptance.

An exaltation of outward achievement, with a corresponding atrophy of the receptive attitude may prove fatal. What will I do when I am no longer victorious, no longer understood, no longer sound and healthy? Without the force of endurance life may embitter me. It may be impossible for me to welcome these moments of misunderstanding, defeat and suffering as precious blessings.

As soon as I forget that the fulfillment of my vowed life rests in the dialogue between active and passive strength, I may become disgruntled enough to seek ways to escape my life call, rather than centering myself in its deepest reality. Loss of my vocation can occur in two ways. One way is to leave my vowed life outright. The other is to stay but to leave my calling inwardly. This latter leave-taking is experienced primarily as resentment, bitterness or cynicism and may spill over into outward behavior. Witnessing for the Holy in community and culture no longer evokes a radiant expression of my best self. Rather it becomes abject, resentful subjection to what seems to be a stern, rigorous, unwelcoming reality.

It is difficult to say whether the life of the religious who leaves his vowed life totally without sufficient reason or the life of a religious who leaves his vocation inwardly is more self-destructive. The resentful religious who stays may complain endlessly about the injustice he has to bear. Not having fostered his power of patience, he may forget that all men face unfairness sometimes. The choice between bearing with these times or becoming embittered by them rests on the wisdom of developing my capacity for resignation and receptivity, when aggressive force alone is not the answer.

A concrete solution to unpleasantness may be possible and, if so, it should be pursued. An equally important consideration is to learn to live with the bad as well as the joyful faces life presents to me. On the one hand, I can be sad about adversity but, on the other hand, I can bless it as my possibility to unfold the right attitude toward self and others, on the deeper level of the spirit.

Every person who desires to face reality from its deepest ground has to develop both active and passive presence to persons, things and events. The strength to do things, to study and write, to keep a classroom of children disciplined and alert, is the easiest to attain, compared to growth in the strength of wise and voluntary resignation when no effective action is possible.

The strength of tolerating others when they oppose me, of living joyfully through misunderstanding and condemnation while others complain, is more difficult to sustain. It is not a consequence of willful self-analysis but of quiet acceptance, not an atmosphere of analytical precision but of calm insight into myself and my life situation.

The strength of respectful acceptance of the un- avoidable, while a necessity for all men, is a special grace of the religious who vowed himself to a life of religious presence to daily reality which radiates to community and culture the source of its own unfold- ing. And yet, paradoxically, some religious seem to have developed only habits of active strength. They are boisterous, delighted and delightful as long as they can actively build and organize. However, at the moment that they are faced with sickness, suspicion, or unjustly forbidden to do certain things, they often do not have the strength to bear with adversity and the patience to await its passing. They cannot cope with their tendencies to rebellion, bitterness, cynicism and disbelief. Some lose their joyfulness and sometimes even their vocation.

Early in religious life it is wise to recognize and unfold my capacity for resignation by welcoming the possibility to bear with unpleasant situations, moments of boredom and feelings of dismay. I may even regard such occasions as openings to dimensions of life of which I would be unaware if I had not experienced any difficulty.

This dialogue with my feelings in tune with my situation and its deepest ground is living with life, not fleeing from it into a utopian dream of perfect contentment. Viewing these unhappy times in light of the

Eternal places the strength of receptivity in its proper perspective as a basis for true participation. Outside of religious presence, outside of faith, my action may degenerate into anxious agitation of no lasting value.

By its very nature, therefore, passive strength is related to the religious attitude, which is reverent receptivity to the self-revelation of the Holy. The beautiful power of resignation to whatever way the Holy chooses to reveal Himself to me sustains the vowed life in adversity and creates room for unique religious participation in world and culture.

Passive strength does not exclude audacious action, bold planning, legitimate protest, standing up for my rights and tenacious striving for betterment of my position, health, development and life situation; it excludes useless worry and agitation, ineffective action, poor timing and exhausting hysterical or compulsive attempts to better or to escape what cannot be improved or avoided at a certain moment of my life. Passive strength implies the receptivity, sensitivity, docility and teachability which endow my planning with prudence, my sensitivity with serenity, my action with sober effectiveness and my words with wisdom.

VI

Purpose of the Participative
Religious Life

We have come to the end of our exploration of the
structures, meanings and aims of the participative re-
religious life. Our reflections on this religious-cultural
phenomenon began in the first book of this series,
PERSONALITY FULFILLMENT IN THE SPIRITUAL LIFE.
We deepened and extended the newly gained insights
in this first volume in the more concrete considerations of the second volume, entitled PERSONALITY FUL-
FILLMENT IN THE RELIGIOUS LIFE. This final volume
of the trilogy contains an elaboration of some of the
fundamental insights that were present germinally in
the two earlier volumes. Continual reflection on these
insights has led to the discovery of new perspectives
not contained in the former essays but related to
them. Having come to the end of these three volumes,
we shall attempt to identify the participative religious
life by a description and discussion of the structure of
its meaning or purpose.

This description is only meant to be final in the sense that it concludes at the end of this trilogy the explorations of the author for the time being. In regard to the question of religious life, every identification remains tentative, not in an absolute sense which would suggest an impossibility to derive fundamental knowledge about religious life, but in a relative sense. While shedding light on the truth, our perspectives are always limited and may always be complemented, deepened, and transformed by new perspectives of other thinkers. With these precautions in mind, we shall try to describe the meaning-structure of the participative life form.

The structure of the meaning of the participative religious life form seems to articulate itself into three constituents which do not exist in isolation but are part of an integral unity. Each articulation is co-determined by the other two. The unitary aim of the participative religious life differentiates itself naturally into three dimensions. We can look upon it first from the perspective of the person who unfolds himself within this life form; secondly, from the mode in which this unfolding person participates in the culture; and finally from the concrete way in which this person incarnates his participation in concrete service.

One dimension cannot function without the others. The person cannot unfold without participation in the culture and such participation cannot be real without its incarnation in some concrete form of service. No service can be truly human without the incarnation of a human mode of participation in the culture and the latter is only possible when one increasingly unfolds himself as a person. For example, the celibate religious can only grow as a cultural participant when he is present religiously to the culture in which he participates and when he incarnates this personal presence in concrete modes of religious-cultural service. Likewise, true religious-cultural participation is impossible without the continual unfolding of his religious-cultural personality.

Service is to be understood here in its fundamental meaning. The concrete expression of any historical-cultural or personal-cultural participation can be called service. As soon as human participation has made itself available in a concrete expression, it can serve the unfolding of mankind and man in some dimension. Cultural participation, no matter how creative and profound, that is not expressed, concretized or made visible to others cannot serve the unfolding of mankind and man. I may be an astute thinker, creatively participating in the contemporary culture of thought, but as long as I do not express my participating thought in a dialogue, lecture, article or book, my cultural participation has not yet become service. The same can be said about my cultural participation in music as a listener or in poetry as a reader. No matter how sincere my participation, as long as it is not embodied in, for example, writing or teaching, it cannot yet be deemed service.

The expression of various modes of cultural participation varies with the kind of participation made serviceable by that expression. The expression of cultural participation in service may vary from cooking a meal to writing a poem, from nursing a patient to composing a symphony, from spiritual direction to teaching mathematics. In each case something concrete, something communicable, has been put at the service of mankind.

Further on, we shall consider the possibility of a service that is no longer an expression of personally lived cultural participation. Because he is an historical being, man is able to use former expressions of cultural participation without involving himself personally in the living human participation that initially gave rise to these expressions. In that case, expressions of others before us become forms of mere functional service as distinguished from personally lived service, which embodies also the personal-cultural participation of the same person who renders the service.

Examples of service that may be devoid of cultural participation would be the "hack" writer, the assembly-line reproducer of paintings, the parroting public speaker or the functional nurse or teacher who merely goes through the motions of her profession with no sense of personal involvement. The service such people render may still be useful, for the operations they

engage in are partly the fruit of the cultural participation of previous generations. The nursing technique
was born with mankind's concern for the sick. The
words of the "hack" writer have been borrowed from
a language that emerged out of the moving thought
and imagination of former writers. The lecture of the
fuctional teacher is composed of concepts which are
the products of the true involvement of other schol-
ars, scientists and authors.

Service which is merely functional imposes a heavy
burden on the recipient. For the recipient himself has
to bring to life the original historical inspiration from
which this expression sprang. His possible failure to
do so may be partly attributed to the person who,
while supposedly serving him, did not enliven his expression by cultural participation in the mode of being that underlies the expression he took over in a
merely functional way. His real task would have been
to restore the inner meaning of the useful expressions
passed on to him by former generations of cultural
participants.

Personal unfolding, cultural participation and true
service are to be seen as a lived unity. For the sake of
clarification, however, we have to differentiate this
unitary structure intellectually and highlight each one
of its constituents. Differentiation of what is a natural unity is desirable in light of the fact that man
possesses the sometimes fatal ability to isolate one
aspect of a life structure from its other aspects and to

live that one aspect in isolation. When he does so, he destroys the life structure concerned and makes it impossible for himself to live harmoniously.

A discussion of the interiorly differentiated structure of the participative religious life may make us aware of the danger of the possible destruction of religious life by emphasizing onesidedly one constituent of its unitary meaning to the detriment of other integral dimensions of the same meaning. As this is a conclusion of our former explorations, this description and discussion may seem to be somewhat repetitious. However, this inconvenience must be withstood for the sake of the gain in clarity, which a synthetic view may bring.

Our descriptive identification of the participative religious life form will differentiate itself into three headings, namely, the personal and spiritual unfolding of the religious celibate, the religious-cultural participation of the religious celibate, and the incarnation of this religious-cultural participation in specific modes of service.

Unique Religious-Cultural Unfolding of the Celibate Religious

In regard to the religious celibate as a unique person, the aim of the participative religious life could be articulated in the following way: The participative life form should always structure itself in such a way that it protects and fosters the highest possible unique religious-cultural unfolding of each religious celibate within the limits inherent in the participative religious life form itself. It should thus foster a personal unfolding that is centered in a vowed, celibate threefold, reverential presence to the Holy as revealing itself in events, self, and others, culture and nature. For Christian religious life the Holy has revealed itself as the Holy Trinity and as Incarnation in Christ who continues to live in his Church. This event of events specifies the reverential presence of the Christian religious.

The personal unfolding of the religious should be in respectful communion with the accumulated wisdom and experience of those who sought and are seeking self-emergence within this fundamental life form to which they gave and are giving shape in the course of human history. This concept of spiritual-historical communion with representatives of the religious life form neither excludes nor includes the possibility or necessity of cultural-periodical condensations of the historical communion of religious in corporate-organizational communities.

Communion and dialogue with the wisdom and experience of the spiritual-historical community of those who lived and are living this life form can incarnate itself in a variety of loose or corporative structures that are in tune with the culture and civilization in which the religious life form is lived. However, a certain type of structure may be necessary within a certain type of civilization. For example, it may be necessary in western civilization that communion between religious be protected and fostered by means of corporate-organizational communities. Western civilization is an organizational civilization. That which is not organized can hardly survive under the competition and pressure of many other well-organized powers and influences.

The religious-cultural unfolding of the celibate religious must be compatible with and conducive to a religious-cultural participation and service which, in turn, fosters the religious-cultural unfolding of each celibate religious. As we have seen, the aim of the participative religious life in its essence is indivisible and unitary. Therefore, the personality development of the religious celibate cannot be at odds with his cultural participation. This indivisibility is one of fundamental orientation and is by no means an indivisibility of the concrete life structures in which the different articulations of this fundamental orientation may be incarnated in daily life. The fundamental orientation is the unitary orientation of man as spirit. But the spirit of man is incarnated spirit and therewith subjected to the laws of time and space.

The timeless and spaceless orientation of the human spirit has to be articulated in a succession of structured times and spaces and lived out in the mundane reality of everyday life. For example, there must be a time and space in which the celibate religious is more available to prayer and study than to service, and there must be a time that he is more available to

322

service than to prayer and study. At such specific times and in such specific places, he does not deny the other constituents of his unitary life orientation. He only emphasizes one more than the other during that period because of the necessity of shifting predominances in his attention and presence, a shift which is bound to his bodily incarnation.

When we say that the participative religious unfolds himself in a way that is compatible with and conducive to his cultural participation and service, we do not imply that the participative religious cannot profit deeply from the wisdom and experience of his brothers in the contemplative religious life. On the contrary, in the dimension of personal religious unfolding he should be illumined by the contemplative religious who witnesses for concentrated presence to the Sacred that is also implicitly at the heart of the personal religious unfolding of the participative religious. The witness of the contemplative religious is meant to call the participative religious back to himself before God, when he is on the verge of destroying the unitary aim of the participative religious life by onesided absorption in service.

Participative religious life should never define itself merely in opposition to the spirituality of the contemplative religious. Each life form and each center of value radiation concentrates on some fundamental value that should be lived in some form by all men, although in less exclusive concentration.

Participative religious life would be very poor in-deed without the gift of witness of the contemplative religious life. Likewise the spirituality of the life form of marriage or the life form of the celibate in the world would be impoverished without the witness of both the contemplative and the participative religious life. The first mode of religious life witnesses for presence to God; the second mode of religious life witnesses for the participation of the culture in this presence.

From what we have described as the personal dimension of the unitary aim of participative religious life, it follows that all structures, rules, customs, and decisions in this life should take into account this dimension. We want to mention here only two main principles that follow immediately from this first constituent of the meaning of this life form. First of all, religious life should create the best possible conditions for the personal and spiritual initiation of each unique person into this life. One of these conditions is to prepare and to make available the most capable religious as masters of religious living. If religious communion has been crystallized in a corporate religious community, as is usually the case in the West, the community should make sure that its initiates are also initiated into dialogue with the best representatives of the spiritual-historical communion of all religious of past and present.

A second guideline for the structuring of religious life, which follows immediately from the first constituent of the aim of religious life, is that each religious community should remain primordially a means or opportunity for continual personal and spiritual self-unfolding of each unique religious celibate in dialogue with the experience and wisdom of the spiritual-historical communion of all religious. Rules, constitutions, and customs should create the best possible conditions for such continual self-unfolding after the period of initial formation in novitiate and juniorate.

Religious-Cultural Participation

The second integral dimension of the unitary structure of the meaning of participative religious life is that of religious-cultural participation. We have explored at length the meaning of religious-cultural participation in the second volume of this series on religious life. In the last book of this trilogy, we have referred repeatedly to the same concept, relating it implicitly and incidentally to the service aspect of participative religious life. It remains to elaborate somewhat on both the unity and the diversity of service and cultural-participation as rooted in the unfolding of the religious celibate in recurrent solitude before God.

The participative religious life should enable each celibate person to witness most effectively in one or the other form of cultural participation, if possible in tune with his best self and with his special talents and predispositions. It should promote a witnessing that is characteristic of the religious participant. His is the witness for a lived and living integration of his presence to the Father in Christ with a wholehearted effective presence to that dimension of cultural unfolding in which he participates.

His witness as a religious-cultural participant binds together the first and the last dimension of the aim of his religious life. Regarding the first dimension, his religious and cultural unfolding within the spiritual, æsthetic and cultural surroundings of his religious home replenishes the richness which animates him in his tireless participation in the culture outside his religious community.

The last dimension of the purpose of religious life, that of service, is integrated in his religious-cultural participation insofar as participation has to be incarnated in some kind of concrete service if it is to be a real presence. If it were only an unincarnated presence, the whole life of the participative religious would evaporate in the thin air of beautiful fantasies, endless dialogues, and lengthy speculations, which would never lead to concrete production.

The style and organization of religious cultural participation should be compatible with and conducive to the unique personal and spiritual unfolding of the religious. Moreover, it should not lastingly interfere with the most fundamental characteristics of his participative religious life form. Otherwise this dimension of the integral meaning of participative religious

326

life would become isolated from the first dimension and therewith lose its ground. Soon his religious-cultural participation would be bereft of inspiration and the religious participant would become a victim of agitated involvement in a variety of actions. He might even deteriorate into a mere public utility engaged in spiritless routines of service.

Since cultural participation and mere service cannot be equated, this may be the place to consider the difference between cultural participation as a source of true service and service which is not inspired by cultural participation.

Human Service and Mere Service

We can begin by enumerating side by side some of the differences between a service that is lived as an expression of cultural participation and a service that is merely service. Subsequently, we may be able to see more clearly what the Christian participative religious has to bring to the human modes of cultural participation that embody themselves in truly human service.

When I participate culturally in my service, I am not merely preoccupied with the flawless execution of the operations that constitute a specific type of service. I want also to participate in the very humane movement of the culture that gave rise to this kind of service. I see this service as a set or series of motions which express, embody and carry on this human concern. For example, when I am a nurse I live this service of the sick as the embodiment of a deeply humane concern for those who suffer, a concern that emerged in the long history of the humanization of man. I participate in that concern. My very participation radiates somehow in the gracious and dedicated style in which I insert myself in the efficient, professional and knowledgeable execution of nursing procedures.

Moreover, in cultural participation, I not only participate in the one human concern that gave rise directly to my specific service, such as care for children in education; I participate also in other cultural constellations of value and meaning which indirectly inspire and animate this specific service. For instance, when I am in service of education, I participate primarily in mankind's loving concern for the life preparation of new generations. At the time, however, I can participate increasingly in other cultural values which indirectly influence my kind of presence in this service. I may participate in mankind's presence to the æsthetic dimension of reality. This will make my behavior as a teacher more gracious, attractive and elevating. I may participate in the parental tenderness for the young which may soften my words and movements as a teacher without detracting from their professional efficiency. I may also participate in mankind's presence to the Sacred or to Christ. Binding my teaching occupation to this mode of religious cultural participation, my mode and style of teaching may be permeated by such reverence and respect that

I awaken in my students a beginning awareness of their own dignity in Christ. These few examples may suffice to indicate how my life of service can be a life of increasing and expanding participation in religious and cultural constellations of values to which humanity has awakened and is to be awakened in the course of the history of its culture.

How different such an inspried service is from a mere service orientation which would open me only to the direct and immediate significance of the practical actions that constitute a specific service operation. To be sure, cultural participation leads to concern that motivates me to strive after the highest possible professional efficiency. The only difference is that *mere service*, while possibly proficient technically, may be lifeless, unanimated, uninspired and no longer an incarnation of true human presence and concern. This harms not only the humanity of those served but also of me who serves them. I cannot with impunity spend most of my waking time in an operation which I have cut off from my living humanity. Mere mechanical interaction with operations that initially emerged from a concerned culture will necessarily deplete and impoverish me. In a sense I become what I do and the way in which I am doing it. After many years of mere service without human engagement, I am likely to experience a diminishment of my humanity. It will become increasingly difficult for me to shift to a human presence in the evening after a day of mere task orientation.

329

When I am called to live the married life form, for instance, it will not be easy for me to assume a loving presence to my husband, wife or children if I did not nourish my humanity during the day within my daily task. This decreased possibility for love may seriously affect my marriage in its deepest aspects. Something similar is true when I live the celibate religious life form. It becomes increasingly difficult to be humanly present to the Lord when there is no humane religious engagement in my work.

Cultural participation within the frame of my service operation engages and actualizes my personality as a whole. In this, service becomes really a process of human and spiritual becoming. In mere service, on the contrary, what is actualized in me are only those peripheral dimensions of my personality which are related directly to the efficient execution of service movements and actions. In animated or spiritualized service, on the other hand, I experience an expansion of my interiority or interior life. Those whom I serve directly or indirectly do not remain objectivated, isolated entitles outside of me, merely defined and classified as patients, students, parishioners, readers, welfare cases or underprivileged minorities. My real concern makes me participate in their subjectivities at least to some degree within the limits of the situation. To that degree they become part of my life, of my living understanding, of my interiority. In this way, I experience a growth in my inner life that would be impossible in mere service, if I were to isolate my interiority from my efficient interaction with others.

From this I can see that cultural participation implies also an increasing participation in the relevant thoughts, moods, feelings and conditions of those whom I serve. This participation enhances the graciousness of my service as well as my efficiency. My participation in that life situation enables me to adapt my service creatively to the living persons I serve. When I am merely an effective and professional service agent, I will unquestionably adapt my service operations to the recipients of my service. In this case, however, it will be merely an adaptation to those outer dimensions of the people served that directly affect and are affected by the set of operations that constitute my service.

Take a simple service like babysitting. I may be a most efficient babysitter who executes exactly all the operations needed to keep a baby clean, protected from things that may harm him, and in bed at the time that is best for him. But I may do so without much participation in the deeper human needs of this child. I may adapt perfectly to him insofar as he needs efficient bodily care while adapting little to his unique individuality. In that case I neither grow as a human being nor expand myself as a human subject. Neither do I help the baby participate more in humanity because of my caring presence. In a human and spiritual sense, it was a lost and empty evening even though it may have been a perfect one in the sense of technical and functional efficiency.

In cultural participation the service person emerges from the human personality as a whole. This emergence, in turn, nourishes the whole personality of the serving person and the whole personality of those who receive his service. In mere service there is a certain isolation of the service-person from the person as a whole. Consequently the real person of neither the service agent nor the service-recipient is reached and enriched.

On the other hand, when my service is animated by my cultural participation, I am potentially more whole and harmonious. There is no split between my deepest religious-cultural participation in humanity and my service operation. I can be totally *there* doing what I am doing and able to deal with those personal needs and desires that are not satisfied by the limited set of service operations in which I am involved daily. Because I can experience my service as an integral expression of my deepest human aspirations, I can gradually integrate other desires into my religious cultural aspirations or I can temporarily sacrifice them in the light of these higher concerns which I lovingly express in my service.

When my service is merely an efficient execution of actions that touch on peripheral needs of society, it is more difficult to fight off dreams and desires that tell me about far more interesting things which I

332

could be doing elsewhere instead of losing my time in teaching, nursing, office work or study. I can be efficient in my service only when I fight these fantasies off and deny them access to my consciousness during my working time. This effort to repress my stubborn needs and feelings absorbs a great amount of energy. Practically I spend double energy during my task. I need energy to concentrate on what I am doing and energy to guard against the intrusion of all these other feelings and desires. This may become exhausting and may even create a certain harshness in my personality and in the style in which I execute my service.

I have to be harsh in regard to my conflicting desires and feelings if I want to keep efficiently present to my task. This harshness toward myself finally shows up in my face, words and movements. Soon I become harsh with others who implicitly appeal to my humanity. They threaten to weaken the harshness which I have to exert against my self in order to operate professionally. It may never occur to me that I can reshape my experiential life in such a way that I shall experience my service as an expression of my best self that participates in the cultural and spiritual unfolding of humanity.

This split in my personality may lead to an alienation and estrangement of myself from the service operation. The isolated service operation may then obtain an autonomous life of its own guided by the inflexible laws of its own mechanics. Soon this isolated service life may dominate and tyrannize the whole of my being. In such a case, my motives for service become extrinsic to the intrinsic meaning and purpose of the service itself. Money, status, power, promotion, and functional efficiency may become the only motivations for my service operation. While such motivations are excellent as side motivations which should bind my work to other aspects and needs of my life, they are pernicious when they become the exclusive motivations. For they cannot integrate the work itself into the aspirations of my most true and profound self that clamors to be a living participant in human culture. The exclusive reign of such extrinsic motives alienates me from my work and my work from me. I cannot live for years in such alienation without losing my vitality and inspiration.

To be efficient in mere service, it is enough that I have a functional affinity to the operations involved in that service. Psycho-physically I must be structured in such a way that this type of operation agrees with me. I have or I do not have this affinity. If I do not have it, I cannot force it. When I am gifted like this, I can develop my gift by training and instruction. However, if I want my service to be a living expression of my cultural participation, then beyond this functional affinity, I need a cultural affinity. The affinity of self to human values is potentially present in every human being. I can grow in it by attempting to live it.

I can awaken to it by meditation and reflection, which foster human motivation. Therefore, the preparation for cultural participation and the repeated restoration of this cultural presence demand time outside the service time itself. I must find daily moments in which I can find and experience myself as a participant in the process of humanization and spiritualization of humanity.

The technical rationalization of service operations today leaves little or no time during the operation itself for being with myself and reawakening the human awareness of what I am doing. The eight-hour work day, while a good and necessary improvement for many reasons, provides far less room for reflection than the fourteen-hour workday of the past period. It is true that people at that time were engaged almost all day in lucrative activities, but a small number of them in the independent professions seem to have worked in a more leisurely fashion allowing for the possibility of reflection. The absence of this possibility today compels us more than ever to find such moments outside the task in the peace and quiet of the religious home. Hopefully, the religious-cultural participant can there regain the meaning and motivation of his daily service as animated by cultural participation.

The Christian religious celibate should be not only a cultural participant but a cultural participant in a special way. One of the values uncovered by humanity during its history of humanization and spiritualization is that of the whole and holy dimension of people, events and things and therewith the same dimension of any kind of service that serves the unfolding of humanity and culture. The Holy is the most fundamental, transcendent value in which I can root all other values that I incarnate in my service. My service reaches its deepest meaning when I unify all the values that inspire and enliven my service in presence to the Holy. This is true for all men. Presence to the Sacred helps man to be really present to what he is doing and prevents self-alienation from his service. Self-centered motives isolate him from his task, from those for whom he works, and from the ground of the Holy from which all service receives its ultimate sacred meaning.

The participative religious lives a life that makes him more present to the Sacred and less preoccupied with certain areas which usually preoccupy a functional society. Because of this enlarged opportunity for deepening himself in religious presence, it is easier for the average man who is a religious to keep this presence alive than for the average man who has not been set free by the vow of celibacy. For the same reason it is easier for the religious celibate to make presence to the Sacred the deepest motivation of his daily task. By his very living, he witnesses for the integration of all other value motivations in the deepest value motivation, that of presence to God.

The Christian religious celibate has encountered the Holy as Christ his Redeemer who lives in the Church. Christ has revealed that the world lives under the dominion of sin. All men belong to this world and all need redemption and salvation. Christ told us that we all are inclined to deviate from the true end of human culture which is to ready itself for salvation by the Lord. Because the world is under the dominion of sin, our best cultural attempts, our most humanitarian services, are soon tainted by pride, self-seeking, and the need to look good in the eyes of others, by anger and aggressiveness, by the need to dominate others, and by avarice and envy. When this happens the process of humanization and spiritualization is retarded. Jesus opposed this tendency to sin and came to redeem us from its dominance. He revealed to us that presence to the Holy is presence to the Father in and through Him.

In the light of His revelation, we know that mankind has defected from the ultimate meaning of its culture, namely, presence to the Father and cooperation with the Holy Sprit in the unfolding of the Father's creation. Therefore, presence to the Father as revealed by Jesus is not only the fundamental mode of life that should inspire, purify and deepen our service but it is also the kind of presence that is easily lost, forgotten, and repressed because of the original sinfulness in which we all share. The Christian religious celibate participates in the culture in order to

337

witness for the redeeming presence of his Lord in this world. He expects that every form of service, no matter how nobly meant and how generously planned, has at its heart the possible taint of human selfishness which affects this service as a whole, which may make it deteriorate, and renders it far less efficacious than it could be.

Sinful motivations that are in all of us diminish the nobility of service. It is presence to the Father in and through Jesus that makes us aware of the original sinfulness that may corrode the works of humanity. This awareness, sustained by grace, motivates us to implore the Lord to purify our motivations and therewith our works.

The Christian celibate religious can be found in a variety of cultural enterprises witnessing to the purifying power of Jesus in this world. He knows that this battle will never be over and that the soul he saves may only be his own. He knows also that the witnessing for the redemption must go on in this sinful world so that hope may not vanish from this earth and that people may not live in the illusion of a mere humanistic salvation. All Christians are called to this witness. Encumbered by many worries and preoccupations, they have set the religious celibate free from care for a family of his own. As a cultural participant he may reawaken in his fellow Christians the awareness of the goodness and the sinfulness of all human motivation so that they may increasingly purify their motivations from this stain. Doing so, they can be more faithful to their task of Christian witnessing, which they share with the participative religious.

Embodiment of Cultural Participation in Service

The third specification of the participative religious life refers to the necessity of a concrete embodiment of personal growth and cultural presence into some kind of service. This can be a service common to the majority of the members of my community, or one in which I participate alone because this is the way I can be of most value to humanity. The unitary aim of the participative religious life implies only that religious-cultural participation be embodied in some type of concrete service. Essentially it does not imply what kind of concrete embodiment it should be.

This latter point is crucial. The greatest danger for any fundamental lasting life form is to confuse the absolute necessity of *some* concrete embodiment in service with the notion of an absolute necessity of a *specific* type of service. A person may discover during his married life or religious life that he cannot function well in the kind of concrete task that has been posited falsely as belonging to the very essence of a fundamental life form like marriage or religious life. The best chance for him to survive spiritually and psychologically as an integrated person may be to change the concrete service in which he embodies his inspiration and presence.

339

We are not saying that one can change the essential unitary aim of the participative religious life which necessarily implies embodiment in some type of concrete service. The only thing one can change without betraying the essence of his fundamental life form is the expression which its concrete embodiment takes. However, when it has been falsely suggested to a participative religious that a certain specific task belongs to the very essence of his lasting life form itself, he may suffer feelings of guilt, failure and insufficiency when rightly asking for another occupation.

A religious may have interiorized the unfounded claims of those who suggest that the type of service in which the majority feel at home should be the type of service in which every good religious should always feel at home. This internalized standard may spiritually and psychologically destroy the person. He may not dare to speak up when he badly needs a change in occupation. He may not even have the background and intellectual ability to find his way out of this confusion. He may be unable to find an experienced spiritual director, therapist or counselor who can relieve the unauthentic guilt feelings which plague him. In trying compulsively to conform to the claim of the majority, the religious may distort his personality and even lead himself into the temptation to betray his fundamental calling to the participative religious life as such.

A concrete form of service like mission work, teaching, social work, nursing, and inner city service presupposes a whole set of conditions which deeply affect and modify the life of the individual. No one can be sure in advance that these conditions will be present for the greater part of his life. It is a lack of wisdom, therefore, to vow oneself lastingly and exclusively to one type of concrete service. This may help to explain why some young people object vehemntly to a lasting commitment to religious life. In many cases they would have no objection if the participative religious life were really a fudnamental life form which includes embodiment of religious-cultural participation in some form of service. But they recoil from the proposal that they should vow themselves lastingly to one detailed form of service.

The modern young man and woman know human psychology well enough to realize that it is unwise and imprudent to commit one life unconditionally to some detailed form of work or to some foreign culture if it means that one can never change this one embodiment of engagement, not even if his personal life unexpectedly were to change. This does not necessarily reflect a lack of generosity on the part of the young. For example, many young men and women out of love for Christ are quite willing to embody their Christian concern for underdeveloped countries in a specific service within these regions. As a matter of fact, they go there and give themselves enthusiastically and wholeheartedly. The only thing they do not think wise is to commit themselves in advance to live there for a life time. The reason for this refusal again is not lack of generosity but the prudent realization that one cannot be sure in advance whether he can always give his best and be his best for himself and others in this type of situation.

When participative religious life as a fundamental lasting life form identifies itself unconditionally and absolutely with the life long execution of one type of service it betrays itself as *fundamental* life form. In that case the participative religious life itself is to blame for the refusal of the young to join it. Insightful counselors of the young may even warn them against joining any participative religious community that suggests that one type of concrete service belongs to the very essence of this fundamental life form. Psychiatry and psychotherapy have presented too much evidence of the havoc that can be wrought in the human person when he imposes on himself such an exclusive frame of work for a life time.

One may ask here if it is wrong for a specific participative community to make available to its members a specific field of service. By no means. Ideally a participative religious community should have one or more fields of preference, such as missions, education, nursing and social work. This field of preference may even take a first place in the community concerned so that each person entering this community can be sure that he will be employed in that field of preference as long as he is able to do so. The spiritual and psychological dangers for person and community enter only at the moment that fanaticism takes over and betrays itself in words like "exclusive," "only," "unconditionally." The fanaticized consciousness is a narrowed consciousness fixated on one type of concrete embodiment of man in the world. The fanaticized consciousness is authoritarian and merciless without respect and compassion. It is a tyrannical consciousness that unwittingly destroys a person for an idea or for the success of a certain type of work. It forces its victims to cooperate in their own destruction by instilling in them guilt feelings when they do not comply at a certain moment of their life with the type of service embodiment that the majority like best. The fanaticized consciousness leads to a streamlined collectivity rigdly organized in service of the one type of embodiment of inspiration that has captivated the whole. Such fanaticism destroys true community. True community can never exist in terms of works only. It always prefers persons to works and is always ready to help the person to be what he can be best.

That various participative communities have various fields of preference which are never made exclusive is a blessing for the religious as a person. It enables potential religious who want to do this kind of work to choose a community where they can be rel-

atively sure that they can live out their religious-cultural presence in this type of service. This blessing
becomes a curse, however, when the field of preference
is rigidly reduced to a tyrannical necessity for all at all
moments of their life no matter what the spiritual,
psychological and physical changes in their abilities
and predispositions. The terrible tragedy is that such
tyranny is interiorized in the form of an unauthentic
repressive conscience which often leads to morbid
guilt feelings. Such repression halts the healthy and
honest awareness that one may no longer be at home
in this specific kind of service.

Authentic participative religious life should assert
not only that its field of preference is never an exclusive field but also it should assert again and again that
no member of the community should feel guilty or
ashamed if he becomes aware that a certain type of
service is no longer the kind that he can live with
spiritual, psychological or physical integrity. He
should feel totally free to ask for and accept another
type of service that is in no way related to the type
of service that became harmful to him. The community should create an atmosphere of mutual respect which prevents anyone from showing dis-
pleasure when another is called to embody his religious-cultural participation in a cultural enterprise
in which the majority is not occupied. Flexibility and
openness protect the fundamental life form as fundamental life form and the personal dignity and spirit-

ual health of those who try to live it. Moreover, it guarantees a greater possibility for the survival of the community concerned in history.

In the first place, priests, religious and lay persons, who are psychologically sophisticated, will not feel obliged in conscience to advise the young to bind themselves lastingly to a religious community which has absolutely identified a fundamental life form with one specific type of service. Consequently, the chance for vocations to the religious life as life form may be rapidly increased.

Secondly, the increase in psychological sophistication may make members of the community aware just how unauthentic an absolute and rigid identification of work and person is. Consequently they may feel forced in conscience to impede the attempt by others to impose one type of service as the essence of the life form itself, for this attempt would harm the spirit of a community and therewith diminish its possibility of survival.

Others again may feel in conscience that they should leave the community at a time of life that they find a special work or culture unbearable. They desire to live the participative religious life itself but feel unable to live it out in this one specific type of service or in a specific foreign culture. If they leave in increasing numbers, their leave-taking is bound to threaten the survival of the community as a whole.

The rigor of only one exclusive type of service —

only foreign missions, only schools, only nursing — diminishes the flexible openness of the community for all kinds of other needs that may arise in the course of history. Historically only those religious communities have survived the centuries that were able to adapt to the changing situation. Those old and venerable communities did have fields of preference, but these fields of preference never became exclusive. Rigorous fixation on only one type of service emerged in the last centuries under the influence of a rationalized functional society. As long as such communities adhere in a forbidding and absolute sense to an exclusive field of concentration their chances for survival in history seem small indeed.

Service and Service Associations

The need to understand in depth the meaning of service in religious life leads us to identify various kinds of service associations. The rationalization of labor in the West led to the emergence of these associations. Certain types of manufacturing demanded that employees work in association in accordance with a rational division of the various aspects and phases of their task. Beginning with industrial enterprises, this principle extended itself to other endeavors, such as education and the arts and sciences.

People would form service associations of administrators and faculty members in a school or of doctors and nurses in a hospital, of singers who assist weekly in liturgical services of a church or of clergy-men who regularly administer to the faithful of a town. The character of such service associations is determined by the immediate demands of the service given.

Service associations are not meant to concern themselves with the fundamental life style of their members. It is true that there have been cases in which companies actually attempted to extend their influence to that private domain. A subtle probing into the relationship between husband and wife in the intimacy of their home was begun. Suggestions were made that a prospective executive should select a wife and arrange his home situation in such a manner that it would enhance his productivity. Fortunately, people resisted this intrusion. In spite of increasing pressures it was still possible to distinguish marriage as a life form from mere service.

To be sure, a wise living of their fundamental life form may make people more relaxed and efficient in their service life. Efficient service, however, is not the first aim and meaning of a fundamental life form. Neither should a service association dictate directly or indirectly by subtle hints, demands and suggestions, what a fundamental life association should be for its associates.

Another type of association that emerged in history was the service life association. The service life association does not restrict itself to that aspect of life that is directly relevant to a service operation. Neither does it concern itself with the fundamental life form that its associates are living. The service life association concerns itself with specific aspects of life as lived outside the fundamental life form and outside the service operation. It concentrates on aspects which can be organized in favor of a better presence to the task itself.

For example, a group of teachers in service of a Catholic school may decide to attend Mass together, to participate together in retreats and days of recollection, which may sustain the inspiration of their Christian educational endeavors. Nurses who are single may decide to live together in the same apartment in order that certain concerns which interfere with their work may be diminished by their shared concern. Singers in a famous choral group may live together under a certain rule which enables them to be available for choir practice in a more disciplined and effective way. People serving the needs of underdeveloped countries may associate in an organization like the Peace Corps which regulates certain aspects of their life in such a way that they can be better available to their task.

We call such associations life associations because they really touch private human life outside the service. We call them service life associations because they touch private life only inso far as it is related to the service. For that reason, people who live their lives in the various fundamental life forms can also be members of such service life associations. Their fundamental life form in and by itself is not touched directly by the demands of the service life association. Here again there are incidents in which the service life association begins to exert subtle pressure on the life form association. But this is all the more reason to defend fiercely the fundamental life association as a last bulwark of human privacy and dignity not yet invaded and perverted by the octopus of rationalized service. When the distinction between these three types of associations is well understood, one can begin to diagnose the possible ills of religious communities which emerged in centuries marked by the rationalization of human service.

Let us take an imaginary example of a community which begins as a service association, changes into a life service association and ends up as a fundamental life association. This imaginary example will be extreme for the sake of demonstrating the dynamics of perversion that may unwittingly enter into a religious life form as they are now threatening to enter the life form of marriage.

A pastor in a small rural town needs generous single ladies willing to staff a school which he wants to erect for Catholic children. He finds a group of young Catholic women who perform that service for him. Soon they form an intimate service association preoccupied with the needs of that school. The pastor can only grant them a small salary. After some time they realize that they can improve their service when they share an apartment near the school that will be paid for by the parish and therewith diminish their cost of living. The service association has become a service life association. Notice that the regulations of their life are still centered around their service. After some years, the pastor may feel that it would be wonderful for his school if he could assure that this group would remain always available and would steadily expand itself. They are already living together. They come together for prayer and Holy Mass in the morning. They seem so involved in the school that they do not think about marriage. Naturally, it strikes him that it would be most convenient for the maintenance and development of his school if these women would form a religious community obliging themselves to serve his educational enterprise. In other words he wants them to bind themselves unconditionally to education by identifying their vow to a fundamental life form with a lifelong commitment to teach.

Though this is a fictitious story it is nonetheless clear that we have here an illustration of the encroachment of service form upon fundamental life form. When a service life form association becomes a fundamental life form association, each person involved should realize that he in fact changes from one more peripheral form of life to a totally different most fundamental form of life. The rules, structures, and customs which centered around one type of service should now be centered first of all around the art of living personally a life that is fundamentally meaningful either in marriage; or religious life.

As we have seen earlier, the unconditional absoluteness with which a human being can commit himself to a fundamental life style cannot be transferred to the type of promise he can give to one specific type of service. When this distinction is not kept in mind, a community carries within itself seeds of destruction. Nobody single, married, or religious, can live his total life to the full only on the basis of service.

The identification of the fundamental life form and service is fostered when a community overextends itself in several types of service operations into which each member is forced indiscriminately. What does this mean practically? It means that the superiors of the community can no longer serve the religious and human unfolding of the members of their community if this would conflict with the demands of the works in which they unconditionally imprisoned themselves. What finally dominates their decisions in regard to their religious may be the impersonal demands of the organizations in which their services are embodied.

This does not mean necessarily that a community should not foster well organized enterprises within which the majority of its members can be effectively employed. The independence and freedom of the fundamental life form demands, however, that the community is not so overextended in one or a few types of work that there is no room left for taking care of the needs of individuals who should be replaced, so that they can temporarily retire or transfer temporarily or lastingly to a totally different kind of work or study. Overextension in a few types of service implies that almost all members are so tightly inserted in a certain number of enterprises that the removal of a person becomes a calamity. He may even feel guilty when he must ask for such a favor.

When service tyrannizes the fundamental life of human beings to this extent, it may show in a strain that painfully marks their personality and behavior. No wonder that young men and women cannot feel attracted to such a life form as they may feel attracted to the life form of marriage. Not only does the vitality within the community go down; but there is also a decrease in vocations.

Another aspect of this deterioration of religious life is a confusion in the young in regard to its purpose. Some realize what the fundamental religious life form really is and enter for that reason. Others somehow entertain the notion that the main aim and concern of religious life as such is the specific type of service the community is temporarily and locally engaged in. They enter to teach, to go to the missions, to nurse, or to do social work. They take religious life in its fundamental meaning as some kind of condition that one has to fulfill if he likes to be engaged in the specific works of this community. This state of affairs leads to a hidden division wthin the community between those who came primarily for religious life and those who came primarily for a specific type of practical engagement.

An interesting illustration can be found in some mission congregations. There was a time that it was practically impossible to work for the Church in the foreign missions as a secular priest or a layman. In some countries the only sure way to go to foreign missions was to join a mission congregation. Some generous men and women not primarily interested in religious life, nevertheless, entered these religious communities because they were deeply interested in work in underdeveloped countries. They considered unconsciously the religious life as a somewhat unfortunate but inescapable condition for the fulfillment of their genuine desire to be religiously active in foreign missions. Later on, with the best intentions they may endanger the fundamental religious life form itself. They may try to define it totally in terms of that one specific enterprise forgetting that the essence of any fundamental life form can never be defined in terms of one or the other concrete enterprise, culture, or country, but only in terms of individual human beings who through their fundamental life form may bear fruit in one or the other type of service in tune with their possibilities.

Again, this does not mean that there should not

353

be religious communities who single out as their field of preference service in foreign missions. Everyone entering such a community should be reasonably sure that he will be sent to the missions if he wants to go there. We only like to stress that this enterprise should never dominate the life of the members in such an exclusive way that it becomes practically for them the ultimate meaning of religious life as such.

Conclusion

We have discussed the articulations of the unitary aim of the participative religious life as a conclusion of our exploration in this trilogy. Let us conclude with some words on the image of the modern participative religious as it emerges before us at the conclusion of these studies.

The participative religious life is a life in which man can achieve his full and ideal stature when he realizes within this style of existence the role God has assigned him from all eternity. God has, so to speak, a specific idea about each of us. That idea is always unique, applicable only to me. Personality development in religious life, therefore, is a matter of actualizing the divine plan insofar as it effects me personally.

In harmony with our very personal being, God has appointed each religious participant a task that no one else can rightly assume. He has assigned every man his irreplaceable role in history, and the more perfectly he unfolds the potential that God has placed at the root of his being, 'the better he serves the ends of Providence.

The participative religious gratefully accepts as a treasure from God's hand the nature he has received. Strengthened by God's grace, he perfects 'the gifts that God has given him. He accepts his shortcomings, such as his oversensitivity, his inclination to anger and violence, his troublesome temperament. He does not try to "break" his character. As the venerable Libermann says, "You don't break iron, you soften it in the fire." If he cannot improve himself immediately or absolutely, a religious lives with himself in peace and humble submission to God. He knows that then his natural imperfection will be compensated for by interior graces of which he may not even be aware. He does not try to be perfect all at once but only attempts to do quietly, peacefully, and sincerely what God asks him to do. Conscious of his deficiencies, he tries to accept them with true humility, without a feeling of inferiority. Inferiority feelings paralyze his self-actualization and rob him of his resiliency.

When the participative religious accepts his nature as it is and is no longer oppressed by anxiety over the faults that stem from it, he is in a position to develop fully the gifts with which God endowed him.

The final aim of his concern with the uninhibited flowering of his potentiality is a desire of the religious participant to arrive at a mature, self-actualizing mode of life. He realizes that only the mature, fully-developed personality can surrender himself in religious cultural participation without losing himself.

A most dynamic element in his unfolding into the mature independence of a fully realized potential is divine grace. The perfect development of a participative religious into final-actualization demands and presupposes the constant influence of grace. Moreover, since the endowment of character and personality flow from the same Eternal Fountainhead as does grace, these two sources of action, far from excluding each other, are mutually complementary and psychologically resonant. God gives grace in accordance with the character and temperament of each participative religious. Hence, each one has to follow his own direction in the unfolding of his presence to God and man. Moreover, the variety of modes of cultural participation for which participative religious are destined require a corresponding variety of graces. Each participative religious under the influence of grace takes on the special form God wants him to acquire and which He has destined for him from all eternity.

Surrender to God's specific design of life for each participative religious is the be-all and end-all of the religious community. Nothing should be feared so much in religious life as thwarting personal grace or handicapping another's life orientation by the external imposition of alien patterns.

The participative religious should not be involved in a multitude of petty devotions or in numerous ascetical practices. Such busy holiness may take him away from the core of his being, hinder his deep personal encounter with God, and repress the essentially personal element of religious life.

To be sure, the participative religious should interiorly distance himself from mundane attachments so that he might enjoy that freedom which is the mark of a truly liberated person. Instead of being anxiously preoccupied with the acquisition of separate virtues one after the other, the participative religious should increasingly live in presence to God in Whom all that is best in every man lies hidden as in its source. The rest follows naturally and spontaneously.

The constant agitation of modern life in which he participates easily inclines him to lose his inner freedom. Hyperactive, tense and anxious, he may be at the mercy of momentary but overwhelming impressions. At times he may live passively instead of actively, being influenced rather than influencing. He should strive to restore an atmosphere of moderation, serenity and equanimity so that he may extricate himself from that raging flow of fleeting impressions which threaten to suck him down into a vortex of agitation.

Once disengaged from the hectic stimuli of stresses and strains, the participative religious can live a life that is activated by those deeper levels of his being where God reveals Himself through the inclination and desires that His own hand has engraved there. Here, too, the truly free religious will at last grow responsive to the grace whereby his Creator strengthens and ennobles his good dispositions and suffuses them with His divinity.

He becomes a manifestation in time of the unique idea which God had of him from all eternity. The true holiness of the participative religious consists, then, in an ever greater realization of what the Creator expected of him, His creature, before time was.

Harm could be done to the life and the task of the participative religious if this highly individual unfolding of his personality were to be distracted by an attempt to imitate another's equally individual experiences and aspirations. Instead of listening too much to others in regard to his own life, the participative religious should prefer to listen to the word of God as it speaks from Holy Scripture and from his own detached and docile heart.

Whatever makes a religious be what he is, his whole capacity in the order of grace and nature is truly a gift and a mandate of the Creator. His plan of life is not of his own choosing. It is God's idea. The path of his religious life is a fascinating exploration in which God's eternal and unique project for him slowly emerges before his fascinated attention.

We may summarize this process of being true to one's self by the word "simplicity." True simplicity has nothing to do with uncouth or gauche behavior, want of intelligence, lack of refinement, or disdain for science and beauty. Simplicity is a courageous fidelity to what is really authentic in us, to what is in accord with God's plan for us. Thus, for example, when Thomas Aquinas wrote his great *Summa* it was an of sublime simplicity, for that mode of thinking and writing was an authentic expression of his personality. Had he forced himself to write out of character in a popular way, he would have been wanting in simplicity.

Everything that goes counter to personal honesty and consistency denotes a lack of simplicity. Paradoxically, there may be instances where a religious may have to be so simple that he seems proud, for mediocre minds may confuse this virtue with a levelling attitude, a lack of originality, an absence of culture and creativity. When a participative religious is heroically faithful to his unique vocation, he may be accused of ambition. He should then not counterfeit simplicity by escaping into the security of the life of "regular fellows"; he should not attempt to be safe at the expense of his integrity.

Since the well-prepared participative religious must take his place not in an abstract world but in an intricate, contemporary environment that may be foreign to his background and preparation, one of his most important character traits must be flexibility. He must be able to adapt himself best to the people around him and even to the uniqueness of each person. He must be sensitive to all the aspects of his life situation, probe its wounds and be alert to every opportunity to alleviate its needs.

In this attempt the modern participative religious cannot afford to be overwhelmed by the variety of problems that clamor for attention and solution. This danger grows in proportion to the complexity of society. He must order and structure the manifold meanings of the cultural situation in which he is engaged before he can respond wisely. A balanced judgment is the necessary counterpart of open-mindedness, lest too great receptivity leave us victims of undigested impressions.

The participative religious should not be carried away by sudden ideas and suggestions that arouse his imagination and take him by surprise. He should not make final decisions as long as he is stirred up emotionally but should wait until equanimity has been restored. This done, the structuring of reality by the participative religious may peacefully proceed. Possessed of a balanced judgment and fully informed through his open-minded presence, he is in a position to engage in realistic planning. This is one of the foundation stones of effective religious-cultural participation.

The participative religious should not engage in impulsive and emotional methods; he should not go adventuring and be satisfied with a hasty and poorly organized approach. Action without thought is like a

360

flower severed from its stem. Feverish activity and the passionate engagement of the most powerful forces is but a shot in the dark unless directed by an observant and reflective mind. The best-equipped army is powerless without intelligence staffs. Therefore, the religious participant has to grow daily in the knowledge of man and matter and has to look to the future as much as to the present.

The participative religious should not only bring maturity, open-mindedness, talents, and practicality to the life situation, he should also be able to interact there with others wisely and respectfully. His first encounter with cultural participants will be with others in the same field, some of whom may be members of his own community. If he reacts with suspicion and unconscious jealousy to the initiative and success of a colleague, he can do immeasurable harm to humanity, for he may dry up a fountain from which many might otherwise have drunk. On the other hand, when he helps his fellow participants develop in ability and grace, applauding their achievements and sympathizing with their adversities, he may do more for God and man than he would have done alone. He should be as much pleased when good is accomplished through his colleagues and confreres as when it is the result of his own endeavors.

Another cardinal feature of the modern religious is his patience with the shortcomings of others. He must be able to be flexible and accommodating to the people, things, and circumstances in his surroundings. He must be aware of that imagination that wants perfection everywhere. This leads to intolerance and fanaticism which is detestible and destructive. Tolerance, respect for individuality, the reluctance to hurt a fellow human being, the disinclination to compel a person to act contrary to his convictions — all demand a refined understanding of man. Therefore the modern religious should daily grow in his understanding of others.

The crowning touch in the character of the cultural participant is a consistent attitude of sympathy and courtesy. He should be a true man or woman of refinement and respect, of mildness, modesty and deference. Kindness, delicacy, politeness, and humility should become a style of life not merely a code of etiquette. A participative religious who has found his position in the world, will be a master of reality who favors practical and systematic approaches when possible and desirable. Keeping himself open for constant changes and rising needs in the situation where he lives and labors will necessitate unending decisions and adaptations on his part. He must be a man of courage and initiative within the limits of his possibilities.

The modern participative religious, then, is a man who develops that unique gift of God, his own personality, as richly as he can — not by repressing his nature and throttling his inclinations, but by upholding his true self with the help of grace. He is receptive and attentive to the ever-changing situation around him, always keeping his emotional balance lest mere impressions and feelings dominate him. He is realistic, precise and practical. He plans his projects carefully and with full understanding of man and situation. Always a gentle person, he cultivates courtesy, politeness and personal neatness. He is full of good will and tolerance toward others, yet courageous in facing hardship and challenge. This ideal of the Christian participative religious grows out of the pages of the New Testament where, without prejudice to His Godhead, the second person of the Blessed Trinity walked among man and loved to call himself "the Son of Man." The new participative religious can only humbly follow Him, patterning his attitudes after the sublime humanity of Christ and partaking of His Divinity through the miracle of Grace — "Another Christ" in the fullest sense of the term.